VIDEOTHERAPY
IN MENTAL HEALTH

VIDEOTHERAPY
IN MENTAL HEALTH

Edited by

JERRY L. FRYREAR, Ph.D.

Clinical Psychologist and Associate Professor
University of Houston at Clear Lake City
Houston, Texas

and

BOB FLESHMAN

Director, Drama Therapy Program
Loyola University of New Orleans
New Orleans, Louisiana

CHARLES C THOMAS • PUBLISHER
Springfield • Illinois • U.S.A.

Published and Distributed Throughout the World by

CHARLES C THOMAS ● PUBLISHER

Bannerstone House

301-327 East Lawrence Avenue, Springfield, Illinois, U.S.A.

© *1981, by* CHARLES C THOMAS ● PUBLISHER

ISBN 0-398-04117-2

Library of Congress Catalog Card Number: 80-20170

Printed in the United States of America
V-R-1

Library of Congress Cataloging in Publication Data

Main entry under title:

Videotherapy in mental health.

   Bibliography: p.
   Includes indexes.
   1. Video tapes in psychotherapy. I. Fryrear,
Jerry L. II. Fleshman, Robert. [DNLM: 1. Psycho-
therapy--Audiovisual aids. 2. Television. WM450.5.V5
V652]
RC455.2.T45V53   616.89'14'028   80-20170
ISBN 0-398-04117-2

For Benjamin

CONTRIBUTORS

JACK S. ANNON, Ph.D., Private Practice; Graduate Affiliate Faculty, Department of Psychology; Clinical Faculty, Department of Psychiatry; Senior Consultant, Sexual Counseling Service, Department of Obstretrics and Gynecology, John A. Burns School of Medicine, University of Hawaii.

PATRICIA G. BALL, Ed.D., Director of Public Affairs, City of Knoxville, Tennessee.

FRED CUTTER, Ph.D., Chief, Psychology Service, Veteran's Administration Medical Center, Fresno, California.

PATRICK H. DOYLE, Ph.D., Associate Professor, Behavioral Sciences, University of Houston at Clear Lake City.

WAYNE D. DUEHN, Ph.D., Professor, Graduate School of Social Work, University of Texas at Arlington.

TOM EMMITT, Director, Telecommunications Center, Camarillo State Hospital, Camarillo, California.

PETER A. FEHRENBACH, M.A., Clinical Psychology Graduate Student, University of Missouri at Columbia.

NANETTE M. FRAUTSCHI, M.A., Clinical Psychology Graduate Student, University of Missouri at Columbia.

RICHARD A. FRY, Ph.D., Psychologist, Marianne Frostig Center of Educational Therapy, Los Angeles, California.

LINDA GREGORIC, M.A., Sociodrama Coordinator, Media and the Arts for Social Services, University of Connecticut.

MICHAEL GREGORIC, Ph.D., Professor of Dramatic Arts and Project Director, Media and the Arts for Social Services, University of Connecticut.

JOHN H. HUNG, Ph.D., Assistant Professor of Health Care Psychology and Director, Behavioral Medicine Clinic, University of Minnesota Health Sciences Center, Minneapolis, Minnesota.

EDWARD JOHNSON, Ph.D., Assistant Professor, Department of Philosophy, University of New Orleans.

RICHARD H. LEE, Ph.D., Teaching Consultant — Family Therapy, Children's Hospital Medical Center, Boston; Faculty, Family Institute of Cambridge; Faculty, Society for Family Therapy and Research; Faculty, Mental Health Continuing Education Consortium, Boston University; Private Practice.

NAZNEEN SADA MAYADAS, D.S.W., Professor, Graduate School of Social Work, University of Texas at Arlington.

SHAUN MCNIFF, Ph.D., A.T.R., Dean of the Arts Institute, Lesley College Graduate School, Cambridge, Massachusetts.

CHRISTINE C. REESE, O.T.R., M.A., A.T.R., Assistant Professor, Arts and Science Division, Shenandoah College, Winchester, Virginia.

CRAIG H. ROBINSON, Ph.D., Private Practice; Clinical Faculty, Department of Psychology; Clinical Faculty, Department of Psychiatry; Consultant, Sexual Counseling Service, Department of Obstretrics and Gynecology, John A. Burns School of Medicine, University of Hawaii.

TED L. ROSENTHAL, Ph.D., Professor, Department of Psychiatry, University of Tennessee Center for the Health Sciences, and Clinical Director, Adult Psychiatry and Alcohol and Drug Unit, MidSouth Hospital, Memphis, Tennessee.

DAVID M. SCHNARCH, Ph.D., Director, Adult Psychotherapy Clinic, and Director of Psychology Internships, Department of Psychiatry and Behavioral Sciences, Louisiana State University Medical Center, New Orleans, Louisiana; Director, Sex and Marital Therapy Program, River Oaks Hospital, New Orleans, Louisiana.

MARK H. THELEN, Ph.D., Professor and Director of Clinical Training, Department of Psychology, University of Missouri at Columbia.

L. ELAINE TOMLINSON, M.S., Consultant, Organizational Management Associates, Inc., New Orleans, Louisiana.

INTRODUCTION

VIDEOTHERAPY in mental health ranges from simple and passive videotaping of a verbal therapy session to elaborate, detailed videotherapy procedures such as closed circuit television in a mental hospital. The purpose of this book is to provide, in a single volume, basic concepts of videotherapeutic intervention and to illustrate videotherapy methods in specific settings and with specific populations. The chapters have as a common theme the therapeutic use of video in mental health. Despite this common theme, the reader will discover a diversity of treatment concepts and a surprising array of treatment methods. Treatment concepts include, among others, video playback for confrontive and informative purposes, creativity, video as an adjunct to other treatment modalities, mastery of video equipment as an occupational skill, video as a tool in social skills training, and video as nonverbal communication between client and therapist.

Part One of the book presents three treatment concepts: video playback, modeling, and creative expression. These three concepts are the most frequent ones underlying videotherapy methods and are treated with critical detail by the chapter authors. These three concepts, in addition to others less well developed, are referred to and discussed throughout the book. Playback, modeling, and creative expression are the foundation of videotherapy.

Part Two of the book is a collection of detailed illustrations of videotherapy methods. The chapters show the diversity of styles of videotherapists. A cross section of professional identities are represented among the authors (psychology, social work, art therapy, communications, etc.) as well as numerous mental health settings (private offices, medical schools, universities, mental health centers, hospitals).

In Part Three we break from a discussion of the practice of

videotherapy per se to other related professional concerns. Chapter 13 addresses the use of video in the training of psychotherapists. Video is becoming a routinely used tool in training centers. It provides an efficient and economical means of presenting information and allows student therapists to see themselves in action.

Chapter 14 is concerned with ethics. The author, a philosopher, eloquently reminds us therapists that the use of video raises a number of ethical questions beyond those inherent in all psychotherapeutic relationships.

Video technology is changing very rapidly. Many formats are available, and new manufacturers appear each year. Because of the rapid change in technology we have not tried to supply a current, soon to be outdated, description of equipment availability and capability. Rather, we have supplied an appendix that lists sources of information helpful to prospective purchasers and users of video. We include books, directories and guides, journals, and addresses of manufacturers.

Video is widely used in mental health, in both therapy and training, and is sure to be more widely used in the future. The cost of the equipment declines as the technology improves, enabling most agencies and even private therapists to purchase a portable unit. There is mounting evidence that video is a valuable therapeutic tool and videotherapy procedures can be powerful intervention techniques.

CONTENTS

xi

Part Three
Professional Considerations

VIDEOTHERAPY
IN MENTAL HEALTH

Part One
Three Basic Videotherapy Concepts

CHAPTER 1

THERAPEUTIC VIDEOTAPED PLAYBACK*

JOHN H. HUNG AND TED L. ROSENTHAL

INTRODUCTION

THE past fifteen years have seen an increasing acceptance of the videotape recorder as a psychotherapeutic tool. Videotaping has been used in diverse ways: to assess and document behavioral changes in therapy (Cline, 1972); to present new and useful information to clients through taped instructions and modeling (Fisher et al., 1976); to identify and analyze behavioral deficits in social skills training (Hersen and Bellack, 1970); as an adjunct in therapist training and supervision (Ingram, 1974); as a storage and retrieval system whereby a therapy session is recorded and later played back to clients (Bailey, 1970), etc. Thus, the videotape recorder has been hailed as "a technological breakthrough" of enormous importance for psychiatry (Alger and Hogan, 1966). Some other of the many videotape applications are covered elsewhere in this book. This chaper will focus on one particularly important aspect, the use of videotape playback in therapy. Specifically, the term *video-tape recorded playback* (VTRP) here refers to any feedback procedure whereby certain aspects of a client's behavior are videotaped and later played back to the client. The amount of material replayed, the conditions under which playback occurs, and the timing of the playback are some of the variables that have been investigated in various studies and will presently be examined in some detail.

Historically, the forebear of therapeutic VTRP appears to be prior work on exposing patients to their own photographs, or to audiotapes of their own voices. Some severe psychotics who

---

*Portions of this chapter are modified and updated versions of an earlier article that appeared in *Advances in Behaviour Research and Therapy, 1*:103-135, 1978. Courtesy of Pergamon Press.

were shown their own photographs were subsequently reported to have undergone an "emotional catharsis" of some therapeutic value (Cornelison and Arsenian, 1960). Success was also reported with replaying the audiotape of a previous therapy session to clients (Abell, 1963; Armstrong, 1964; Geocaris, 1960; Kidoff, 1963). Shortly thereafter the videotape recorder became available to the scientific community. There quickly appeared a deluge of reports on VTRP applications: in therapy with psychotic inpatients (Cornelison and Tausig, 1964; Moore, Chernell and West, 1965); for a patient with characterological problems (Geertsma and Revich, 1965); in group therapy with institutionalized patients (Stoller, 1965; 1967); and in individual, group, marital, and family therapy with outpatients (Alger, 1966; Alger and Hogan, 1966). This early research is examined in an excellent review by Bailey and Sowder (1970) and will not be discussed here.

In the first survey of VTRP, Danet (1968) enthusiastically concluded that the technique had great potential in therapy, despite the very preliminary nature of the research and his reservations about possible deleterious effects of VTRP. When discussing the use of self-confrontation by audio— and videotape, Holzman (1969) criticized the ad hoc nature of most theoretical explanations accounting for VTRP effects. This concern was echoed by Bailey and Sowder (1970), who underscored the lack of any clear theoretical and conceptual framework: "The underlying theoretical rationale is usually nebulous or not mentioned at all. . . ." Noting that most studies contained serious methodological and design deficiencies, they concluded that insufficient data existed to support the therapeutic effectiveness of VTRP and warned against possible harmful effects from its indiscriminate use. Soon after, Griffiths (1974) concluded that most findings in the literature were merely "post hoc rationalizations based on uncontrolled clinical observations of the sequalae of feedback." The only exception to these cautious assessments was found in a recent survey by Sanborn, Pyke, and Sanborn (1975), who concluded that VTRP was a highly successful therapeutic tool. However, critics of this survey (Gur and Sackeim, 1978) have noted that it was noncritical, most cursory, and failed to address the conceptual bases of the technique.

In view of the host of VTRP studies during the past decade, the present writers recently examined VTRP research since Bailey and Sowder's (1970) review. Our appraisal (Hung and Rosenthal, 1978) suggested that no empirical evidence supports the *independent* use of VTRP. Subsequently, further research on the topic has been reported. The present chapter summarizes our previous review and updates the area. Thus, fifty-two VTRP studies are critically reviewed, theorectical conceptions of VTRP are examined, and VTRP is discussed from a social learning theory standpoint.

VTRP: EMPIRICAL FINDINGS

VTRP Applications with Defined Populations

Marital and Family Therapy

In marital and family therapy, VTRP content has ranged from a segment of the therapy session (Alger and Hogan, 1969: Kaswan and Love, 1969) to samples of game playing (Edelson and Seidman, 1975), and role plays of problems solving (Alkire and Brunse, 1974; Jacobson, 1977; Patterson and Hops, 1972; Silk, 1972) or interpersonal interactions (Bernal, 1969; Duehn and Mayadas, 1975; Durrett and Kelly, 1974; Eisler, Hersen and Agras, 1973). Table 1-I lists the important features of these eleven studies. VTRP length ranged from two to sixty-eight minutes, with the mean duration at thirty minutes. In about half of the studies, playback was immediate. Over 80 percent used VTRP in conjunction with other treatment (e.g., modeling, role playing, counseling and instructions in behavioral principles) or having clients rate the playback after viewing it. Most studies were highly inadequate in design and measurement procedures. Thus, several advocates of VTRP proposed that it is a superb tool based on purely subjective evaluations (Alger and Hogan, 1969; Berger, 1970). Most studies lacked comparison or control groups to allow valid conclusions to be drawn about VTRP effects. Nearly half failed to include objective and reliable outcome measures. All but two (Edelson and Seidman, 1975; Eisler et al., 1973) of eleven marital and family therapy studies are ridden with faulty procedures, se-

TABLE 1-I

FEATURES OF MARITAL AND FAMILY THERAPY STUDIES

Authors	N in VTRP	Total N	Content	Length (min.)	Imm. vs Delay	Type of conjoint treatment	Type of comparison group(s)	Equal time?	Type of dependent measure	Potential therapist bias?	Follow-up?	Results
Alger & Hogan (1969)	150	150	therapy	15	I	none	none	NA	impressions	yes	no	+ good addition
Patterson & Hops (1972)	2	2	prob. solving	7	I	rate VTRP, modeling	none	NA	beh. rating	no	no	+ useful tool
Silk (1972)	50	50	prob. solving	20	D	instruction role-playing	none	NA	self-report	yes	no	+ 70% reported improvement
Eisler et al. (1973)	6	6	interaction	2	I	none	irrelevant TV; VTRP + instructions	NA	beh. rating	no	no	– little effect alone
Alkire & Brunse (1974)	12	24	role-play	60	D	discussion, role-playing	hospital treatment	no	self-report	?	no	+ increase self-concept
Duehn & Mayadas (1975)	10	10	interaction	?	I	modeling, beh. therapy	none	NA	none	yes	no	– inconclusive
Edelson & Seidman (1975)	24	76	interaction	2	I	focused feedback	feedback only; no feedback	yes	self-report	yes	no	+ improvement
Jacobson (1977)	20	20	prob. solving	?	I	beh. couns.	none	NA	beh. rating	no	no	+ improvement

TABLE 1-I (Continued)

Authors	N in VTRP	Total N	Content	Length (min.)	Imm. vs Delay	Type of conjoint treatment	Type of comparison group(s)	Equal time?	Type of dependent measure	Potential therapist bias?	Follow-up?	Results
Bernal (1969)	2	2	parent-child interaction	15	D	instruction, beh. couns.	none	NA	beh. rating	no	2 yr	+ improvement
Kaswan & Love (1969)	30	30	interview	?	D	rate VIRP, post VIRP discussion	parent couns.; child therapy	?	impression, beh. index	yes	6 wk	+ improvement
Durrett & Kelley (1974)	5	10	parent-child interaction	50	D	beh. couns. modeling	standard counseling	?	beh. rating	no	1 yr	+ improvement

verely limiting any firm conclusions about VTRP effects.

In one of the methodologically clearest marital therapy studies (Edelson and Seidman, 1975), couples were videotaped at initial interview and assigned to the following conditions: (1) focused verbal feedback, with the therapist providing constructive comments on partners' interaction pattern during the interview; (2) focused feedback plus VTRP of session; or (3) no feedback control. VTRP plus focused feedback produced more change in interpersonal perceptions — assumed to affect marital satisfaction — than both other conditions, which did not differ. These results are consistent with Eisler et al. (1975), who found that VTRP *plus* focused feedback improved nonverbal marital interaction, but no evidence favored the independent use of VTRP.

A study by Alkire and Brunse (1974) warns of potentially harmful effects in using VTRP. They found a very high casualty rate among spouses given VTRP: of nine couples, two men commited suicide and four other couples separated. Design limitations in this study notwithstanding, its results urge caution in deciding whether or not to use VTRP for marital therapy where, on the whole, the extant data do not really allow one to draw meaningful conclusions about the value of VTRP as an *independent* therapeutic device.

In the related family therapy area, all three parental counseling studies obtained favorable VTRP effects. The difference in success rates between marital and family treatment may stem from their distinctive procedures rather than the population studied. Thus, successful family therapy outcomes occurred when VTRP effects were bolstered by discussions after or during the playback, or by having clients rate the VTRP. This issue of qualifying boundary conditions in VTRP use is emphasized below.

Treatment of Alcoholism

With alcololics, VTRP content either has focused on the patient's behavior while intoxicated, or on the constrast between inebriated and sober states. Typically, an "alcohol interview" is filmed during which the patient must drink enough

(120 cc) to affect blood alcohol level and thinking processes. This interview is subsequently replayed (Faia and Sheen, 1976; Feinstein and Tamarin, 1972; Paredes and Cornelison, 1968; Paredes, Ludwig, Hassenfeld, and Cornelison, 1969b; Schaefer, Sobell, and Mills, 1971; Vogler, Compton and Weissback, 1975; Vogler, Weissback, Compton and Marten, 1977). Some studies also included a segment of the person's sober behavior in VTRP (Baker, Udin and Vogler, 1973; Sobell and Sobell, 1973). Playback was always delayed, usually presented at the next session the following day or week, with VTRP durations ranging from five to 180 seconds. Most studies combined VTRP with other treatments, such as discussions led by therapists (Faia and Sheen, 1976; Feinstein and Tamarin, 1972) or counseling in the use of behavioral principles and techniques (Baker et al., 1973; Sobell and Sobell, 1973; Vogler et al., 1975; Vogler et al., 1977). Table 1-II lists the main features of nine alcohol studies.

Early research contains the kinds of procedural shortcomings previously noted and failed to clarify VTRP effects. More recent work is methodologically clearer, and includes comparison groups as well as objective behavioral measures, such as drink preference, sip magnitude, intersip time, interdrink time, and total volume of liquor consumed (Baker et al., 1973; Schaefer et al., 1971; Vogler et al., 1975; Vogler et al., 1977). Faia and Sheen (1976) took recidivism rate as an outcome measure, and Sobell and Sobell (1973) also added such indices of daily functioning as vocational status, use of therapeutic support, and friends' evaluation of general adjustment.

VTRP used alone failed to create any gains. Even when VTRP plus discussions appeared helpful *during* treatment, there was rapid deterioration after therapy ended (Faia and Sheen, 1976; Feinstein and Tamarin, 1972). Although replays of own drunkeness may have motivating properties (Sobell and Sobell, 1973), its independent use without further therapist guidance has failed to demonstrate significant benefits. Those methodologically sound studies finding the most improvement combined VTRP with other methods into multifaceted programs (Baker et al., 1973; Sobell and Sobell, 1973; Vogler et al., 1975). Thus, when joined with alcohol education, training in

TABLE 1-II

FEATURES OF ALCOHOLISM STUDIES

Authors	N in VTRP	Total N	Content	Length (min.)	Imm. vs Delay	Type of conjoint treatment	Type of comparison group(s)	Equal time?	Type of dependent measure	Potential therapist bias?	Follow-up?	Results
Paredes & Cornelison (1968)	7	7	drunk beh.	90	D	discussion, comments	none	NA	impressions	yes	7 mo	+ improvement
Paredes et al. (1969b)	66	66	drunk beh.	11	D	none	none	NA	impressions	yes	no	−low self-esteem
Schaefer et al. (1971)	13	32	drunk beh.	30	D	none	no-VTRP; hosp. treat.	no	beh. indices	?	1 yr	−more attrition
Feinstein & Tamarin (1972)	1	1	drunk beh.	120	D	discussion	none	NA	impressions	yes	2 wk	−deterioration after termin.
Baker et al. (1973)	10	40	drunk & sober beh.	90	D	beh. couns.	beh. couns.; stand. treat.; modeling	yes	beh. indices	?	6 wk 6 mo	+ improvement
Sobell & Sobell (1975)	35	70	drunk & sober beh.	90	D	psychotherapy, beh. couns.	conventional treatment	?	beh. indices impressions	?	no	+ potential use
Vogler et al. (1975)	23	42	drunk beh.	180	D	beh. couns.	beh. couns.; beh. therapy	no	beh. indices	?	1 yr	+ improvement
Faia & Sheen (1976)	22	46	drunk beh.	20	D	discussion	discussion only	yes	beh. indices	yes	1 yr	−high recidivism

TABLE 1-II (Continued)

Authors	N in VTRP	Total N	Content	Length (min.)	Imm. vs Delay	Type of conjoint treatment	Type of comparison group(s)	Equal time?	Type of dependent measure	Potential therapist bias?	Follow-up?	Results
Vogler et al. (1977)	23	80	drunk beh.	20	D	beh. couns.	beh. couns.; beh. therapy	no	beh. indices	yes	1 yr	–no difference between groups

alternative responses to stressors, and guidance in self-control, VTRP appears to be beneficial. However, the additive effects of VTRP remain unclear since research has not yet compared how its presence versus absence affects the outcomes of multicomponent programs.

VTRP With Inpatients

Most hospitalized inpatients given VTRP were diagnosed as chronic schizophrenics. Table 1-III lists the key features of these studies. Typically, patients were shown a replay of a therapy session (Bailey, 1970; Braucht, 1970; Ennis, 1973; McNiff and Cook, 1975; Robinson and Jacobs, 1970; Shean and Williams, 1973) or an interview (Griffiths and Hinkson, 1973; Paredes, Gottheil, Tausig and Cornelison, 1969a; Resnikoff, Kagan and Schauble, 1970). Sometimes playback focused on patients' behavior while roleplaying (Edelstein and Eisler, 1976; Muzekari and Kamis, 1973). With more severely impaired psychotics, VTRP presented the patient's expressive characteristics and styles (Berger, 1973; Berman, 1972; Muzekari, Weinman and Kreiger, 1973). Except for one study giving playback the next day (Bailey, 1970), all replays were immediate, with VTRP durations ranging from four to sixty (mean = 20) minutes. Seven of fourteen studies surveyed gave VTRP in conjunction with other techniques, such as post-VTRP discussion (McNiff and Cook, 1975; Paredes et al., 1969a; Resnikoff et al., 1970), psychotherapy (Berger, 1973; Muzekari et al., 1973; Shean and Williams, 1973), and modeling plus instructions (Edelstein and Eisler, 1976).

The independent test of VTRP in over half of the inpatient research, and inclusion of comparison and control groups in 79 percent of the cases, reflect better methodology than the marital therapy studies. However, the failure of over half the studies to obtain rigorous or convergent measures of VTRP effects, and the failure of all but two studies (Griffiths and Hinkson, 1973; Shean and Williams, 1973) to provide follow-up measures, again limits the conclusions one can draw.

Methodological considerations aside, the fourteen studies surveyed yielded rather equivocal findings. Five found no differences between patients receiving identical treatment with or

TABLE 1-III

FEATURES OF STUDIES ON PSYCHIATRIC INPATIENTS

Authors	N in VTRP	Total N	Content	Length (min.)	Imm. vs Delay	Type of conjoint treatment	Type of comparison group(s)	Equal time?	Type of dependent measure	Potential therapist bias?	Follow-up?	Results
Paredes et al. (1969a)	13	40	interview	20	I	post-VTRP questions	no VTRP; VTRP of others	?	impressions clinical. test	yes	no	– no difference in clin. data
Bailey (1970)	8	24	group therapy	30	D	none	no VTRP; no-treatment	yes	self-report (Q-sort)	yes	no	+ more verbally productive
Braucht (1970)	44	73	group dis.	20	I	none	no-VTRP	yes	self-report self-rating	?	no	+ increased accuracy of self-concept
Resnikoff et al. (1970)	1	1	interview	9	I	post-VTRP discussion	none	NA	impressions	yes	no	+ heightened psychological clarity
Robinson & Jacobs (1970)	20	40	therapy	60	I	none	therapist led discussion	yes	self-rating; beh. rating	yes	no	+ improvement
Berman (1972)	15	45	identify self	14	I	none	no VTRP; VTRP of others	yes	clin. tests	yes	no	–no difference between groups

TABLE 1-III (Continued)

Authors	N in VTRP	Total N	Content	Length (min.)	Imm. vs Delay	Type of conjoint treatment	Type of comparison group(s)	Equal time?	Type of dependent measure	Potential therapist bias?	Follow-up?	Results
Berger (1973)	40	40	distorted self-image	varied	I	psychotherapy	none	NA	impressions	yes	no	+ good adjunct
Ennis (1973)	24	48	group therapy	varied	I	none	verbal feedback group therapy	?	self-rating; beh. indices	?	no	– no difference between groups
Griffiths & Hinkson (1973)	10	30	interview	?	I	none	no VTRP; VTRP of others	yes	self-report; self-rating	yes	2 wk	– changes disappeared in 2 wk
McNiff & Cook (1973)	?	?	art therapy	15	I	group dis. & hosp. milieu	none	NA	impressions	yes	no	+ improvement
Muzekari & Kamis (1973)	20	80	model-building	4	I	none	no VTRP; modeling	yes	beh. indices	yes	no	+ increased task oriented verbal beh.
Muzekari et al. (1973)	24	36	phy. char. & expression	?	I	group therapy	social interaction	yes	self-report; beh. indices	yes	no	– no difference between groups
Shean & Williams (1973)	16	48	group therapy	?	I	group therapy	group therapy only; no treatment	yes	beh. ratings	yes	3 mo	+ improvement
Edelstein & Eisler (1976)	1	1	role-play	?	I	modeling & instructions	modeling instructions	NA	beh. indices	yes	no	+ improvement

without VTRP (Berman, 1972; Ennis, 1973; Griffiths and Hinkson, 1973; Muzekari et al., 1973; Paredes et al., 1969a). Excluding reports making unsupported claims, most studies yielding positive results found VTRP only effective when conjoined with other treatment strategies. In two instances in which independent judges felt there was improvement, patients did not perceive any change (Robinson and Jacobs, 1970; Shean and Williams, 1973). Two studies found that VTRP may affect the process, but not outcome, of therapy (Bailey, 1970; Muzekari and Kamis, 1973). This finding, taken together with the success found when VTRP was used along with modeling and instructions (Edelstein and Eisler, 1976), suggest that VTRP may facilitate interaction among chronic schizophrenics, and serve as a *first* step in teaching patients useful behaviors. Once again, it appears that unless combined with further guidance, there is no evidence that VTRP per se has helped inpatients.

Improving Social Competencies

In the past five years, VTRP has been used to teach social skills to the relatively unimpaired, most of them college undergraduates. Tape content typically contained role plays of specific target behaviors, such as asserting oneself (Aiduk and Karoly, 1975; Duehn and Mayadas, 1976; Galassi, Kostka and Galassi, 1974; Scherer and Freedberg, 1976), poise in dating (Melnick, 1973), personal problem solving (Arnkoff and Stewart, 1975), interpersonal interactions (Cavior and Marabotto, 1976), or giving a speech (Blount and Pedersen, 1970; Curran and Gilbert, 1975; Fino, 1974). Playback duration ranged from five to thirty minutes and was always immediate (*see* Table 1-IV). Seven of the ten studies combined VTRP with other interventions.

VTRP in this relatively new area reflects greater scientific rigor, compared to work previously discussed. Thus, all studies included comparison groups, and most obtained objective response indices such as duration of eye contact, observer ratings of affect and assertiveness, and probe scenes for generalization of behavior changes. However, over half the studies still lacked adequate controls, and 80 percent lacked follow-up checks, sug-

TABLE 1-IV

FEATURES OF SOCIAL SKILLS TRAINING STUDIES

Authors	N in VTRP	Total N	Content	Length (min.)	Imm. vs Delay	Type of conjoint treatment	Type of comparison group(s)	Equal time?	Type of dependent measure	Potential therapist bias?	Follow-up?	Results
Blount & Pedersen (1970)	25	50	teaching	7	I	none	no VTRP	yes	self-report self-rating	yes	no	- no differences between groups
Melnick (1973)	19	59	role-play	15	I	participant modeling	modeling; PM; rfn; attent.; test-retest	yes	beh. indices self-report	?	?	+ VTRP + PM is best
Fino (1974)	?	?	speech	5	I	vary self-perception	no VTRP	yes	self-report	yes	no	- no effect
Galassi et al. (1974)	16	32	role-play	30	I	modeling, role-play	test-retest	no	beh. indices	yes	no	+ improvement
Aiduk & Karoly (1975)	12	48	role-play	?	I	none	no-treatment; beh. rehears.	yes	self-report	yes	no	- all conditions improved
Arnkoff & Stewart (1975)	14	56	prob. solving	?	I	none	modeling + VTRP; modeling; test-retest	yes	beh. ratings	yes	no	+ improved quality of information
Curran & Gilbert (1975)	16	35	role-play	10	I	beh. couns.	sys. desen.; min. contact	yes	self-report; beh. indices	no	yes	+ improvement

TABLE 1-IV (Continued)

Authors	N in VTRP	Total N	Content	Length (min.)	Imm. vs Delay	Type of conjoint treatment	Type of comparison group(s)	Equal time?	Type of dependent measure	Potential therapist bias?	Follow-up?	Results
Cavior & Marabotto (1976)	12	36	interacting	15	I	rating of VTRP	self-monitor; external agent monitoring	yes	independent beh. ratings	?	no	+ improvement
Duehn & Mayadas (1976)	1	1	role-play	?	I	beh. rehears., modeling, homework	beh. rehears.; modeling; homework	NA	beh. indices	yes	6 mo	+ improvement
Scherer & Freedberg (1976)	56	137	role-play	1-3	I	beh. rehears. + feedback	no VTRP	yes	self-report	?	1 yr	–no differences between groups

gesting that better methodology is still needed.

Nearly half the research yielded negative findings. Used alone, VTRP had no effect (Blount and Pedersen, 1970; Fino, 1974) but brought significant gains if part of a comprehensive program (Curran and Gilbert, 1975; Duehn and Mayadas, 1976; Galassi et al., 1974; Melnick, 1973) or if combined with self-ratings while viewing VTRP (Cavior and Marabotto, 1976). This last paper also addressed the importance of clients' set when viewing VTRP: when instructed to monitor negative aspects of their behavior, clients changed it more than when attending to neutral or positive conduct. It appeared that calling attention to problematic behavior can help clients to reduce it.

VTRP has also led to effects different from, but complementary to, modeling Arnkoff and Stewart, 1975; Edelstein and Eisler, 1976; Melnick, 1973). Yet, VTRP plus behavioral rehearsal was no better than assertion training alone (Scherer and Freedberg, 1976). Again, no data favor its exclusive use, but VTRP may have value as part of a braoder program. Thus far, it has augmented modeling but not role-playing outcomes (cf. Rosenthal and Bandura, 1978).

Other Therapeutic Settings

VTRP has also been tested with miscellaneous problems (*see* Table 1-V), in some cases rather creatively. Thus, Feldman and Paul (1975) systematically presented audio-visual stressor tapes to epileptics until seizures were elicited. Then, on a split screen, patients viewed both the stressor material plus a replay of themselves entering seizure while watching the stressor. This procedure sought to help clients identify triggering events of seizures and to learn adaptive coping strategies. With attempted suicides, patients' physical condition, the steps taken to save them, and their family's reactions were videotaped in the emergency room and later replayed to the patient (Resnik, Davison, Schnyler, and Christopher, 1973). A man who feared to see himself in the mirror observed his videotaped image played back, first malfocused and then progressively clearer, until he could face the sight of himself calmly (Lautch, 1970). Likewise a teenage anorexic filmed in the same brief, standard interview was repeatedly confronted with her excessively thin body (Gottheil, Backup, and Cornelison, 1968). Thus, much the same operations were applied in diverse cases for different purposes. The frequency of VTRP sessions ranged from one twenty-minute episode (Alker et al., 1976) to fifty-four exposures (Gottheil et al., 1969). Over half the studies used delayed playback, and 62 percent gave some other treatment, usually dyadic psychotherapy.

Methodological issues again greatly limit the conclusions to be drawn. Only half the studies took objective outcome data or follow-up measures, and few (25%) did both. Five of eight papers were case reports, all but one of which had no comparison groups. Not surprisingly, all five case reports found favorable VTRP results, but two of the three experiments with comparison groups obtained negative findings (Alker, 1976; Van Noord, 1973). The only experiment to find VTRP benefits based them on an unvalidated measure of self-actualization, derived from Maslow's theory, i.e. a questionable index (Smith, 1972). Hence, anecdotal reports aside, the just-cited research does not offer solid proof that VTRP, alone or with psychotherapy, has treatment value.

VTRP Research Methodology

In research up to their review, Bailey and Sowder (1970) found three commom procedural flaws: (1) adequate control groups were lacking to address confounding variables, e.g. differences among therapists and among general modes of treatment; (2) the validity and reliability of assessment procedures were questionable; and (3) failure to conduct follow-up studies. We find these flaws are still frequent and severely limit the results of work after 1970. Hence, this section examines the following aspects of method in some length: presence of comparison and control groups; temporal confounds among conditions; value of dependent measures; potential therapist bias; and follow-up measures.

Comparison and Control Groups

Of all studies, 33 percent did not compare VTRP to other

TABLE 1-V

FEATURES OF STUDIES ON MISCELLANEOUS PROBLEMS*

Author	Subjects or target beh.	N in VTRP	Total N	Content	Length (min.)	Imm. vs Delay	Type of conjoint treatment	Type of comparison group(s)	Equal time?	Type of dependent measure	Potential therapist bias?	Follow-up	Results
Gottheil et al. (1969)	anorexia nervosa	1	1	interview	54 sessions	D	post-VTRP questions	none	NA	beh. indices	yes	yes	+ increased weight
Creer & Miklich (1970)	temper tantrums	1	1	role-play	10	D	none	app. & inapp. behavior	NA	?	yes	no	+ improvement
Lautch (1970)	fear of self-image	1	1	self-image	18 sessions	D	systematic desensitization	none	NA	impressions beh. indices	yes	yes	+ improvement
Smith (1971)	undergrad. students	16	16	group activity	?	I	none	no VTRP	yes	self-report	yes	no	+ attitude improved
Resnik et al. (1973)	attempted suicide	2	2	ER activity	?	D	psychotherapy	none	NA	impressions	yes	no	+ potential use of VTRP
Van Noord (1973)	student clients	?	?	affective reactions	?	I	stimulated recall	traditional therapy	?	self-report beh. ratings	yes	no	- no difference between group
Alker et al. (1973)	undergrad. students	21	61	interview	20	I	none	no VTRP; test-retest	no	self-report	yes	yes	- no improvement
Feldman & Paul (1976)	epileptics	5	5	stressor/ seizures	varies	D	presenting stressor, therapy	none	NA	impressions beh. indices	yes	yes	+ improvement

*From *Advances in Behaviour Research and Therapy*, 1:103-185, 1978. Courtesy of Pergamon Press.

treatments but made the criterion of effectiveness pre- to post therapy gains; 88 percent of these found VTRP successful. If at least one comparison group was included, the overall success rate drops to 50 percent. Of thirty-five studies with some comparison group, thirteen only used other treatment(s), e.g. dyadic psychotherapy or modeling, yielding 62 percent success for VTRP. The remaining twenty-two studies included at least one control group, most commonly by giving all clients an identical therapy but with versus without VTRP. Thus *joint* outcome effects were usually tested but not those of VTRP itself, as suggested by Bailey and Sowder (1970). Only twelve of fifty-two total studies did provide a no treatment control group (Aiduk and Karoly, 1975; Alker et al., 1975; Arnkoff and Stewart, 1975; Baker et al., 1973; Bailey, 1970; Berman, 1972; Edelson and Seidman, 1975; Griffiths and Hinkson, 1972; Muzekari and Kamis, 1972; Schaefer et al., 1971; Scherer and Freedberg, 1976; Shean and Williams, 1973). Of these, five yielded unfavorable results, the remaining seven found VTRP effective, but sometimes only in a limited fashion. Thus, adequately controlled research at best suggests a 58 percent success rate, notably lower than the 88 percent reported in studies without comparison groups. Furthermore, reported success rates seem directly related to the degree of adequate controls, reiterating that control groups are needed in future VTRP research.

Temporal Inequalities Among Conditions

Excluding three using a multiple baseline design, of thirty-two studies that compared VTRP to some other treatment, only 61 percent clearly kept therapy time constant across conditions. Six studies omitted but another six failed to equate the duration of guidance among treatment variations (Alker et al., 1976; Alkire and Brunse, 1974; Galassi et al., 1974; Schaefer et al., 1971; Vogler et al., 1975; Vogler et al., 1977). When unequal, more time was always given to VTRP clients, in one case double that for the comparison group (Galassi et al., 1974). Failure to equalize treatment times makes extra therapist contact a confound and nullifies the purpose of comparison or control groups. However, reports with time equated did not differ in VTRP success rate (58%) from those in which VTRP clients had longer contact (60%). In themselves, temporal inequalities did not seem to affect the results, but gained importance in conjunction with the use or omission of control groups: 56 percent of the nine studies with adequate control variations that equalized time reported success, somewhat below the 69 percent aggregrate success rate. Therefore, it seems important to hold time constant in future research.

Dependent Variables

The outcome measures fall into three classes: clinical observations, behavioral data, and self-reports. One-fifth of the studies based conclusions just on therapists' subjective impressions. This invites experimenter bias and ignores both reliability and validity, as illustrated when therapist-judged "improvement" was not paralled by gains on behavioral and psychometric indices (Paredes et al., 1969a). Twelve studies took clients' self-reports, i.e. attitude ratings or inventory responses as outcome measures. Sometimes, VTRP brought behavioral gains but not improved self-reports (Robinson and Jacobs, 1970; Shean and Williams, 1973), at other times the reverse occurred (Muzekari et al., 1973). This lack of concordance plus some questionable constructs, for example self-actualization (Smith, 1970) and existential "temporal relatedness" (Alker, 1973), raises doubts about how validly the self-reports measured therapy gains.

The remaining research (53%) used behavioral measures. Thus, the number of sips per drink, volume per sip, and indices of daily functioning, e.g. number of work days missed due to drinking, were used to assess outcome in treating alcoholism (Vogler et al., 1975). Such behavioral indices as percentage of eye contact or number and nature of nonverbal gestures have served as dependent measures in social skills training (Galassi et al., 1974). Independent observers often rate clients' behavior. Thus, in terms of validity, reliability, and objectivity, such data seem the most convincing evidence for change.

The best success rate was found in studies using clinical impressions of VTRP gains (90%). Next were studies using behavioral measures (79%). The worst outcomes were based on self-report data (42%), which seems surprising until one recalls the dubious construct and predictive validity of certain self-report measures, e.g. "temporal relatedness" mentioned earlier. At present, the behavioral data seem the most meaningful measures. Clinical impressions invite inflated optimism through experimenter bias. Until such time as replicably valid inventory devices may be developed and earn wide use, self-reports depend too much on the idiosyncracies of specific instruments and hence may inflate *or* mask treatment gains. However, joint use of both behavioral and rating measures can, at this stage, augment purely overt response data and encourage the search for means to track covariation between public and private events (Bandura, 1977b; 1978; Rosenthal, 1978).

Potential Experimenter Bias

If therapists' subjective judgments serve as outcome measures, and if clinicians know the research or what treatment each client receives, the danger exists that personal expectations will lead therapists to act differently in line with which treatments they favor or discount. Yet, of twenty-nine studies potentially open to therapist bias, only two took clear precautions to control for it (Curran and Gilbert, 1975; Durrett and Kelly, 1974). Yea or nay on this control issue was not stated in ten studies, but the remaining seventeen failed to guard against therapist bias. This shortcoming needs much more attention in future VTRP research.

Follow-up Measures

Only nineteen studies gave data on follow-up, and if so, it was usually conducted either six months after treatment ended (Baker et al., 1973; Curran and Gilbert, 1975; Kaswan and Love, 1969; Paredes and Cornelison, 1968; Sobell and Sobell, 1973) or at one year later (Jacobson, 1977; Lautch, 1970; Schaefer et al., 1971; Scherer and Freedberg, 1976; Vogler et al., 1975; Vogler et al., 1977). The remaining studies had follow-up at one week (Alker et al., 1976), two weeks (Griffiths and Hinkson, 1973), two months (Faia and Sheen, 1976), three months (Shean and Williams, 1973), two years (Bernal, 1969; Gottheil et al., 1969), or three years (Feldman and Paul, 1976). VTRP success rate was lower in studies giving (61%) than those omitting (73%) follow-up data. Since immediate VTRP outcomes appeared to deteriorate over time (Feinstein and Tamarin, 1972; Griffiths and Hinkson, 1973), we find need for follow-up measures to evaluate both immediate *and* long-term VTRP effects more systematically.

Common Thrusts in VTRP Use

Closer examination of all fifty-two studies reveals certain common factors and highly consistent patterns of VTRP applications (*see* Tables 1-I; 1-V). This section deals with these qualifying conditions.

VTRP Content

Playback content falls into four categories. A majority of studies gave clients VTRP of some target response, either undesirable (24%), e.g. own drunkeness, or positive (31%), e.g., client role-playing assertiveness in hypothetical situations. VTRP of client during the therapy, being interviewed, or interacting with a significant other occurred in 38 percent of the studies. A last few (7%) contained no specific scenario, and clients just observed their own images.

VTRP success appears to reflect playback content. The worst results emerged if clients only viewed their own images or saw undesirable aspects of their own behavior; neither format exceeded 50 percent positive findings. Studies giving VTRP of rather global events, e.g. conduct during the last verbal therapy session, reported a better (63%) success rate. Replaying clients' desirable role-playing efforts brought the best results (81% of studies were successful).

Research on Objective Self-awareness suggests the confronting one's own image usually creates an unpleasant affective state (Duval and Wicklund, 1972; Wicklund, 1975). Hence, this pattern of results may stem from the valence of VTRP content. Just looking at one's videotaped image or viewing one's undesirable behavior can be aversive. Less of this occurs when VTRP contains relatively nonspecific activity. When VTRP depicts positive behavior instead, positive affect may be created. Other things equal, more favorable content seems more likely to create favorable results. However, 85 percent of studies giving VTRP of undesirable acts also used role playing as a conjoint treatment, restricting a conclusion based on the subjective valence of VTRP because the contributions of positive affect and explicit symbolic rehearsal cannot be distinguished.

VTRP Duration

Length of playback ranged from two (Edelson and Seidman, 1975) to 180 minutes (Vogler et al., 1975), with a mean of thirty-four minutes. A point-biserial correlation between VTRP duration and treatment outcome for all thirty-five studies specifying duration was not significant (r_{pb} = .21, p > .05), yet duration seems to play an important role in VTRP effects. Mean playback duration in reports with favorable outcomes was 37.9 minutes, versus 21.2 minutes in studies not finding benefits. Furthermore, two-thirds of the studies used VTRP lasting 20 minutes or less, while one-third used VTRP lasting 30 minutes or more. Only one study used VTRP·lasting over 20 but under 30 minutes (Vogler et al., 1977). Comparing the success rates for long (30 minutes or more) and short (20 minutes or less) durations reveals that 82 percent of long VTRP studies claimed positive findings compared to 57 percent using short VTRP. Thus, longer VTRP exposure seems to have more chance of producing gains. In view of the nonsignificant point-biserial, perhaps no linear relationship exists between outcome and duration. VTRP may instead depend on whether a minimum, "threshold" length is reached, but further increasing duration need not produce extra gains. The extant data suggest that playback should run at least 20 to 30 minutes and that, other things equal, durations of 40 minutes or more produce the strongest VTRP effects.

VTRP Timing

Playback was given immediately after recording in 61 percent of total studies. The remainder delayed VTRP from one day to one week, except for Kaswan and Love's (1969) two-week delay. Delayed playback studies reported a higher success rate (80%) than did immediate playback studies (61%). Among delayed playback studies, there were comparable success rates for those giving VTRP one day following one week later. Superficially, a *dichotomy* between delayed versus immediate timing seems to delay VTRP effects. Yet, this contrast is confounded with playback duration, the average length of which for immediate VTRP was 15 minutes, compared to 54 minutes for delayed playback. Given other evidence that outcomes improve if therapeutic social influence is promptly implemented by performance trials (Rosenthal, Hung, and Kelley, 1977), perhaps the only safe conclusion is that longer duration, delayed playback is more likely to produce gains than shorter, immediate VTRP.

Combined versus Exclusive Use of VTRP

Some 33 percent of studies gave VTRP alone. The remaining majority joined VTRP with other treatments, ranging from verbal psychotherapies to such behavioral techniques as modeling, role playing, focused therapist feedback, instructions on self-management principles, and therapist-led discussions. The role of VTRP has also varied from that of primary treatment, with minor additions, to being just one of many components in a multifaceted program (*see* Tables 1-I; 1-V). Studies making VTRP the sole therapy yielded a 65 percent success rate, versus 71 percent for those combining VTRP with other techniques, giving no clear evidence that increasing treatment elements enhances success. Yet, 86 percent of studies including post-VTRP discussions, self-rating the VTRP, or focused therapist feedback in treatment reported success, suggesting that certain procedures united with VTRP create better joint results than VTRP alone (65%). The existing data do not permit a systematic evaluation of many specific combinations, but some data suggest that VTRP may be more helpful if used with demonstrations by models (Edelstein and Eisler, 1976; Melnick, 1973; Walter, 1975) than in a program already containing role playing by clients as a key component (Aiduk and Karoly, 1975;

Melnick and Stocker, 1977; Scherer and Freedberg, 1976). Thus, when VTRP is redundant with other treatment elements, it also adds the least.

Context of VTRP Presentation

Except for a few studies in which clients were simply confronted with their own images on videotape (Berger, 1973; Berman, 1972; Lautch, 1970; Muzekari et al., 1973) or merely observed themselves in a drunken state (Paredes et al., Schaefer et al., 1971), over 88 percent of the research used VTRP to support *additional* contacts between client and therapist. These interactions fall into five categories (*see* Tables 1-I; 1-V): individual or group psychotherapy (32%); modeling and/or role playing (23%); therapist-led discussion (19%); counseling in behavioral principles and techniques (16%); and interviews by the therapist (10%). Only half of the interview VTRP studies reported success; 63 percent of studies using therapist-led discussions and 69 percent of those using psychotherapy reported VTRP benefits. Behavioral counseling and modeling/role playing yielded success rates of 86 percent and 90 percent respectively. Thus, VTRP effects appear to depend on the context in which client-therapist interactions occur: The best results were found when the therapist provided clients with specific and structured guidance on how to modify selected behaviors. With guidance more ambiguous, such as in verbal psychotherapy and free discussions, or nonexistent, as in standardized interviews, less therapeutic gain occurred.

Client Characteristics

None of the studies systematically explored individual differences. Yet, it seems reasonable to assume that some clients would benefit more from VTRP than others. Thus, where personality variables relating to clients' reactions have been tested, some results have been encouraging. For example, low defensive subjects viewed themselves more negatively during VTRP feedback than high defensive subjects (Kimball and Cundick, 1977). Likewise, in a nontherapy study, the accuracy of evaluating VTRP of one's own behavior was related to observer's use of defense mechanisms, as measured by an objective inventory (Kipper and Ginot, 1979). Thus, subjects characterized by "projective" styles distorted their self-perceptions the most. Another recent study using VTRP as preparatory material for a stressful medical examination found that it reduced anxiety only for patients characterized as "sensitizers" and not for "repressors" (Shipley, Butt, and Horwitz, 1979). These results further suggest that VTRP may have new, medicopsychological applications that merit serious study, especially if client variables are also taken into account. Further research is needed to identify types of clients who might benefit most from VTRP, and those most prone to harm (Alkire and Brunse, 1974).

The Current State of VTRP

With a few exceptions (Audik and Karoly, 1975; Arnkoff and Stewart, 1975; Baker et al., 1973; Bailey, 1970; Berman, 1972; Edelson and Seidman, 1975; Griffiths and Hinkson, 1973; Muzekari and Kamis, 1973; Scherer and Freedberg, 1978; Shean and Williams, 1973), most of the fifty-two studies reviewed reflect one or more shortcomings raised by Bailey and Sowder (1970). The empirical data provide no support for VTRP as an *independent* therapy. Conjoined with other techniques, VTRP may be effective, for diverse reasons in different settings. Even then, adding other treatment components precludes evaluating VTRP's unique effects, of any.

Another longstanding deficiency has been the lack of a clear theoretical framework to guide research. Even with improvements in design, most current studies approach the topic with no coherent orientation for selecting VTRP options. Plausible explanations of why VTRP may work within some boundary conditions but not others are next examined.

CONCEPTIONS OF VTRP

The main current viewpoints on VTRP effects fall within three major categories: explanations based on affect, explanations based on information, and VTRP as artifact. These conceptions are next reviewed, followed by a discussion of a cognitive-behavioral interpretation.

Explanations Based on Affect

Anxiety

One's videotaped image may serve as a powerful emotional stimulus (Berger, 1970; Yenawine and Arbuckle, 1971). Exposure to objective audiotape feedback has been shown to increase anxiety, as measured by galvanic skin response indices (Holzman, Rousy, and Snyder, 1966). Geertsma and Revich (1975) proposed that VTRP works by evoking strong affect in observers both from characteristics of the videotaped image and from the playback's psychological content. The resultant affect, i.e. anxiety, can elicit adaptive ego functions, which adjust future behavior to produce better self-perceptions. However, this view never addressed the negative consequences that arousal may produce, such as hampering performance of desirable behavior. Thus, casting VTRP as a powerful affective stimulus, which it may be, does not really explain how it works.

Self-confrontation

Some writers propose that VTRP forces patients to acknowledge aspects of their unacceptable behavior that they had previously been unwilling or unable to perceive. This conception prompted the use of VTRP to confront attempted suicides (Resnik et al., 1973), anorexics (Gottheil et al., 1969), and alcoholics (Berger, 1970; Vogler et al., 1975). Holzman (1969) sought to base a theoretical explanation on empirical data. Citing evidence for a changed ratio of bone-to-air conduction specific to hearing one's own voice, he proposed that by giving cues distinctive from what is normally heard when we talk, VTRP produces de-automatization (Gill and Brenman, 1959). This "shake-up" temporarily disrupts habitual activities and can be followed by either improvement or decrement in the organization of behavior. A confrontation view does not assume VTRP is sufficient by itself, but rather that it "primes" clients for subsequent treatment. How it primes further therapy, and the conditions favoring use of confrontation, need to be specified.

Objective Self-awareness

Wicklund (Duval and Wicklund, 1972; Wicklund, 1975) proposed a sequence of events, starting with awareness of oneself as an object, and ending in possible behavioral change. Seeing oneself on VTRP, and even the knowledge of being videotaped, can instigate a state of objective self-awareness, leading to self-evaluation and comparison of self with some standard. When such comparisons bring awareness that a negative, undesirable discrepancy exists, the self-aware state becomes aversive. Unless able to excape it, people's behavior may change to reduce the noxious discrepancy. Some indirect evidence supports this theory (Ickes et al., 1973), and Wicklund (1975) discusses diverse behavior changes produced by experimental manipulations of objective self-awareness. In contrast to informational views, the resultant changes come not from the impact of new information but from the salient effects of refocusing attention to self. Thus, objective self-awareness may offer an empirically based, theoretical explanation of how VTRP can augment other treatment effects.

Explanations Based on Information

Informational views assume that by presenting cues about aspects of self that people did not know or denied, VTRP can alter one's perceptions and cognitions, which mediate overt changes.

Nonspecific Feedback

"Feedback" has often acquired an explanatory, rather than a purely descriptive, status. Kanfer (1967) proposed that when immediate feedback is available through self-monitoring, clients can identify the consequences of their behavior and help control it. Thus, VTRP offers some unique advantages by allowing immediate recovery and review of objective data about interactions in therapy (Hollander and Moore, 1972). From a communication viewpoint, VTRP helps reveal communications inconsistencies that have previously gone unnoticed (Permulter et al., 1967; Spivack, 1974). Alger and Hogan (1969) termed this the "second chance phenomenon." Beyond imparting information that is unbiased and less prone to the distortions inherent in personal relationships, VTRP also allows people to perceive themselves much as others see them. Successful outcomes from such feedback depend on three conditions: that one lacked prior knowledge about the troublesome facets of one's behavior; that one is guided by perceiving social reactions; and that one has the skills to alter conduct to more acceptable forms.

This global feedback view seems unsatisfactory because it lacks support for its implicit assumption that the more people know about their behavior, the better they will make it. Even when the correct meanings (i.e., what is *wrong*) are extracted and processed from the information imparted by VTRP, successful action (i.e., what to *do*) need not occur unless available in the person's behavioral repertoire (cf. Rosenthal and Bandura, 1978). Typically, feedback only produces behavioral gains if combined with other guidance (Kanfer, 1967; Schaefer et al., 1971; Sobell and Sobell, 1973). No doubt VTRP can play a feedback role, but its impact will depend on its content as well as on how clients discriminate, interpret, and weigh the information (Kimball and Cundick, 1977). Little empirical evidence supports a feedback explanation cast in these global terms.

Self-concept Changes

VTRP may change self-concept in a favorable direction, thus creating positive outcomes (Boyd and Sisney, 1967). After VTRP, psychiatric patients improved their attitudes towards self (Boyd and Sisney, 1967), and student teachers rated themselves more favorably (Blount and Pedersen, 1970). However, alcoholics who saw VTRP of their own drunken behavior verbalized lower self-esteem (Paredes et al., 1969b), a pattern common in objective self-awareness research (Ickes et al., 1973). Thus, VTRP may affect self-concept, but the direction of change depends on the content of playback: observing one's positive behavior may improve, and one's negative conduct decrease, perceptions of self-worth.

After VTRP, ratings among real, ideal, and public selves (Boyd and Sisney, 1967) and between own and independent judges' ratings of subjects' self-concepts (Braucht, 1970) converged significantly. To the extent that some clients suffer from distorted self-perceptions, VTRP may shift deviant self-views closer towards social reality. Even so, no data verify that a more realistic self-concept, greater "self-actualization" (Smith, 1970), or better existential "temporal relatedness" (Alker, 1973) are valid indices of therapy gain. Again, without better specifying such relevant parameters as the content and context of VTRP and how they operate, an explanation based on self-concept changes seems too sketchy to be satisfactory.

Actor-Observer Differences in Attributions of Causality

Attribution research suggests that actors (people who engage in some behavior) mainly attribute their conduct to situational factors, but observers attribute the same act more to actors' enduring dispositions (Jones and Nisbett, 1971). This disparity stems from differences in the information available about an event and can be varied by changing the actor's and observer's viewpoints (Storms, 1973). Ronchi and Ripple (1972) have proposed that VTRP produces attributional changes: it increases belief in one's personal causality. A recent reconceptualization of actor-observer differences in causal attributions suggested that VTRP content and context variables may be important in determining VTRP effects (Monson and Snyder, 1977). The importance of context is further supported by the consistent finding that people tend to assign causality to self when efforts produce positive outcomes but to external factors when outcomes are negative (Johnson, Feigenbaum, and Weiby, 1964; Jones, Davis, and Gergen, 1961).

Thus, attribution research suggests that insofar as VTRP allows actors to become observers of their own behavior, they may reassess their personal causality. A revised view of own role and options may then alter self-regulatory standards and overt behavior. Research has shown that shifting attributions can change behavior (Kopel and Arkowitz, 1978; Mahoney and Arnkoff, 1978; Nisbett and Schachter, 1966). There is also evidence that new behavior is more likely to persist if ascribed to oneself rather than external forces (Freedman and Fraser, 1966; Lepper, 1973; Uranowitz, 1975). Thus, by turning actors into observers, VTRP may modify self-perceptions with consequent effects on overt behavior. This may be one plausible mechanism to explain why change occurs, but the context and content of VTRP, as these govern the process events assumed to be critical, need further exploration and specification.

VTRP Viewed as Artifact

Psychologists are rarely loathe to question the reality of the Emperor's new clothes. At least two conceptions dispute that VTRP itself is the spur to changes it may appear to sponsor.

Recording per se

In all VTRP studies, clients knew they were being videotaped. Might the fact of being recorded and not VTRP be responsible for any resultant effects? This notion is supported by the objective self-awareness research and data on self-monitoring (Ernst, 1973; Nelson, Lipinski, and Black, 1975). By simply calling attention to misbehavior, might not the person monitor it more closely and correct its defects? Apparently not, based on designs that included audiovisual recording without playback for control purposes but found it brought no significant improvement (Alker et al., 1976; Bailey, 1970; Blount and Pedersen, 1970; Griffiths and Hinkson, 1973; Melnick and Stocker, 1977; Paredes et al., 1969a; Schaefer et al., 1971). Lack of empirial support aside, a pure self-monitoring view is strained to predict favorable outcomes with clinical patients, who are typically poor at monitoring their internal states and other people's expressive behavior (Snyder, 1974).

"Nonspecific" Factors

Fino (1974) proposed that VTRP has little value in itself, but that nonspecific factors not part of VTRP, but associated with its therapy use, are responsible for any gains obtained. Since few studies have controlled for sheer contacts with therapists — or kept them blind to the design — one can argue that TLC from an expert plus the *novelty* of VTRP may alter patients' motivation, and thereby the process and outcome of treatment (cf. Rosenthal, 1976). Also, clinicians aware of an experiment's plan may put forth special efforts when testing a new treatment. Granting that "nonspecific" factors may contribute to VTRP effects, similar reservations will apply to most treatment efforts. Acknowledging social influence components need not preclude some active role for presenting specific VTRP under defined conditions.

Toward a Cognitive-behavioral Interpretation

None of the conceptions discussed so far seem entirely adequate. Their divergent emphases notwithstanding, almost all assume that VTRP primes people for further guidance by changing their perspective (especially regarding themselves). This is consistent with the data that VTRP has its maximum impact when conjoined with other therapies. However, most extant views either implicitly assume VTRP is a meaningful category of events (no more the case than would be giving "books" as aids to treatment) or narrow attention to one of several sets of relevant boundary conditions. This section examines some of these important emphases and seeks to integrate them into a more inclusive formulation.

Among cognitive-behavioral viewpoints, social learning theory offers a framework with particular relevance to the mechanisms underlying VTRP effects. In this approach, overt action and covert self-expectations are assumed to stem from four main sources of information (Bandura, 1977a), three of which nearly always concern VTRP use: "performance ac-

complishments" occur when clients enact the behavior being
videotaped; "vicarious exposure" occurs in the VTRP session
when clients observe themselves; and "verbal persuasion" is
present whenever clients take part in post-VTRP discussions or
receive therapists' comments. Performance, observation, and
social influence from others jointly determine the cognitive
standards and expectations that help regulate behavior.

Bandura (1977b, 1978) also proposed that perceived "self-
efficacy" is a critical mediator linking therapy events to outcome changes. Self-efficacy involves predictions about what a
person can or cannot do, as distinguished from outcome expectations about the incentive *effects* an action will create if actually performed. Both self-efficacy and outcome expectations
govern overt conduct. In turn, both are steered by personal
cognitions or predictions about reality — based on information
accessible to the person. Thus, VTRP showing that in some
contexts one can perform acts ordinarily avoided may raise
one's perception that one could perform similar behavior in
naturalistic transfer settings. Feedback about the deficiencies or
noxious aspects of one's typical conduct, and observation of its
social impact on interaction partners, may alter outcome expectations. Such cognitive shifts invite new or more rigorous self-
standards and efforts toward adaptive behavior. Both kinds of
information also offer guidance that can be augmented by new
in vivo trials, by therapist discussions and coaching, by modeling demonstrations, and by many other treatment strategies.

In applying such reasoning to VTRP effects, it is crucial to
specify the *meaning* (message-value) of playback. VTRP content and context play very important roles. For example, clients
who perceive themselves as acting fearful versus gauche versus
adept in a situation will use the same VTRP cues differently.
Likewise, a context of relative spontaneity versus therapist-
dictated response versus challenge by a natural interaction
partner, e.g. spouse, can endow the same VTRP events with
unlike meanings. Also, since VTRP self-observation is a form
of self-modeling, data on vicarious processes are pertinent here.
Rosenthal and Bandura (1978) caution that presenting a demonstration does not assure that the episode will have impact:
attention losses, encoding or retention problems, and incentive

factors can all interfere with modeled guidelines. For example, VTRP may produce no outcome gains because it is misunderstood, lacks personal relevance, or is too stressful for the observer. Clients' phenomenological stance when viewing VTRP is also important. Observers told to empathize with a model reacted unlike peers who were asked to be detached onlookers (Aderman, Brehm, and Katz, 1974). Thus, how people are oriented to observe themselves and to discriminate message content will affect the meaning clients extract from VTRP (Cavior and Marabotto, 1976). Likewise, the teaching value of guided practice with corrective feedback has been emphasized in modeling research, and again affected outcomes in empirical VTRP studies. All these considerations were largely ignored in most prior reports, perhaps explaining the historical lack of a unifying framework for VTRP research. By distinguishing among such influences as the content, context, and supplementary guidance aspects of VTRP applications, a cognitive-behavioral stance invites more effective use of the technique and more informative research on its potentialities and their boundary conditions.

CONCLUSION

A critical review of fifty-two VTRP studies reiterates our earlier (Hung and Rosenthal, 1978) appraisal: No empirical data support the *independent* use of VTRP; therapeutic gains only emerged if it was used as one facet of composite treatment programs. When found helpful, VTRP content typically depicted desirable aspects of clients' conduct, playback duration was usually thirty minutes or longer, exposure to VTRP was in main delayed, and playback was accompanied or followed by structured therapist guidance.

Consistent with empirical outcomes, a survey of explanatory formulations found no theoretical basis for why VTRP, *unless further defined* by more specific criteria, should prove beneficial. Despite considerable research, as yet there are no convincing proofs that VTRP per se has value, nor credible reasons for why it should. A cognitive-behavioral framework to organize and clarify the boundary conditions governing VTRP effects appears promising.

The foregoing is not meant to eliminate the therapeutic use of VTRP but rather to warn against its applications in global, nonspecific form. Properly combined with other techniques, it can play a useful part. Thus, conjoined with corrective feedback or other guidance, VTRP was useful in family therapy, in behavioral programs for alcoholics, and supplemented modeling (but not role playing) in social skills training. Such factors as VTRP content, client characteristics, the context in which clients receive VTRP, and the nature of concurrent interventions all seem worthy of further study. Thus many new directions (e.g., methods to help assure that clients will interpret playback as intended; the serial provision of repeated VTRP episodes as progress markers to demonstrate clients' improvement over time, etc.) appear open to exploration. Finally, evidence that apt cueing *without* overt task practice can foster important changes (Goldfried, 1979; Hung, Rosenthal and Kelley, 1980) may help clarify the extent to which VTRP promotes cognitive reorganization or restructuring under defined limiting conditions.

BIBLIOGRAPHY

Abell, R. G. A new technique for facilitating insight into dissociated material. *Science and Psychoanalysis, 6*:247-254, 1963.

Aderman, D., Brehm, S. S., & Katz, L. H. Empathic observation of an innocent victim: The first world revisited. *Journal of Personality and Social Psychology, 29*:342-347, 1974.

Aiduk, R., & Karoly, P. Self-regulatory techniques in the modification of nonassertive behavior. *Psychological Reports, 36*:895-905, 1975.

Alger, I., & Hogan, P. Enduring effects of videotaped playback experience on family and marital relationships. *American Journal of Orthopsychiatry, 39*:86-94, 1969.

Alker, H. A. The incommmeasurability of humanistic and behavioristic approaches to personality change — an empirical response. *Cornell Journal of Social Relations, 8*:105-118, 1973.

Alker, H. A., Tourangeau, R., & Staines, R. Facilitating personality changes with audiovisual self-confrontation and interviews. *Journal of Consulting and Clinical Psychology, 44*:720-728, 1976.

Alkire, A., & Brunse, A. J. Impact and possible casualty from videotape feedback in marital therapy. *Journal of Consulting and Clinical Psychology, 42*:203-210, 1974.

Arnkoff, D. B., & Stewart, J. The effectiveness of modeling and videotape feedback on personal problem solving. *Behaviour Research and Therapy, 13*:127-133, 1975.

Armstrong, R. C. Playback techniques in group psychotherapy. *Psychiatric Quarterly Supplement, 38*:247-252, 1964.

Bailey, K. G. Audiotape self-confrontation in group psychotherapy. *Psychological Reports, 27*:439-444, 1970.

Bailey, K. G., & Sowder, W. T. Audiotape and videotape self-confrontation in psychotherapy. *Psychological Bulletin, 74*:127-137, 1970.

Baker, T. B., Udin, R., & Vogler, R. E. The effects of videotaped modeling and self-confrontation on the drinking behavior of alcoholics. *International Journal of the Addictions, 10*:779-793, 1973.

Bandura, A. *Social learning theory.* Englewood Cliffs, N. J.: Prentice-Hall, 1977(a).

―――. Self-efficacy: Towards a unifying theory of behavioral change. *Psychological Review, 84*:191-215, 1977(b).

―――. Reflections on self-efficacy. *Advances in Behaviour Research and Therapy, 1*:238-269, 1978.

Berger, M. M. *Videotape techniques in psychiatric training and treatment.* New York: Brunner-Mazel, 1970.

―――. A preliminary report on multi-range immediate impact video self-confrontation. *American Journal of Psychiatry, 130*:304-306, 1973.

Berman, A. L. Videotape self-confrontation of a schizophrenic ego and thought processes. *Journal of Consulting and Clinical Psychology, 39*:78-85, 1972.

Bernal, M. E. Behavioral feedback in the modification of brat behaviors. *Journal of Nervous and Mental Diseases, 148*:375-385, 1969.

Blount, H. P., & Pedersen, D. M. Effects of videotape playback of a person on his self-concept. *Psychological Reports, 26*:667-670, 1970.

Boyd, H. S., & Sisney, V. Immediate self-image confrontation and changes in self-concept. *Journal of Counseling Psychology, 31*:291-294, 1967.

Braucht, G. N. Immediate effects of self-confrontation on the self-concept. *Journal of Consulting and Clinical Psychology, 35*:95-101, 1970.

Cavior, N., & Marabotto, C. M. Monitoring verbal behaviors in a dyadic interaction. *Journal of Consulting and Clinical Psychology, 44*:68-76, 1976.

Cline, D. W. Videotape documentation of behavioral change in children. *American Journal of Orthopsychiatry, 42*:40-47, 1972.

Cornelison, F. S., & Arsenian, J. A study of the response of psychotic patients to photographic self-image experience. *Psychiatric Quarterly, 34*:1-8, 1960.

Cornelison, F. S., & Tausig, T. N. A study of self-image experience using videotapes at Delaware State Hospital. *Delaware State Medical Journal, 36*:229, 1964.

Creer, T. L., & Miklich, D. R. The application of a self-monitoring procedure to modify inappropriate behavior: A preliminary report. *Behaviour*

Research and Therapy, 8:91-92, 1970.

Curran, J. P., & Gilbert, F. S. A test of the relative effectiveness of a systematic desensitization program and an interpersonal skills training program with date anxious subjects. *Behavior Therapy,* 6:510-521, 1975.

Danet, B. B. Self-confrontation in psychotherapy reviewed. *American Journal of Psychotherapy,* 22:245-258, 1968.

Duehn, W. D., & Mayadas, N. S. The use of video feedback and operant interpersonal learning in marital counseling with groups. *Group Psychotherapy and Psychodrama,* 28:157-163, 1975.

———. The use of stimulus/modeling videotapes in assertion training for homosexuals. *Journal of Homosexuality,* 1:373-381, 1976.

Durrett, D. D., & Kelley, P. A. Can you really talk to your child? A parental training program in communication skills towards the improvement of parent-child interaction. *Group Psychotherapy and Psychodrama,* 27:98-109, 1974.

Duval, S., & Wicklund, R. A. *A theory of objective self-awareness.* New York: Academic Press, 1972.

Edelson, R. I., & Seidman, E. Use of videotape feedback in altering interpersonal perceptions of married couples: A therapy analogue. *Journal of Consulting and Clinical Psychology,* 45:244-250, 1975.

Edelstein, B. A., & Eisler, R. N. Effects of modeling and modeling with instructions and feedback on the behavioral components of social skills. *Behavior Therapy,* 7:382-389, 1976.

Eisler, R. M., Hersen, M., & Agras, W. S. Effects of videotape and instructional feedback on nonverbal marital interaction: An analogue study. *Behavior Therapy,* 4:551-558, 1973.

Ennis, D. L. The effects of videotape feedback versus verbal feedback on the behavior of schizophrenics in group psychotherapy. *Dissertation Abstracts International,* 34:2926-2927, 1973.

Ernst, F. Self-recording and counterconditioning of a self-mutilative compulsion. *Behavior Therapy,* 4:144-146, 1973.

Faia, C., & Sheen, G. Using videotapes and group discussions in the treament of male chronic alcoholics. *Hospital and Community Psychiatry,* 27:847-851, 1976.

Feinstein, C., & Tamarin, J. Induced intoxication and videotape feedback in alcoholism treatment. *Quarterly Journal of Studies on Alcohol,* 33:408-416, 1972.

Feldman, R. C., & Paul, N. L. Identity of emotional triggers in epilepsy. *Journal of Nervous and Mental Disease,* 162:345-353, 1976.

Fino, M. J. The effects of message, videotape, and self-esteem variables on subjects' perceptions of recorded behavior in a self-confrontation situation. *Dissertation Abstracts International,* 34:3493, 1974.

Fisher, T. J., Reardon, R. C., & Burck, H. D. Increasing information seeking behavior with a model-reinforced videotape. *Journal of Counseling Psychology,* 23:234-238, 1976.

Freedman, J. L., & Fraser, S. C. Compliance without pressure: The foot-in-the-door technique. *Journal of Personality and Social Psychology,* 4:195-202, 1966.

Galassi, J. P., Galassi, M. D., & Litz, M. C. Assertive training in groups using video playback. *Journal of Counseling Psychology, 21:*390-394, 1974.

Galassi, J. P., Kostka, M. D., & Galassi, M. D. Assertive training: A one-year followup. *Journal of Counseling Psychology, 22:*451-458, 1975.

Geertsma, R. H., & Revich, R. S. Repetitive self-observation by videotape feedback. *Journal of Nervous and Mental Desease, 41:*29-41, 1965.

Gill, M. M., & Brenman, M. *Hypnosis and related stress.* New York: International Universities Press, 1959.

Goldfried, M. R. Anxiety reduction through cognitive-behavioral intervention. In P. C. Kendall & S. D. Hollon (Eds.), *Cognitive-behavioral intervention: Theory, research and procedures.* New York: Academic Press, 117-152, 1979.

Gottheil, E., Backup, C. E., & Cornelison, F. S. Denial and self-image confrontation in a case of anorexia nervosa. *Journal of Nervous and Mental Disease, 148:*238-250, 1969.

Griffiths, R. D. P. Videotaped feedback as a therapeutic technique: retrospect and prospect. *Behaviour Research and Therapy, 12:*1-8, 1974.

Gur, R. C., & Sackein, H. A. Confrontation and psychotherapy: A reply to Sanborn, Pyke, and Sanborn, *Psychotherapy: Theory, Research and Practice, 15:*258-265, 1978.

Hersen, M., & Bellack, A. S. A multiple-baseline analysis of social skills training in chronic schizophrenics. *Journal of Applied Behavior Analysis, 9:*239-245, 1976.

Hollander, C., & Moore, C. Rationale and guidelines for the combined use of psychodrama and videotape self-confrontation. *Group Psychotherapy and Psychodrama, 25:*75-83, 1972.

Holzman, P. S. On hearing and seeing oneself. *Journal of Nervous and Mental Disease, 148:*198-209, 1969.

Holzman, P. S., Rousy, C., & Snyder, C. On listening to one's own voice: Effects of psychophysiological responses and free associations. *Journal of Personality and Social Psychology, 4:*432-441, 1966.

Hung, J. H., & Rosenthal, T. L. Therapeutic videotaped playback: A critical review. *Advances in Behavioural Research and Therapy, 1:*103-135, 1978.

Hung, J. H., Rosenthal, T. L., & Kelley, J. E. Social comparison standards spur immediate assertion: "So you think you're submissive?" *Cognitive Therapy and Research 4:*223-234, 1980.

Ickes, W. J., Wicklund, R. A., & Ferris, C. B. Objective self-awareness and self-esteem. *Journal of Experimental Social Psychology, 9:*203-219, 1973.

Ingram, D. B. Videotape self-confrontation in teaching communication skills. *Dissertation Abstracts International, 35:*1772-1773, 1974.

Jacobson, N. S. Problem solving and contingency contracting in the treatment of marital disorder. *Journal of Consulting and Clinical Psychology, 45:*92-100, 1977.

Johnson, T. J., Feigenbaum, R., & Weiby, M. Some determinants and consequences of the teacher's perceptions of causation. *Journal of Educational Psychology, 55*:237-246, 1964.

Jones, E. E., & Nisbett, R. E. *The actor and the observer: Divergent perceptions of the causes of behavior.* New York: General Learning Press, 1971.

Jones, E. E., Davis, K. E., & Gergen, K. J. Roleplaying variations and their informational value to person perception. *Journal of Abnormal and Social Psychology, 63*:302-310, 1961.

Kanfer, F. Self-monitoring: Methodological limitations and clinical applications. *Journal of Consulting and Clinical Psychology, 35*:148-152, 1970.

Kaswan, J., & Love, L. Confrontation as a method of psychological intervention. *Journal of Nervous and Mental Disease, 148*:224-237, 1969.

Kidorf, I. W. A note on the use of tape recording during the therapy session. *International Journal of Group Psychotherapy, 13*:211-213, 1963.

Kimball, H. C., & Cundick, B. F. Emotional impact of videotape and reenacted feedback on subjects with high and low defenses. *Journal of Counseling Psychology, 24*:377-382, 1977.

Kipper, D. A., & Ginot, E. Accuracy of evaluating videotape feedback and defense mechanisms. *Journal of Consulting and Clinical Psychology, 47*:493-499, 1979.

Kopel, S., & Arkowitz, H. The role of attribution and self-perception in behavior change: Implications for behavior therapy. *Genetic Psychology Monographs, 92*:175-212, 1975.

Lautch, H. Videotape recording as an aid to behavior therapy. *British Journal of Psychiatry, 117*:207-208, 1970.

Lepper, M. R. Dissonance, Self-perception and honesty in children. *Journal of Personality and Social Psychology, 25*:65-74, 1973.

Mahoney, M. J. *Cognition and behavior modification.* Cambridge, Mass.: Ballinger, 1974.

Mayadas, N. S., & O'Brien, D. E. The use of videotape in group psychotherapy. *Group Psychotherapy and Psychodrama, 26*:107-119, 1973.

McNiff, S. A., & Cook, C. C. Video art therapy. *Art Psychotherapy, 2*:55-63, 1975.

Melnick, J. A comparison of replication techniques in the modification of minimal dating behavior. *Journal of Abnormal Psychology, 81*:51-59, 1973.

Melnick, J., & Stocker, R. B. An experimental analysis of the behavioral rehearsal with feedback technique in assertiveness training. *Behavior Therapy, 8*:222-228, 1977.

Monson, T. C., & Snyder, M. Actors, observers and the attribution process: Toward a reconceptualization. *Journal of Experimental Social Psychology, 13*:89-111, 1977.

Moore, F. J., Chernell, E., & West, M. J. Television as a therapeutic tool.

Archives of General Psychiatry, 12:217-220, 1965.

Muzekari, L. H., & Kamis, E. The effect of videotape feedback and modeling on the behavior of chronic schizophrenics. *Journal of Clinical Psychology, 29*:313-316, 1973.

Muzekari, L. H., Weinman, B., & Kreiger, P. A. Self-experiential treatment in chronic schizophrenia. *Journal of Nervous and Mental Disease, 157*:420-427, 1973.

Nelson, R. O., Lipinski, D. P., & Black, J. L. The effects of expectancy on the reactivity of self-recording. *Behavior Therapy, 6*:337-349, 1975.

Nisbett, R. E., & Schachter, S. Cognitive Manipulations of pain. *Journal of Experimental Social Psychology, 2*:227-236, 1965.

Paredes, A., & Cornelison, F. S. Development of an audiovisual technique for the rehabilitation of alcoholics. *Quarterly Journal of Studies on Alcohol, 29*:84-92, 1968.

Paredes, A., Gottheil, E., Tausig, T. N., & Cornelison, F. S. Behavioral changes as a function of repeated self-observation. *Journal of Nervous and Mental Disease, 148*:449-456, 1969.

Patterson, G. H., & Hops, H. Coercion, a game for two: Intervention strategies for marital conflict. In R. E. Ulrick and P. Mounjoy (Eds.), *The experimental analysis of social behavior.* New York: Appleton-Century-Crofts, 1972.

Permulter, M. S., Loeb, D. G., Gumpert, G., O'Hara, F., & Higbie, I. S. Family diagnosis and therapy using videotape playback. *American Journal of Orthopsychiatry, 37*:900-905, 1967.

Resnik, H. L. P., Davison, W. T., Schnyler, D., & Christopher, P. Videotape confrontation after attempted suicide. *American Journal of Psychiatry, 130*:460-463, 1973.

Resnikoff, A., Kagan, N., & Schauble, P. G. Acceleration of psychotherapy through simulated videotape recall. *American Journal of Psychotherapy, 24*:102-111, 1970.

Robinson, M., & Jacobs, A. Focused videotaped feedback and behavior change in group psychotherapy. *Psychotherapy: Theory, Research, and Practice, 7*:169-172, 1970.

Ronchi, D., & Ripple, R. E. *Videotape playback: To see ourselves as others see us.* Paper presented at the American Educational Research Association, Chicago, Illinois, 1972.

Rosenthal, T. L. Modeling therapies. In M. Hersen, R. M. Eisler, & P. M. Miller (Eds.), *Progress in Behavior Modification* (Vol. 2). New York: Academic Press, 1976, 53-97.

———. Bandura's self-efficacy theory: Thought *is* father of the deed. *Advances in Behaviour Research and Therapy, 1*:203-209, 1978.

Rosenthal, T. L., & Bandura, A. Psychological modeling: Theory and practice. In S. L. Garfield and A. E. Bergen (Eds.), *Handbook of psychotherapy and behavior change,* 2nd ed. New York: John Wiley and Sons, 1978.

Rosenthal, T. L., Hung, J. H., & Kelley, J. E. Therapeutic social influence:

Sternly strike while the iron is hot. *Behaviour Research and Therapy,* *15*:253-259, 1977.

Sanborn, D. E., Pyke, H. F., & Sanborn, C. J. Videotape playback and psychotherapy: A review. *Psychotherapy: Theory, Research and Practice, 12*:179-186, 1975.

Schaefer, H. H., Sobell, M. B., & Mills, K. C. Some sobering data in the use of self-confrontation with alcoholics. *Behavior Therapy, 2*:28-39, 1971.

Schaefer, H. H., Sobell, M. B., & Sobell, L. C. Twelve month follow-up of hospitalized alcoholics given self-confrontation experiences by videotape. *Behavior Therapy, 3*:283-285, 1972.

Scherer, S. E., & Freedberg, E. J. Effects of group videotape feedback on development of assertive skills in alcoholics: a follow-up study. *Psychological Reports, 39*:983-992, 1976.

Shean, G., & Williams, E. Y. The effects of videotape feedback in the behavior of chronic psychotic patients. *Psychotherapy: Theory, Research, and Practice, 10*:163-166, 1973.

Shipley, R. H., Butt, J. H., & Horwitz, E. A. Preparation to reexperience a stressful medical examination: Effect of repetitious videotape exposure and coping style. *Journal of Consulting and Clinical Psychology, 47*:485-492, 1979.

Silk, S. The use of videotape in brief joint marital therapy. *American Journal of Psychotherapy, 26*:417-424, 1972.

Smith, O. Changes in self-actualization and self-concept as result of the use of visual feedback in marathon sensitivity training. *Dissertation Abstracts International, 31*:3280, 1971.

Snyder, M. Self-monitoring of expressive behavior. *Journal of Personality and Social Psychology, 30*:526-537, 1974.

Sobell, M. B., & Sobell, L. C. Individualized behavior therapy for alcoholics. *Behavior Therapy, 4*:49-72, 1973.

Sobell, M. B., Sobell, L. C., & Mills, K. C. Alcoholics treated by individualized behavior therapy: One year treatment outcome. *Behaviour Research and Therapy, 11*:599-618, 1973.

Spivack, J. D. Interpersonal process recall: Implications for psychotherapy. *Psychotherapy: Theory, Research, and Practice, 11*:235-238, 1974.

Stoller, F. H. Closed circuit TV used for psychotherapy. *Modern Hospitals, 60*:105, 1965.

———. Group psychotherapy on TV: An innovation with hospitalized patients. *American Psychologist, 22*:158, 1967.

Storms, M. D. Videotape and the attribution process: Reversing actors' and observers' points of view. *Journal of Personality and Social Psychology, 27*:167-175, 1973.

Uranowitz, S. Helping and self-attribution, a field experiment. *Journal of Personality and Social Psychology, 31*:852-854, 1975.

Van Noord, R. W. Stimulated recall with videotape and simulation in counseling and psychotherapy: A comparison of effects of two methodologies with undergraduate student clients. *Dissertation*

Abstracts International, 34:3073-3074, 1973.

Vogler, R. E., Compton, J. V., & Weissback, T. A. Integrated behavior change techniques for alcoholics. *Journal of Consulting and Clinical Psychology, 43*:233-243, 1975.

Vogler, R. E., Weissback, T. A., Compton, J. V., & Martin, G. T. Integrated behavior change techniques for problem drinkers in the community. *Journal of Consulting and Clinical Psychology, 45*:267-279, 1977.

Walter, G. A. Effects of Videotaped training inputs on group performance. *Journal of Applied Psychology, 60*:308-312, 1975.

Wicklund, R. A. Objective self-awareness. In L. Berkowitz (Ed.), *Advances in experimental social psychology* (Vol. 8). New York: Academic Press, 1975.

Yenawine, G., & Arbuckle, S. Study of the use of videotape and audiotape as techniques in counselor education. *Journal of Counseling Psychology, 18*:1-6, 1971.

CHAPTER 2

DEVELOPMENTS IN THERAPEUTIC VIDEOTAPE AND FILM MODELING*

MARK H. THELEN, RICHARD A. FRY, PETER A. FEHRENBACH, and NANETTE M. FRAUTSCHI

THE use of videotape and film modeling in therapy was the logical outgrowth of the documented effects of live modeling (Bandura, 1969; Geer & Turtletaub, 1967; Sarason, 1968). Film and videotape modeling have advantages over live modeling because they provide the opportunity to capture "naturalistic" modeling sequences that would be difficult to create in clinic settings, and they permit greater control over the composition of the modeling scenes because the film or videotape can be reconstructed until the most desirable scenes are produced. These media also allow for the convenient use of multiple models, repeated observations of the same model, reuse of the films or videotapes with other clients, and self-administered treatment sessions. Lastly, more clients can be treated, and there is less demand on the professional's time per client.

This chapter examines the research on videotape and film modeling, herein referred to as symbolic modeling (SM), in the treatment of clinical and clinical like, i.e. analogue, problems. Anxiety reduction is a frequent treatment goal. There is a growing body of research on SM methods, which are designed to reduce the anxiety in phobias, dental and medical stress, and test anxiety. However, SM is not limited to anxiety states. The most prolific area of SM research has been in the treatment of interpersonal skills deficits where anxiety may be a factor but where learning social skills is important. In addition, there have been a few studies on other clinical problems, for example

---

*This chapter is an adaptation of an article entitled "Therapeutic Videotape and Film Modeling: A Review," published in the *Psychological Bulletin, 86*:701-720, 1979. Copyright 1979 by the American Psychological Association. Reprinted by permission.

alcoholism, drug abuse, etc.

In the following sections, the therapeutic effectiveness of SM is examined. Procedural and conceptual issues germaine to SM research are discussed. Finally, attention is given to methodological considerations, which are critical to eventually discerning the effects of SM in a variety of therapeutic settings and with various clinical populations.

EFFECTS OF THERAPEUTIC SYMBOLIC MODELING

Table 2-I summarizes the studies that have investigated therapeutic SM. The studies are grouped according to the behavior under investigation beginning with phobias, followed by test anxiety, dental and medical stress, interpersonal skills, and other clinical problems. The second column in Table 2-I notes the subjects (adults and children) and the target behavior under investigation. In the third column, studies are reported that included a no treatment, attention, or placebo control. The treatment group was either SM alone or SM plus one or more treatment components, e.g. instructions or behavioral rehearsal. Column 4 lists the results of studies involving a comparison treatment that was composed of one or more components. As with column 3, the SM condition included either SM alone or SM plus one or more additional components. The last two columns of Table 2-I contain information pertinent to generalization and maintenance: whether or not these factors were assessed and, if so, whether the results were affirmative or negative. Finally, the table presents the time interval between the treatment intervention and the assessment of maintenance.

The results, as they are summarized in Table 2-I, pertain to between-group differences, usually based on posttest differences or differences in change scores between groups. The symbol "less than" (<) denotes less *improvement* in the clinical behavior, and the symbol "greater than" (>) is meant to indicate greater *improvement* in the clinical behavior. For example, the first study listed in Table 2-I is by Bandura and Barab (1973). The table shows that SM was greater than an irrelevant film. This should by interpreted to mean that the SM group improved more than the control group, that is the SM group

TABLE 2-I

RESULTS OF SYMBOLIC MODELING STUDIES

Authors	Subjects	Symbolic Modeling vs. Control	Symbolic Modeling vs. Comparison Treatment	Generalization	Maintenance
PHOBIAS					
Bandura & Barab (1973)	Adults, snake fear	SM > irrelevant film on B, physiological, & SR*		Yes	Not assessed
Bandura, Blanchard, & Ritter (1969)	Adults, snake fear	SM + relaxation > no treatment on Att, B, & SR*	SM + relaxation > desensitization on SR & = desensitization on B; SM + relaxation < live modeling + participation on Att, B, & SR*	Yes	1 mo. Yes
Bandura & Menlove (1968)	Children, dog fear	SM > irrelevant film on B*;		Yes	1 mo. Yes
Denney & Sullivan (1976)	Adults, spider fear	SM > no treatment on B & SR* SM + relaxation > no treatment on B & SR*	SM > spider only film on B & SR	Not assessed	Not assessed
Hill, Liebert, & Mott (1968)	Children, dog fear	SM > no treatment on B		Not assessed	Not assessed
Kornhaber & Schroeder (1975)	Children, snake fear	SM > no treatment on Att & B*		Not assessed	Not assessed
Lewis (1974)	Children, water fear	SM > irrelevant film on B SM + guided participation irrelevant film on B	SM < guided participation on B SM + guided participation > guided participation on B; SM + guided participation > SM on B	Yes	Not assessed
Lira, Nay, McCullough, & Etkin (1975)	Adults, snake fear	SM > no treatment on Att & = no treatment on B & SR	SM > snake only film on Att & = snake only film on B & SR; SM < rehearsal on B & = rehearsal on Att & SR	Not assessed	2 mos. Yes

TABLE 2-I (Continued)

Authors	Subjects	Symbolic Modeling vs. Control	Symbolic Modeling vs. Comparison Treatment	Generalization	Maintenance
Morris, Spiegler, & Liebert (1974) Spiegler, Liebert, McMains, & Fernandez (1969)	Adolescents, snake fear	SM > irrelevant film on SR*	SM > snake only on SR*	Not assessed	Not assessed
Experiment I	Adults, snake fear	SM > no treatment on B*a		Not assessed	1 mo. Yes
Experiment II	Adults, snake fear	SM > no treatment on B		Not assessed	Not assessed
Experiment III	Adults, snake fear		SM + relaxation > relaxation on B	Yes	1 wk. Yes
Weissbrod & Bryan (1973)	Male children, snake fear		SM > SM with snake replica on B	Not assessed	2 wks. Yes
TEST ANXIETY					
Andrews (1973)	Adults, test anxiety	SM + relaxation > no treatment on B & = no treatment on SR		Not assessed	Not assessed
Jaffe & Carlson (1972)	Adults, test anxiety	SM > no treatment on B & SR*		Not assessed	Not assessed
Malec, Pack, & Watkins (1976)	Adults, test anxiety	SM > no treatment on SR*		Not assessed	Not assessed
Mann (1972)	Adults, test anxiety	SM > no treatment on B & SR; SM + relaxation > no treatment on B & SR	SM = SM + relaxation on B & SR	Not assessed	6 wks. Yes
DENTAL/MEDICAL STRESS					
Machen & Johnson (1974)	Preschoolers, dental fear	SM > control on B	SM = desensitization on B	Not assessed	Not assessed
Melamed, Hawes, Heiby, & Glick (1975)	Children, dental fear	SM ˙> irrelevant film on B & staff rating & = irrelevant film on physiological & SR		Not assessed	Not assessed

TABLE 2-I (Continued)

Authors	Subjects	Symbolic Modeling vs. Control	Symbolic Modeling vs. Comparison Treatment	Generalization	Maintenance
Melamed & Siegel (1975)	Children, hospital fear	SM > irrelevant film on physiological, B, SR*, & parent ratings*		Not assessed	3 wks. Yes*
Melamed, Weinstein, Hawes, & Katin-Borland (1975)	Children, dental fear	SM > irrelevant task on B & staff rating & = irrelevant task on SR		Not assessed	Not assessed
Shaw & Thoresen (1974)	Adults, dental fear	SM + relaxation > assessment only on B, SR*, & Att*	SM + relaxation > audiotape discussion on B, Att*, & SR*; SM + relaxation > desensitization on Att* & = desensitization on B & SR	Not assessed	3 mos. Yes
Vernon (1973)	Children, anesthesia fear	SM > control on B* & = control on parent rating		Not assessed	4 wks. Yes*
Vernon (1974)	Children, innoculation fear	SM > control on B* & = control on staff rating		Not assessed	Not assessed
Vernon & Bailey (1974)	Children, anesthesia fear	SM > control on B & = control on staff rating		Not assessed	Not assessed
Wroblewski, Jacob, & Rehm (1977)	Adults, dental fear	SM = placebo on B & SR	SM < SM + relaxation on B* & = SM + relaxation on SR	Not assessed	2 wks. Yes*

INTERPERSONAL SKILLS[b]

Authors	Subjects	Symbolic Modeling vs. Control	Symbolic Modeling vs. Comparison Treatment	Generalization	Maintenance
Burrs & Kapche (Note 1)	Adult psychiatric pts., social skills deficit	SM + 3 components = no treatment on SR & staff rating		No	1 mo.[c] No
Curran (1975)	College students, dating anxiety	SM + 4 components > waiting list on B & = waiting list on SR	SM + 4 components = desensitization on B & SR; SM + 4 components > relaxation on B & = relaxation on SR	Not assessed	Not assessed
Curran & Gilbert (1975)	College students, dating anxiety	SM + 6 components > minimal contact on B* & SR	SM + 6 components > desensitization on B* & = desensitization on SR	Not assessed	6 mos. Yes
Curran, Gilbert, & Little (1976)	College students, dating anxiety		SM + 5 components > sensitivity training on B & SR*	Not assessed	Not assessed

TABLE 2-I (Continued)

Authors	Subjects	Symbolic Modeling vs. Control	Symbolic Modeling vs. Comparison Treatment	Generalization	Maintenance
Eisler, Hersen, & Miller (1973)	Adult male psychiatric pts., unassertiveness	SM + rehearsal > test-retest on B*	SM + rehearsal > rehearsal on B*	Not assessed	Not assessed
Evers & Schwartz (1973)	Preschoolers, social isolation		SM < SM + praise on B*	Not assessed	4 wks.
Evers-Pasquale & Sherman (1975)	Preschoolers, social isolation	SM > control film on B		Not assessed	No
Galassi, Galassi, & Litz (1974)	College students, unassertiveness	SM + 3 components > assessment only on B* & SR		Not assessed	4 wks.
Galassi, Kostka, & Galassi (1975)	Follow-up of Galassi et al. (1974)			Not assessed	Yes
Goldstein, Martens, Hubben, VanBelle, Schaaf, Wiersma, & Goedhart (1973)				Not assessed	Not assessed
Experiment I	Adult neurotics, dependence	SM > assessment only on B*		Not assessed	1 yr.
Experiment III	Adult schizophrenics, independence	SM > assessment only on B; SM + instructions > assessment only on B	SM = instructions on B; SM = SM + instructions on B; SM + instructions = instructions on B	Not assessed	Yes*
Gottman (1977)	Preschoolers, social isolation	SM + control film on B & status		Not assessed	6 wks.
Gottman, Gonso, & Schuler (1976)	Children, low sociometric status	SM + 2 components > attention control on status* & = attention control on B		Not assessed	No; 6 wks.; Yes*d
Gutride, Goldstein, & Hunter (1973)	Adult psychiatric pts., social interaction	SM + 3 components > assessment only on B* & SR*		No	Not assessed
Hersen, Eisler, & Miller (1974)	Adult psychiatric pts., unassertiveness	SM + 2 components > test-retest on B*	SM + 2 components > rehearsal on B*	Yes*	Not assessed

TABLE 2-I (Continued)

Authors	Subjects	Symbolic Modeling vs. Control	Symbolic Modeling vs. Comparison Treatment	Generalization	Maintenance
Hersen, Eisler, Miller, Johnson, & Pinkston (1973)	Adult psychiatric pts., unassertiveness	SM + components > test-retest on B* & = test-retest on SR; SM + rehearsal > test-retest on B* & = test-retest on SR	See footnote[e]; SM + 2 components > SM + rehearsal on B* & = SM + rehearsal on SR	Not assessed	Not assessed
Jaffe & Carlson (1976)	Adult male psychiatric pts., asocial behavior	SM + rehearsal > attention control on B* & staff ratings*	SM + rehearsal = instructions + rehearsal on B & < instructions + rehearsal on staff ratings*	Yes*	1 mo. Yes*
Jakibchuk & Smeriglio (1976)	Preschoolers, social isolation	SM + self-guiding comments control film on B; SM R self-guiding comments > assessment only on B; SM + narration = control film on B; SM + narration = assessment only on B[f]	SM + self guiding comments > SM + narration on B[f]	Not assessed	3 wks. Yes
Keller & Carlson (1974)	Preschoolers, social isolation	SM > control film on B		Not assessed	3 wks. No
McFall & Twentyman (1973)	College students, unassertiveness	SM + rehearsal > assessment only on SR	SM + rehearsal = audiotaped modeling + rehearsal on SR	Yes	2 wks. Yes
O'Connor (1969)	Preschoolers, social isolation	SM > control film on B		Not assessed	Not assessed
O'Connor (1972)	Preschoolers social isolation	SM > control film on B; SM + shaping > control film on B	SM > shaping on B; SM + reinforcement > reinforcement on B; SM + reinforcement = SM on B	Not assessed	3 wks. Yes
Rathus (1973)	College students, unassertiveness	SM + 2 components > placebo on B & SR*; SM + 2 components > assessment only on B & SR*		Not assessed	Not assessed
Thelen, Fry, Dollinger, & Paul (1976)	Male delinquents, interpersonal behavior	SM + rehearsal > control tapes on staff ratings & = control tapes or teacher ratings		Not assessed	2 wks. No
OTHER CLINICAL PROBLEMS					
Baker, Udin, & Vogler (1975)	Adult males, alcoholism		SM < self confrontation + behavioral counseling on B	Not assessed	6 wks.[g] No

TABLE 2-I (Continued)

Authors	Subjects	Symbolic Modeling vs. Control	Symbolic Modeling vs. Comparison Treatment	Generalization	Maintenance
Reeder & Kunce (1976)	Adults, heroin addiction	SM > no treatment on B	SM + discussion > lecture + discussion on B	Not assessed	Yes[h]
Thomas (1974)	Children, classroom attention			Not assessed	Not assessed
Van Camp (1972)	Adults, marital conflict	SM = practice on B & SR		Not assessed	Not assessed
Wincze & Caird (1976)	Adult females, sex anxiety	SM > waiting list on SR*	SM < systematic desensitization on SR*	Not assessed	Not assessed

Note: SM = symbolic modeling, B = behavioral measure, SR = self report measure excluding attitude measures, Att = attitude measure, > indicates greater improvement, − indicates no differences, < indicates less improvement, * indicates that the results were mixed.

a. An SM without narration group = no treatment on B; and SM + narration group > no treatment on B.

b. When a condition consisted of two or more components, in addition to SM, only the number of components is indicated. The following components were used in one or more of the studies: instructions, rehearsal, feedback, homework, relaxation, discussion, reinforcement, and communication training.

c. Similar results were obtained at a 3 month follow-up.

d. Post test data collected 6 weeks after intervention.

e. SM + rehearsal + instructions > rehearsal + instructions on B* & = rehearsal + instructions on SR; SM + rehearsal + instructions > rehearsal + instructions on B* & = rehearsal on SR; SM + rehearsal > on B* & = rehearsal on SR;
SM + rehearsal < rehearsal + instructions on some B measures and > rehearsal + instructions on other B measures, & = rehearsal + instructions on SR.

f. Because of its importance in this study, narration is reported as a separate component. It is not considered as a separate component for the other studies.

g. Similar results were obtained at a 6 month follow-up.

h. Post test data collected 90 days and 180 days after intervention.

showed greater fear reduction. An equal sign (=) indicates no differences between groups.

In this section, an overview will be presented of the kinds of clinical and analogue problems to which SM has been applied. In a later section, the methodological problems associated with these studies will be discussed.

Phobias

As can be seen in Table 2-I, research on phobias has been done with both adults and children. The target behaviors have included fears of animals, spiders, and water. The purpose of the SM treatment is to reduce anxiety so that the subject will be able to perform the feared task, e.g. touch a snake.

The third column in the table reveals that SM, both with or without added components, was effective in reducing phobic behavior in comparison with untreated subjects and those who observed an irrelevant film. The fourth column reveals that SM compares favorably with other treatment components, especially if SM was combined with relaxation or guided participation. The last two columns of Table 2-I show that, when assessed, generalization and maintenance effects were obtained.

Test Anxiety

Four studies have been reported that appraised the effects of SM, often including vicarious relaxation, on test-anxious adults. Table 2-I reveals that generally positive effects have been obtained for SM in comparison with control groups; however, no research has compared SM with other treatment components. None of these studies reported an assessment of generalization, and only one study (Mann, 1972) assessed the maintenance of the treatment effects. Mann found that changes were maintained six weeks after treatment. The research in this area is too sparse to offer much useful information for the practicing clinician.

Dental/Medical Stress

In contrast to the experimental nature of the phobia research and the limited work on test anxiety, a number of applied studies have used SM to alleviate stress and disruptiveness in dental and medical patients, typically among people who have had no prior dental work or surgery. Prior to the actual dental work or surgery, the modeling film or videotape is shown to each treatment subject. Looking at the column on Table 2-I that compares SM with control groups, it can be seen that all but one of the studies (Shaw & Thoreson, 1974) used SM alone, and the studies typically did not involve other components. It appears that SM is often effective in comparison with controls according to behaviorally based measures, but the results are less clear for measures obtained from staff ratings, peer ratings, and self-reports.

As shown in column 4, only three studies (Machen & Johnson, 1974; Shaw & Thoreson, 1974; Wroblewski, Jacob, & Rehm, 1977) have investigated the effect of SM relative to other treatment components, e.g. desensitization. Given the mixed findings of these few studies, a definite statement about the relative effectiveness of SM and other treatments is not possible.

Generalization as such has not been assessed by researchers in this area; however, the dependent measure was often taken in the natural setting so that additional measures to assess generalization were probably not necessary. Maintenance of treatment effects, ranging from three weeks to three months, was appraised in four studies (Melamed & Siegel, 1975; Shaw & Thoreson, 1974; Vernon, 1973; Wroblewski et al., 1977) and all of these studies found at least some indication of maintenance.

Interpersonal Skills

SM has been used extensively to facilitate assertiveness, social interaction, and the development of other appropriate social skills. This area of research contains the largest number of studies involving SM. Studies have been done with children, adolescents, college students, and adult psychiatric patients. The third column of Table 2-I shows that SM alone generally resulted in greater improvement than controls, although two studies found no differences in the effects of SM and control conditions on the social interaction of isolated preschoolers

(Gottman, 1977; Jakibchuk & Smeriglio, 1976). With five exceptions SM plus other treatment components, often three or four in number (*see* footnote b in Table I), typically resulted in greater improvement than a control condition. In three of these five studies, the failure to obtain significant differences between a treatment condition including SM and a control condition was based on self-report measures (Burrs & Kapche, 1969; Curran, 1975; Hersen et al., 1973).

Of the studies that compared the effects of SM plus other components with a control group, nearly all (13 of 15 studies) contained rehearsal: four, a discussion component; three, a homework component; two, a reinforcement component; and one, a communication training component. Eight of the thirteen studies that contained SM plus rehearsal included other components as well. There is a need to independently manipulate SM and other treatment components, especially rehearsal, to appraise their separate and joint effects. Additionally, definitive statements about the individual and combined effects of treatment components are difficult to make because of differences in dependent measures and the frequent use of multicomponent treatment packages.

Most of the studies that compared SM with other treatments involved SM plus one or more additional components. The two components most frequently combined with SM were rehearsal (8 studies) and instructions (7 studies). Of the seventeen group comparisons involving SM plus one or more additional components in which a behavioral measure was used, the condition that included SM resulted in greater improvement than the comparison treatment in eleven instances and was equal to the comparison treatment in six instances. However, with the self-report measures, conditions that contained SM resulted in greater improvement than the comparison treatment in only one (Curran, Gilbert, & Little, 1976) of the ten instances. It appears that SM plus additional components compares favorably with alternative treatments based on behavioral measures, but few differences have been found on self-report measures. Two explanations are offered for this finding (differences on behavioral but not self-report measures). First, the behavioral measures were typically obtained during role-play situations that were similar if not identical to those used in the treatment sessions. Changes in pre-post measures, then, may reflect increased role-playing skills due to practice or merely improvement in those situations used in training rather than a general improvement of social skills. These changes would not be reflected on more global measures, such as self-report measures. Second, if training resulted in changes in general social skills, it may require a period of time for these changes to be incorporated in a person's self-perception and self-report. Hersen and Bellack (1976) have labeled this phenomenon "attitudinal lag."

Also shown in the fourth column of Table 2-I are five studies in which the comparison treatment included SM. These studies indicate that SM plus praise is more effective than SM alone in increasing social interaction among socially isolated children (Evers & Schwartz, 1973). However, O'Connor (1972) found that shaping did not make a similar additive contribution to SM alone. Instructions, when included in a treatment package including SM plus rehearsal, facilitated the development of assertive behaviors more than just SM plus rehearsal (Hersen et al., 1973). However, SM plus instructions was equivalent to SM alone in increasing independent behavior (Goldstein et al., 1973). Also, Jakibchuk and Smeriglio (1976) reported that treatment conditions which included SM plus first person, self-guiding comments were superior to those which included SM plus narrative, third-person comments in the sound track. This study will be discussed further in a later section. Because of insufficient research on any one component and differences in the dependent measures and populations employed, the practitioner is offered limited guidance regarding which components most effectively combine with SM.

In research on interpersonal skills, generalization has usually not been assessed. Of those studies which assessed generalization, three found that SM, at least as one component, facilitated generalization (Hersen, Eisler, & Miller, 1974; Jaffe & Carlson, 1976; McFall & Twentyman, 1973), whereas two studies failed to find such effects (Burrs & Kapche, 1969; Gutride, Goldstein, & Hunter, 1973). However, as with the dental/medical research, studies involving social isolation in preschoolers have assessed the subjects' behavior in the natural settings, during children's interactions at nursery school. Generalization to home or other settings has not been assessed. The results concerning maintenance are also very mixed. Of the thirteen studies that assessed maintenance, eight found some evidence for maintenance, and five obtained negative results.

Other Clinical Problems

This section of Table 2-I contains five studies that focused on problems not incompassed by the previous sections. Since no problem area was investigated more than once, it is impossible to make any definitive observation with respect to the influence of SM. However, we can expect increased attention to the use of SM with substance abuse and marital problems.

CONCEPTUAL AND PROCESS CONSIDERATIONS

Attention is given in this section to variables and processes that have been studied within the context of SM research and that have relevance to theoretical and applied considerations. Attending to the process considerations may facilitate theorizing regarding modeling and a further refinement of the applications of SM and may aid the clinician in decision making regarding the composition of the material.

Model-Observer Similarity

Model-observer similarity has drawn the attention of many researchers. Two variables in particular, model age in relation to observer age and the presentation of a coping versus a mastery model, have received considerable attention.

Bandura and Barab (1973) reported that adults showed as much snake-fear reduction after observing a child model as subjects who observed a peer model. Fear measures included behavioral, self-report, and physiological measures. Similarly, Weissbrod and Bryan (1973) exposed children to a same age or a younger age model and found no difference between the two groups on a behavioral approach to snakes measure. The reader will note that neither of the above two studies contained a model who was older than the subjects. Kornhaber and Schroeder (1975) addressed this question by exposing snake-fearing children to either a child or an adult model. Those subjects who observed a child model demonstrated greater fear reduction on a behavioral avoidance test than those who observed an adult model, but there were no differences on an attitude measure. Furthermore, Kornhaber and Schroeder found that children who observed an adult model did not show greater fear reduction than did a no-treatment control group. Although these studies are limited in number, they are reasonably consistent. With adult subjects, it appears that observing a same age or child model facilitates fear reduction. Similarly, children experience the same degree of fear reduction when exposed to peer-aged or younger models. However, the observation of adult models has minimal effects upon children. Children may see older models as superior and more capable and, therefore, may not imitate their approach behavior in a fearful situation. On the other hand, when adults observe children or when children observe younger children, they may be motivated to perform the approach response (Bandura & Barab, 1973). Bandura and Barab reported that adult subjects who observed an adult model showed a positive correlation between fear extinction (based on autonomic responses) and behavioral improvement, which they interpreted as vicarious extinction. In contrast, the adult subjects who observed a child model demonstrated little relationship between fear extinction and behavioral improvement, which suggests that motivational factors served to influence approach behavior. In other words, "if that kid can do it so can I." No applied research has been done on the effects of model-subject age differences when both model and subject are adults.

A related issue with respect to model-observer similarity is whether so-called "coping" models, who are presented as initially having difficulties (e.g., anxiety) and then overcoming their problems, are more effective than "mastery" models, who demonstrate the desirable behavior with skill from the outset. In the studies just reviewed, coping models were often used, but the coping-mastery variable was infrequently manipulated. However, a few studies shed light on this problem.

In a study with snake-avoiding college females, Meichenbaum (1971) suggested that the coping-mastery variable might relate to the broader question of model similarity, which has been shown to enhance imitation (Rosekrans, 1967). In the Meichenbaum study, the coping models displayed initially hesitant behavior, but later fearlessly interacted with the target snake, whereas the mastery models were fearless throughout the modeling sequences. Meichenbaum found that the subjects who observed the coping models improved more than subjects in the mastery condition. A similar procedure was used to alleviate interview anxiety in psychiatric patients (Bruch, 1975). Bruch's results were not as consistent as Meichenbaum's, but he reported improvement of subjective anxiety according to self-ratings among the coping subjects as compared with the mastery subjects. Working in the area of anxiety associated with surgery, Vernon (1974) reported that subjects who observed a model who showed some degree of pain were subsequently rated as experiencing less pain than were subjects who observed a model who did not demonstrate pain. Perhaps a study that fails to demonstrate effects is as important as affirmative studies. Lira, Nay, McCullough, and Etkin (1975) reported that adult female subjects who observed a fearless "expert" model were uninfluenced by that model as compared with a control group based on behavioral and self-report measures. Meichenbaum (1971) acknowledged, however, that the greater effectiveness of the coping model in his study could have stemmed from the modeling of coping techniques that were an inherent feature of the coping condition, rather than from the perceived similarity between observer and model per se. In consideration of this point, Kornhaber and Schroeder (1975) presented models who did not demonstrate deep breathing, which was central to Meichenbaum's coping model. With this confound removed, Kornhaber and Schroeder found greater change in evaluative attitudes toward snakes among those who observed a fearless model, but they obtained no differences on a behavioral measure. Also, Jaffe and Carlson (1972) found no differences on behavioral and self-report measures of test anxiety between adults who observed a calm model and adults who observed an anxious model. These findings are generally consistent with

Kornhaber and Schroeder's (1975) suggestion that with model coping skills removed, the greatest effect of a coping model may be on attitudes rather than on overt behavior.

A number of other researchers have adopted the Meichenbaum procedures in their applications of SM to clinical problems. The more focal problems of phobias and stress associated with dental and medical procedures have been responsive to the coping manipulations. Lewis (1974) found water-phobic subjects to be significantly improved at the posttreatment assessment after they observed a coping model. Hill, Liebert, and Mott (1969) and Spiegler, Liebert, McMains, and Fernandez (1969) combined the mastery and coping procedures by depicting an "expert" model who demonstrated competent dog or snake handling to an initially apprehensive, i.e. coping model. The second model then imitated the first model. Both research groups found moderate support for the combined modeling approaches based on behavioral measures. In her studies of dental anxiety (Melamed, Hawes, Heiby, & Glick, 1975; Melamed, Weinstein, Hawes, & Katin-Borland, 1975) and anxiety associated with surgery (Melamed & Siegel, 1975), Melamed used coping models to successfully reduce the disruptive behavior of children undergoing these procedures. Except for Gottman (Gottman, 1977; Gottman, Gonso, & Schuler, 1976), who obtained weak effects, most studies have reported positive effects using a coping model with interpersonal problems (Evers & Schwarz, 1973; Evers-Pasquale & Sherman, 1975; Jakibchuk & Smeriglio, 1976; O'Connor, 1969, 1972; Thelen et al., 1976).

Narration

Based on current theorizing (Bandura, 1977), narration should facilitate attention to the model and verbal labeling of the critical model behavior, and thereby increase the effectiveness of modeling interventions. Jakibchuk and Smeriglio (1976) reported that SM plus narration failed to significantly affect the social behavior of isolated preschool children in comparison with two control groups. However, researchers have reported that SM plus narration diminishes snake fears in adults

(Spiegler et al., 1969), social isolation among preschoolers (Evers-Pasquale & Sherman, 1975; Keller & Carlson, 1974; O'Connor, 1969, 1972), and anesthesia fear among children (Vernon & Bailey, 1974). Since SM alone often has a favorable effect, it is of questionable value to demonstrate that SM plus narration has a favorable effect. Perhaps the greater question is whether narration has an incremental effect over SM alone. In a relevant study, Morris et al. (1974) found that SM plus narration was no better than SM alone on a self-report measure of snake fear among adolescents.

Although the effect of adding narration to SM is uncertain, Jakibchuk and Smeriglio (1976) reported a timely study in which they compared narration with the influence of self-guiding model comments on the social isolation behavior of preschool children. Children exposed to SM plus self-guiding comments by the model improved more than children in two control conditions and in an SM plus narration condition. These findings are consistent with the earlier work of Meichenbaum (1971), who reported that a model's self-verbalization facilitated reduction of snake fear among female undergraduates. It may be that self-verbalization facilitates the conversion of the model's behavior into perceptual-cognitive images, as described by Bandura (1977). Perhaps model self-verbalizations are expecially facilitative when the model behavior is relatively complex, because they would enhance the clarity of the model behavior.

Context and Complexity of Model Behavior

The context of the videotape or film may be critical to the client's attention to the model. It is suggested that the model context needs to be sufficiently simple to insure attention to the critical model behaviors, but it should also contain enough contextual cues to facilitate generalization to other settings. Furthermore, as the complexity of the target behavior increases, such as with interpersonal behavior, there may be greater need to both simplify and amplify the target behaviors. An example of such simplification of complex target behaviors is Hersen et al.'s (1973) reliance on eight response modalities characteristic of assertive responses. These included a lengthy reply, a request for behavior change, consistent eye contact, a refusal to comply with unreasonable requests, a fully audible speaking voice, an assertive affect, a quick latency of response, and overall assertiveness. Elaborative or focusing narration, self-guiding comments, or instructions may be used in conjunction with simplified target behavior to increase further the subject's attentiveness to relevant materials. By these means, the client's attention is directed to the subtleties of the interpersonal interactions, which may otherwise go unnoticed in daily naturalistic modeling.

In the course of developing modeling films for interpersonal skills, it is important to avoid overwhelming the client. Even with simplification and elaboration it is possible to overload the client with too many significant points of focus. Burrs and Kapche (1969) failed to achieve successful results using SM with psychotic inpatients. In his criticism of their study, Goldstein (1973) cited their research as an attempt to cover too much ground in short videotapes. However, when combined with role playing, SM may be effective with more complex skills, e.g. requesting new behavior, whereas instructions may be adequate for less complex skills, e.g. eye contact (Eisler et al., 1973; Hersen et al., 1974; Hersen et al., 1973).

Uncertainty, Arousal, and Model Warmth

Other factors are also very likely to be relevant to the matter of attention to and imitation of the model. For example, Yussen & Levy (1975) found that subjects who observed a warm live model attended to the model and recalled the model's behavior more than did subjects who observed a neutral live model. Others have suggested that uncertainty in the observer may increase attention to and subsequent imitation of a model (Marlatt, 1972; Thelen, Dollinger, & Kirkland, 1979; Thelen, Paul, Dollinger, & Roberts, 1978). If this is the case, it is likely that clients will profit most from SM when they actively seek information regarding appropriate behavior, e.g. shortly before a stressful medical procedure. On the other hand, if a client experiences extreme anxiety in anticipation of a stressful event or if the model's behavior creates a great deal of anxiety in the client, the client may avoid attending to the model.

Retention

Since most researchers failed to collect data on maintenance, there is relatively little material relevant to the question of retention. The behavioral rehearsal and practice components that were so frequently used in the interpersonal skills research might be expected to facilitate not only immediate imitation of the model but also the retention of the modeled behavior (Bandura, 1977). However, there is no research that documents the influence of rehearsal and practice following observation of symbolic model on the retention of that behavior. Research by Thelen, Fryrear, and Rennie (1971) with a nonclinical target behavior, i.e. standards of self-reward, suggests that the influence of observing a model can have long-term effects. Given the limited research, a practitioner who used modeling tapes or films might wish to do a follow-up to assess whether the therapeutic changes were maintained.

Model Consequences

When constructing modeling materials, model reinforcement can easily be incorporated. Model consequences have been extensively researched (Thelen & Rennie, 1972) and are important to the theorizing of Bandura (1977), who ascribed both informational and incentive functions to this variable. Many of the studies that focused on anxiety-related problems did not contain model consequences, perhaps because of the assumption that the absence of negative consequences following the demonstration of the feared act in itself serves as positive model reinforcement. Model consequences were included in some of the studies on social isolation in preschoolers (Evers & Schwarz, 1973; Evers-Pasquale & Sherman, 1975; O'Connor, 1969, 1972), assertion (McFall & Twentyman, 1973), and in some of the dental and medical stress studies (Melamed, Hawes, Heiby, & Glick, 1975; Melamed, Weinstein, Hawes, & Katin-Borland, 1975). Although all of these studies showed some positive effects for SM, none of them manipulated the model-consequences variable. Therefore, this research does not establish that model consequences have an additive effect over the influence of SM alone. However, it is likely that in some instances model reward increases the effects of observing a model.

Acquisition vs. Disinhibition

Yet another aspect of Bandura's (1977) theory of imitation is his distinction between two effects of modeling, disinhibition and the acquisition of behavior. A behavior that has previously been acquired may not be performed because of fear or anxiety. Observation of a model engaging in the behavior without negative consequences or with positive consequences may disinhibit the behavior or increase its frequency. On the other hand, new patterns or sequences of behavioral components are also exhibited by observers following observation of a model. In this manner novel behaviors are acquired.

It is important to both application and theory to determine if SM primarily facilitates anxiety reduction and disinhibition or the acquisition of skills. Of course, it is possible that SM has an important influence in both areas. The treatment components that researchers have combined or compared with SM may give some clues as to their thinking regarding this matter. Research on the use of SM with phobias, test anxieties, and dental/medical stress used primarily relaxation and desensitization as additional components and as comparison treatments. One might infer that researchers see these problems as primarily involving anxiety and inhibition. In contrast, the components, e.g. rehearsal, used by most researchers of interpersonal problems reflect an assumption of a skills deficit. However, two recent studies raise a question as to the extent that skills deficits are the cause of some interpersonal problems studied. Schwartz and Gottman (1976) found that low-assertive college students were as able as moderate- and high-assertive college students to write out what they thought a good assertive response might be. Even more significantly, when asked to role play an assertive response for a hypothetical unassertive friend, the low-assertive students were as assertive as the moderate- and high-assertive students. Consistent with the above, Nietzel and Bernstein (1976) found that high demand instructions made unassertive college students more assertive than low demand instructions. Both of the above studies suggest that assertive responses were in the behavioral repertoires of the low-assertive college students. However, since both studies were with college students, similar conclusions regarding other clinical populations are not possible. For example, it is likely that unassertive psychiatric inpatients have a more severe behavioral deficit than do unassertive college students (Hersen & Bellack, 1976).

Morris et al. (1974) have suggested that phobias have a cognitive and an emotional component. The cognitive component involves information about alternative responses and expected outcomes that might ensue. The emotional aspect involves autonomic processes. According to Morris et al. (1974), the cognitive aspect should dominate in the anxiety of relatively normal people with snake fears because of their lack of experience and their faulty beliefs. They found that high school children with snake fears who observed a symbolic model showed more fear reduction than a control group based on a cognitive (worry) measure but not an emotionality (autonomic reactions) measure. Based on these findings, one might infer that SM is better suited to change cognitions and not so effective in changing autonomic reactions. These findings are generally consistent with a study by Bandura and Menlove (1968), in which they demonstrated that highly emotion-prone subjects in a multiple model condition showed less reduction in dog fear than subjects who were not highly emotion prone. Morris et al. worked with relatively normal subjects, who may be more similar to the moderately emotion-prone subjects than to the highly emotion-prone subjects in the Bandura and Menlove study. One implication of these findings may be that SM is not as effective with more severe clinical problems that involve a strong anxiety component.

Multiple Models

Another facet of an SM treatment that is easily incorporated is the use of multiple models. The purpose of using multiple models is to increase the odds that the observer will select at least one model to imitate, to provide multiple exposures to the target behavior, to increase the treatment stability, and to facilitate generalization of the behavior. Many of the studies reviewed in Table 2-I employed multiple models, and this was especially likely in those studies which assessed generalization. However, only Bandura and Menlove (1968) actually manipulated the number of models. In their study the usual posttreatment, follow-up, and generalization comparisons failed to differentiate the dog-fearing children who observed multiple models from those who observed a single model. However, more children in the former group completed the behavioral approach test than did children in the single model group. Since multiple models are readily incorporated in an SM treatment, and since multiple models logically seem to facilitate generalization, practitioners might wish to incorporate this feature into their SM treatment, despite the limited research.

METHODOLOGICAL CONSIDERATIONS

One could write an entire volume on methodological concerns in this area of research; only some of the more critical matters are discussed here. These points generally pertain to a number of studies rather than to one or two isolated studies. The following discussion concerns (a) subject selection, (b) defining the treatment or the independent variable, (c) control groups, (d) the criterion measures of change, and (e) generalization and maintenance.

Subject Selection

No study can be better than the accuracy of the clinical population sampled. Some researchers in the area of interpersonal skills problems obtained subjects through psychology classes, which is probably not as desirable as obtaining subjects through newspaper advertisements (Little, Curran, & Gilbert, 1977). Psychology students are a relatively homogeneous population, and they are seldom completely naive concerning the experimental hypotheses. Inferences from studies that used college students to more diverse populations are highly risky. A strength in the research on dental/medical fears is that the subjects were drawn from the clinical setting in which the problem was demonstrated.

Another related problem is the tendency in SM research to use people who have relatively minor clinical problems. This is most apparent in the research on snake phobias. As Morris et al. (1974) suggested, the efficacy of SM with relatively normal snake phobics may not obtain when SM is applied to a more clinical population. Therefore, practitioners should be cautious when applying SM with highly disturbed people.

Definition of the Independent Variable

The composition of the treatment is another critical area. Although some of the studies compared SM alone with one or more control conditions, the prominent tendency, especially in the studies on interpersonal skills, has been to include a multitude of additional components in treatment conditions that contained SM. The net result is that one knows relatively little about the individual influence of SM as a separate component and relatively little about what SM might contribute to an intervention that contains one or more other components. Few studies were designed to identify the influence of the specific components (cf. Goldstein et al., 1973; O'Connor, 1972). As a result, practitioners have little guidance concerning which components most effectively combine with SM and with which clinical groups.

Comparisons With Control Groups

If one wishes to attribute changes to a treatment, one must rule out effects that may be attributed to assessment, attention, placebo, or demand characteristics. In general, the research on dental or medical stress and interpersonal skills controlled for the influence of assessment, attention, and placebo. The research on phobias and test anxiety often contained only a no-treatment control, which does not allow one to rule out the influence of nontreatment variables. However, when the primary purpose of a study is to compare SM with other treatment techniques, an instruction/demand control may not be critical.

Many of the studies on interpersonal skills that used role playing (rehearsal) as part of the treatment package also used role playing to assess possible changes in interpersonal behavior but did not control for practice in role playing. It is possible that any assessed changes in these studies stemmed from the increased competence of the treatment subjects at role playing, whether it pertained to assertiveness or to other behaviors. Therefore, if role playing is a part of the treatment and assessment, it is important to control for role playing as a general skill that can be learned.

Assessment

The matter of assessment in research on SM is both critical and complicated. A number of different methods have been used to assess the effect of the SM intervention, including self-report, physiological, and a variety of behavioral measures. Many researchers assessed behavioral changes in role-playing situations, whereas others assessed behavior by creating circumstances relevant to the behavior under investigation and unobtrusively observed the subject's responses. Other behavioral measures that have been employed include direct observation in natural settings by trained observers and general ratings from informed acquaintances of the subjects. At some point the practitioner must decide which of these measures is most relevant to his or her clinical situation.

Much of the research on SM contained a number of measures to assess the effects of the intervention, and most researchers in this area generally support the idea of multiple dependent measures. However, there is a poor relationship between some of these measures of assertion (Rich & Schroeder, 1976) and of anxiety (Paul & Bernstein, 1973). Table 2-I reveals discrepant findings between the various types of dependent measures within a number of studies, e.g. discrepancies between self-report and behavioral measures, as well as mixed results on a given type of measure, e.g. discrepancies between multiple self-report measures. When a large number of measures are obtained, significant differences are more likely a function of chance.

Once the dependent variables have been selected, the clinician must determine the amount of change that constitutes clinical significance. The research on SM with dental and medical stress illustrates this well. There was consistent, statistically significant improvement in the behavior ratings of the SM groups, but the results of staff ratings and self-report questionnaires were mixed. If there is no improvement in the opinions of staff and subjects, are the behavioral ratings that important?

A number of researchers have questioned the reliability and validity of the assessment methods used in SM research. For example, evidence has been presented indicating that the behavioral avoidance tests used to assess target anxiety in phobics are subject to a variety of uncontrolled situational and procedural influences (Bernstein & Nietzel, 1973). Bernstein and Nietzel argued that such influences as demand characteristics and instructional differences potentially obscure the relationship between treatment variables and anxiety. This is especially true when such influences result in the inclusion of less phobic subjects, who may respond more readily than "true" phobics to posttreatment demands for approach behavior (Bernstein & Paul, 1971). Role-playing procedures used to assess assertiveness and heterosexual anxiety may be similarly influenced by instructionally mediated demand (Nietzel & Bernstein, 1976), thus limiting the validity of such procedures. The reliability and validity of most self-report measures of assertiveness have also been criticized (Rich & Schroeder, 1976), and such tests may be insensitive to treatment effects (*see* Table 2-I). Finally, Gottman (1977) criticized naturalistic observation assessment procedures employed in previous studies of SM with socially isolated preschoolers. These studies were criticized for the lack of detail in the coding systems employed, the failure to adequately control observer bias, the use of error-prone time sampling procedures, and the failure to control for interobserver reliability "decay" and observer "drift."

One last point deserves mention. Only three of the studies reviewed in Table 2-I used a physiological measure to assess change. Even though there are problems with physiological measures, in that correlations between physiological measures are low and are sometimes inconvenient to obtain, greater use of such measures seems to be indicated. This is especially true when treating anxiety-related problems and might eventually help to clarify the controversy concerning the relative roles of anxiety and skills deficit in the various areas studied. In summary, it is important to incorporate multiple measures into an assessment of the effects of SM, and in general, more serious consideration of assessment problems is needed in future research.

Generalization and Maintenance

Ultimately, a clinical intervention is no better than the extent to which the effects are maintained in the client's natural environment. Since nearly all of this research, except that on dental and medical stress, was not carried out in a naturalistic setting, it is important to address the question of generalization. The second to last column in Table 2-I shows the small number of studies that assessed generalization. Even some of the studies that assessed generalization did so in a way that leaves much to be desired. Many of the researchers appraised generalization within a context that more closely approximated the treatment situation than the natural environment. For example, some of the phobia research appraised generalization by introducing a snake different from the one used for treatment. What does this tell us about the subject's response to a snake that he or she happens upon in the yard on a Sunday afternoon? Similarly, a frequent method of assessing generalization in assertion research has been to introduce role-playing scenes that are different from those used for treatment. Surely this measure of generalization more closely approximates the treatment situation than the natural environment. The time has come to assess generalization outside the treatment setting and in settings more like the natural environment. The dental and medical research represents a clear exception to this problem. Since treatment and data collection typically occur within the natural environment, the question of generalization becomes less of a problem.

The question of maintenance has received about as little attention as generalization (*see* the last column of Table 2-I). When a maintenance measure was obtained, it often followed treatment by a few days, and these researchers typically did not assess the duration of the changes in the natural environment. In short, duration without generalization is of little value.

SUMMARY AND CONCLUSIONS

The use of videotape and film modeling in clinical and analogue settings was reviewed. Most of the research has been on phobias, test anxiety, dental and medical stress, and interpersonal skills. A number of methodological problems with previous research were noted. Nonetheless, the use of SM as a treatment device, perhaps combined with other components, has a promising future. At this point, the need is for studies with more clinical or disturbed populations, for studies that systematically vary the treatment components, that carefully use multiple measures to assess change, and that appraise both generalization and maintenance in natural settings or settings that closely approximate the natural environment. Until such time as this kind of research is conducted, practitioners will need to use discretion in the application of SM.

REFERENCES

Andrews, J. A study of the effects of a filmed, vicarious, desensitization procedure in the treatment of manifest anxiety and test anxiety in community college students. *Dissertation Abstracts International*, 1973, *33*, 5399-5400.

Baker, T. B., Udin, H., & Vogler, R. The effects of videotaped modeling and self-confrontation on the drinking behavior of alcoholics. *International Journal of the Addictions*, 1975, *10*, 779-793.

Bandura, A. *Principles of behavior modification.* New York: Holt, Rinehart and Winston, Inc., 1969.

———. *Social learning theory.* Englewood Cliffs, N. J.: Prentice-Hall, 1977.

Bandura, A., & Barab, P. Processes governing disinhibitory effects through symbolic modeling. *Journal of Abnormal Psychology*, 1973, *82*, 1-9.

Bandura, A., Blanchard, E., & Ritter, B. Relative efficacy of desensitization and modeling approaches for inducing behavioral, affective, and attitudinal changes. *Journal of Personality and Social Psychology*, 1969, *13*, 173-199.

Bandura, A., & Menlove, F. Factors determining vicarious extinction of avoidance behavior through symbolic modeling. *Journal of Personality and Social Psychology*, 1968, *8*, 99-108.

Bernstein, D. A., & Nietzel, M. T. Procedural variation in behavioral avoidance tests. *Journal of Consulting and Clinical Psychology*, 1973, *41*, 165-174.

Bernstein, D. A., & Paul, G. L. Some comments on therapy analogue research with small animal "phobias." *Journal of Behavior Therapy and Experimental Psychiatry*, 1971, *2*, 225-237.

Bruch, M. Influence of model characteristics on psychiatric inpatients' interview anxiety. *Journal of Abnormal Psychology*, 1975, *84*, 290-294.

Burrs, V., & Kapche, R. *Modeling of social behavior in chronic hospital patients.* Unpublished manuscript, California State College (Long Beach), 1969.

Curran, J. P. Social skills training and systematic desensitization in reducing dating anxiety. *Behaviour Research and Therapy*, 1975, *13*, 65-68.

Curran, J. P., & Gilbert, F. S. A test of the relative effectiveness of a systematic desensitization program and an interpersonal skills training program with date anxious subjects. *Behavior Therapy*, 1975, *6*, 510-521.

Curran, J. P., Gilbert, F. S., & Little, L. M. A comparison between behavioral replication training and sensitivity training approaches to heterosexual dating anxiety. *Journal of Counseling Psychology*, 1976, *23*, 190-196.

Denney, D. R., & Sullivan, B. J. Desensitization and modeling treatments of spider fear using two types of scenes. *Journal of Consulting and Clinical Psychology*, 1976, *44*, 573-579.

Eisler, R. M., Hersen, M., & Miller, P. M. Effects of modeling components of assertive behavior. *Journal of Behavior Therapy and Experimental Psychiatry*, 1973, *4*, 1-6.

Evers, W., & Schwartz, J. Modifying social withdrawal in preschoolers: The effects of filmed modeling and teacher praise. *Journal of Abnormal Child Psychology*, 1973, *1*, 248-256.

Evers-Pasquale, W., & Sherman, M. The reward value of peers: A variable influencing the efficacy of filmed modeling in modifying social isolation in preschoolers. *Journal of Abnormal Child Psychology*, 1975, *3*, 179-189.

Galassi, J. P., Galassi, M. D., & Litz, M. C. Assertive training in groups using video feedback. *Journal of Counseling Psychology*, 1974, *21*, 390-394.

Galassi, J. P., Kostka, M. D., & Galassi, M. D. Assertive training: A one year follow up. *Journal of Counseling Psychology*, 1975, *22*, 451-452.

Geer, J., & Turtletaub, A. Fear reduction following observation of a model. *Journal of Personality and Social Psychology*, 1967, *6*, 327-331.

Goldstein, A. P. *Structured learning therapy: Toward a psychotherapy for the poor.* New York: Academic Press, 1973.

Goldstein, A. P., Martens, J., Hubben, J., VanBelle, H. A., Schaaf, W., Wiersma, H., & Goedhart, A. The use of modeling to increase independent behavior. *Behavior Research and Therapy*, 1973, *11*, 31-42.

Gottman, J. The effects of a modeling film on social isolation in preschool children: A methodological investigation. *Journal of Abnormal Child Psychology*, 1977, *5*, 69-78.

Gottman, J., Gonso, J., & Schuler, P. Teaching social skills to isolated children. *Journal of Abnormal Child Psychology*, 1976, *4*, 179-197.

Gutride, M., Goldstein, A., & Hunter, G. The use of modeling and role playing to increase social interaction among asocial psychiatric patients. *Journal of Consulting and Clinical Psychology*, 1973, *40*, 408-415.

Hersen, M., & Bellack, A. S. Social skills training for chronic psychiatric patients: Rationale, research findings, and future directions. *Comprehensive Psychiatry*, 1976, *17*, 559-580.

Hersen, M., Eisler, R., & Miller, P. An experimental analysis of generalization in assertive training. *Behaviour Research and Therapy*, 1974, *12*, 295-310.

Hersen, M., Eisler, R., Miller, P., Johnson, M., & Pinkston, S. Effects of practice, instructions, and modeling on components of assertive behavior. *Behavior Research and Therapy*, 1973, *11*, 443-451.

Hill, J. H., Liebert, R., & Mott, D. Vicarious extinction of avoidance behavior through films: An initial test. *Psychological Reports*, 1968, *22*, 192.

———. Modeling therapy for test anxiety: The role of model affect and consequences. *Behaviour Research and Therapy*, 1972, *10*, 329-339.

Jaffe, P. G., & Carlson, P. M. Relative efficacy of modeling and instructions in eliciting social behavior from chronic psychiatric patients. *Journal of Consulting and Clinical Psychology*, 1976, *44*, 200-207.

Jakibchuk, Z., & Smeriglio, V. L. The influence of symbolic modeling on the social behavior of preschool children with low levels of social responsiveness. *Child Development*, 1976, *45*, 912-919.

Kornhaber, R., & Schroeder, H. Importance of model similarity in extinction of avoidance behavior in children. *Journal of Consulting and Clinical Psychology*, 1975, *43*, 601-607.

Lewis, S. A comparison of behavior therapy techniques in the reduction of fearful avoidance behavior. *Behavior Therapy*, 1974, *5*, 648-655.

Lira, R., Nay, W., McCullough, J., & Etkin, M. Relative effects of modeling and role playing in the treatment of avoidance behaviors. *Journal of Consulting and Clinical Psychology*, 1975, *43*, 608-618.

Little, L. M., Curran, J. P., & Gilbert, F. S. The importance of subject recruitment procedures in therapy analogue studies on heterosexual-social anxiety. *Behavior Therapy*, 1977, *8*, 24-29.

Machen, J., & Johnson, R. Desensitization, model learning, and the dental behavior of children. *Journal of Dental Research*, 1974, *53*, 83-87.

Malec, J., Pack, T., & Watkins, J. T. Modeling with role playing as a treatment for test anxiety. *Journal of Consulting and Clinical Psychology*, 1976, *44*, 679.

Mann, J. Vicarious desensitization of test anxiety through observation of videotaped treatment. *Journal of Counseling Psychology*, 1972, *19*, 1-7.

Marlatt, G. A. Task structure and the experimental modification of verbal behavior. *Psychological Bulletin,* 1978, *78,* 335-350.

McFall, R. M., & Twentyman, C. T. For experiments on the relative contributions of rehearsal, modeling, and coaching to assertion training. *Journal of Abnormal Psychology,* 1973, *81,* 199-218.

McGuire, D., Thelen, M. H., & Amolsch, T. Interview self-disclosure as a function of length of modeling and descriptive instructions. *Journal of Consulting and Clinical Psychology,* 1975, *43,* 356-362.

Meichenbaum, D. Examination of model characteristics in reducing avoidance behavior. *Journal of Personality and Social Psychology,* 1971, *17,* 298-307.

Melamed, B., Hawes, R., Heiby, E., & Glick, J. Use of filmed modeling to reduce uncooperative behavior of children during dental treatment. *Journal of Dental Research,* 1975, *54,* 797-801.

Melamed, B., & Siegel, L. Reduction of anxiety in children facing hospitalization and surgery by use of filmed modeling. *Journal of Consulting and Clinical Psychology,* 1975, *43,* 511-521.

Melamed, B., Weinstein, F., Hawes, R., & Katin-Borland, M. Reduction of fear-related dental management problems with use of filmed modeling. *Journal of the American Dental Association,* 1975, *90,* 822-836.

Morris, L. W., Speigler, M. D., & Liebert, R. M. Effects of a therapeutic modeling film on cognitive and emotional components of anxiety. *Journal of Clinical Psychology,* 1974, *30,* 219-223.

Nietzel, M. T., & Bernstein, D. A. Effects of instructionally mediated demand on the behavioral assessment of assertiveness. *Journal of Consulting and Clinical Psychology,* 1974, *44,* 500.

O'Connor, R. Modification of social withdrawal through symbolic modeling. *Journal of Applied Behavior Analysis,* 1969, *2,* 15-22.

———. Relative efficacy of modeling, shaping, and the combined procedures for modification of social withdrawal. *Journal of Abnormal Psychology,* 1972, *79,* 327-334.

Paul, G. L., & Bernstein, D. A. *Anxiety and clinical problems: Systematic desensitization and related techniques.* Morristown, New Jersey: General Learning Press, 1973.

Rathus, S. A. Instigations of assertive behavior through videotape mediated assertive models and directed practice. *Behaviour Research and Therapy,* 1973, *11,* 57-65.

Reeder, C. W., & Kunce, J. T. Modeling techniques, drug abstinence behavior, and heroin addicts: A pilot study. *Journal of Counseling Psychology,* 1976, *23,* 560-562.

Rich, A. R., & Schroeder, H. E. Research issues in assertiveness training. *Psychological Bulletin,* 1976, *83,* 1081-1096.

Rosekrans, M. A. Imitation in children as a function of perceived similarity to a social model and vicarious reinforcement. *Journal of Personality and Social Pyschology,* 1967, *7,* 307-315.

Sarason, I. Verbal learning, modeling, and juvenile delinquency. *American*

Psychologist, 1968, *23,* 254-266.

Schwartz, R. M., & Gottman, J. M. Toward a task analysis of assertive behavior. *Journal of Consulting and Clinical Psychology,* 1976, *44,* 910-920.

Shaw, D. W., & Thoresen, C. E. Effects of modeling and desensitization in reducing dentist phobia. *Journal of Counseling Psychology,* 1974, *21,* 415-520.

Speigler, M., Leibert, R., McMains, M., & Fernandez, L. Experimental development of a modeling treatment to extinguish persistent avoidance behavior. In R. Rubin and C. Franks (Eds.), *Advances in behavior therapy.* New York: Academic Press, 1969.

Thelen, M. H., Dollinger, S. J., & Kirkland, K. D. Imitation and response uncertainty. *The Journal of Genetic Psychology,* 1969, *135,* 139-152.

Thelen, M. H., Fry, R. A., Dollinger, S. J., & Paul, S. C. Use of videotaped models to improve the interpersonal adjustment of delinquents. *Journal of Consulting and Clinical Psychology,* 1976, *44,* 492.

Thelen, M. H., Fryrear, J. L., & Rennie, D. L. Delayed imitation of self-reward standards. *Journal of Experimental Research in Personality,* 1971, *5,* 317-322.

Thelen, M. H., Paul, S. C., Dollinger, S. J., & Roberts, M. C. Response uncertainty and imitation: The interactive effects of age and task options. *Journal of Research in Personality,* 1978, *12,* 370-380.

Thelen, M. H., & Rennie, D. L. The effect of vicarious reinforcement on imitation: A review of the literature. In B. A. Maher (Ed.), *Progress in Experimental Personality Research,* New York: Academic Press, Inc., 1972.

Thomas, G. M. Using videotaped modeling to increase attending behavior. *Elementary School Guidance and Counseling,* 1974, *9,* 35-40.

VanCamp, J. Modification of adult aggressive behavior by using modeling films. *Dissertation Abstracts International,* 1972, *32,* 7327.

Vernon, D. T. A. Use of modeling to modify children's responses to a natural, potentially stressful situation. *Journal of Applied Psychology,* 1973, *58,* 351-356.

———. Modeling and birth order in responses to painful stimuli. *Journal of Personality and Social Psychology,* 1974, *29,* 794-799.

Vernon, D. T. A., & Bailey, W. The use of motion pictures in the psychological preparation of children for induction of anesthesia. *Anesthesiology,* 1974, *40,* 68-72.

Weissbrod, C., & Bryan, J. Filmed treatment as an effective fear reduction technique. *Journal of Abnormal Child Psychology,* 1973, *1,* 196-201.

Wincze, J. P., & Caird, W. K. The effects of systematic desensitization and video desensitization in the treatment of essential sexual dysfunction in women. *Behavior Therapy,* 1976, *7,* 335-342.

Wroblewski, P. F., Jacob, T., & Rehm, L. P. The contribution of relaxation to symbolic modeling in the modification of dental fears. *Behavior*

Research and Therapy, 1977, *15,* 113-115.

Yussen, S. R., & Levy, V. M., Jr. Effects of warm and neutral models on the attention of observational learners. *Journal of Experimental Child Psychology,* 1975, *20,* 66-72.

CHAPTER 3

VIDEO ENACTMENT IN THE EXPRESSIVE THERAPIES

SHAUN MCNIFF

I HAD the unique experience of having virtually every expressive theapy session that I conducted over a five-year period (1973-1978) recorded on videotape. The Addison Gallery of American Art at Phillips Academy in Andover, Massachusetts was at that time exploring how it could make the museum environment of use to the various mental health centers in its community. The Gallery was also actively involved in sponsoring and creating media art works. Christopher Cook, the director of the Gallery, and I thought that through a museum-sponsored video art therapy program we could offer a new service to the hospitals and clinics within the area while also conducting research into the artistic application of video to psychotherapy.

We believe that a creative use of the media would greatly expand the more conventional role of videotape in therapy. Just as contemporary artists were at the time demonstrating how television stereotypes could be replaced by more personal and evocative transformations of video, we set out to show that this could also be done within psychotherapy.

VIDEO

The Addison Gallery program provided extraordinary opportunities for research. Every week we had at least two portapaks available for our use. The Gallery also hired a skilled videotape operator and editor to work in cooperation with our expressive therapists. In addition to these technical resources we were able to save all of the significant tapes that we made over the five-year period for the purpose of studying the development of our work. The attractive environment of the museum and the outside grounds of the academy were supportive of artistic approaches to video. We were able to work within a visually evocative context, which helped to motivate artistic responses within our expressive therapy sessions. Virtually all of our work was done within groups. With the assistance of graduate student trainees from Lesley College we, however, were able to work on a one-to-one basis within our groups. Since the Addison Gallery program has been documented within the book *The Art Museum as Educator* (Newsome and Silver, 1978), attention will be focused here on the general operational principles that we discovered about the artistic use of videotape in psychotherapy.

SELF CONFRONTATION

As with many other forms of video therapy, the fundamental element of our expressive art therapy work was the process of self-confrontation by client and therapist alike. The basic emotional response that most of us have when engaged with videotape is the feeling that we will be "seen" by others and by ourselves. This anticipation tends to arouse the emotional polarities of self-disparagement and self-interest. We are either attracted to the monitor, as Narcissus was to his mirror image, or we find it very difficult to look forthrightly at our behavior. Although there might occasionally be a person who can approach the videotape presentation of the self with studied objectivity, I have found this to be rare in exposing hundreds of clients, graduate students, and professional clinicians to their self-image as recorded on the videotape. On the basis of our experience we can say with certainty that videotape playback arouses strong emotions in virtually all people who are unaccustomed to seeing themselves on a television monitor.

Self-confrontation is the basis of videotherapy. The immediate replay of real-life process made possible through video technology allows this confrontation to happen in a way that cuts through verbal defenses, perceptual denial, wishful and idealized self-images, and inaccurate perceptions of group process. Because of its ability to forcefully penetrate a person's defenses, videotape self-confrontation can be a very threatening and potentially shattering experience. This threat makes it essential to consider how the medium can be introduced gradually and with respect for the feelings of clients as well as therapists.

The arts offer many opportunities for desensitizing people to videotape and becoming progressively involved in different aspects of self-confrontation. We will often first expose people to videotape by recording hand movements during a dance therapy session, or by showing hands at work creating visual art objects, writing, or making gestures during a conversation. Typically, people's curiosity and desire to see more are sparked as they find themselves trying to determine whose hands are being shown and as they watch for their own. For the person who is intimidated by a camera, hand gestures tend to be less threatening and less difficult to express in a graceful fashion. We have found that this first exposure to videotape inspires most people to become more aware of the nonverbal communication and expression constantly taking place within the group.

Because early validation seems to be essential if people are to be encouraged to participate spontaneously in the videotaping of the ongoing expressive therapy process, we will have our first sessions recorded by a skilled camera person who understands the videotherapy experience. We try to avoid confronting people with less desirable behaviors in the beginning sessions because we are at that time more concerned with fostering familiarity and comfort with this medium of self-analysis. We have found it necessary to avoid highly emotional situations in the early stages of videotherapy. Too much emotion too early makes it difficult or virtually impossible for people to sort out and understand their feelings. In our first sessions we try to emphasize the supportive role of videotape. We use it to validate expression rather than to create further inhibitions and obstacles to artistic spontaneity. Throughout all of our experiences with videotape we have consistently found that the playback procedure intensifies the emotional process either positively or negatively and that these feelings become the content of psychotherapeutic sharing and analysis.

The self-confrontation of the therapist during the videotherapy experience is as real as that of the client. Within an expressive art therapy context therapists have the opportunity not only to evaluate their personal behavior but also to assess their effectiveness in either furthering or inhibiting the artistic self-expression of others. Observing myself working on video-tape throughout a five-year period had a profound impact on my self-learning. The videotape playback allowed me to study closely my facial and bodily expressions when interacting with another person in both comfortable and stressful situations. I was also able to evaluate my tone of voice, the texture and rhythm of my speech, and the continuity of my behavior from session to session. Videotape provided the opportunity for a very intense and penetrating form of self-supervision that confronted me with both unattractive and pleasing aspects of my style of interacting with others, traits that had not become manifest within conventional forms of supervision and training.

THE ARTS AS VIDEO SUBJECT MATTER

Within my expressive therapy work, videotape has generally been used in the service of the other arts. Dance/movement therapy, music/sound therapy, dramatic improvisation, and other, more *process-oriented* expressive therapies can be greatly assisted by videotape. Through the playback experience we can evaluate behaviors and time-dependent experiences that before the introduction of recording media could be held in conscious-ness only through the use of self-selected memories. Psycho-therapy is in essence a process of enacting the story of one's life as it occurs in the present and as it has existed in the past. the arts dramatize and augment the significance of interpersonal enactments by extending the scope of communication to in-clude all of the expressive modalities of mind and body. Be-cause the expressive therapies focus on the movement of the individual in space and time, together with the kinesis of human interactions, they have benefited extensively from video-tape recording. Videotape has also served as a bridge between the different arts in that the artistic dimensions of movement, language, sound, and vision are integrated into the video enactment. Videotherapists who are presently interested in recording only the verbal interactions of clients and therapists within conventional psychotherapeutic procedures can greatly extend the scope of self-confrontation and observation by engaging other expressive modalities.

The nonverbal forms of expression that might be exhibited within a brief, ten-minute videotape of an interpersonal interaction present an extensive body of information for diagnostic analysis. The research of William Condon (1966), who has isolated individual film frames of behavior to trace the body messages that are given within otherwise undetected expressions, shows that careful scrutiny of the closer intervals of the film/video recording will reveal important information about the individual. I have often felt that a ten or fifteen minute playback to a small group of people can present an excessive amount of perceptual data for analysis, and we have had to select certain aspects of the tape upon which to focus our attention. This ability of videotape to repeatedly offer endless amounts of information about interpersonal process to a large extent accounts for why we were able to use the equipment in session after session with clients and find that they rarely tired of the playback experience. We have worked with institutionalized adult clients who, after five years of videotherapy experience, still find the process to be of personal interest and therapeutic value. As therapists we find that the videotaping of sessions is on ongoing form of self-learning. Time spent with videotape is accumulative in the sense that clients and therapists become more sophisticated in viewing the playback and more selective in perceiving tapes of group interactions. Our lives are constantly changing, and videotape rarely loses its appeal as a means of observing these transformations. Video playback functions as an ongoing mirror for our changing selves.

THE RITUAL OF PLAYBACK

As I look back on our experience over the years with videotape in the expressive art therapies, the strongest association that I have to the work is the ritualistic aspect of playback. The viewing of the tape of our group activity brought us together regularly at the end of each session. The playback tended to take on ceremonial qualities in that it was a predictable form of closure for each session. Viewing the tape inevitably brought the group together in an intimate way that did not always characterize our activity in earlier stages of the expressive therapy session. Because of the regularity of the playback structure we knew that even if we went off and worked completely on our own, the camera would probably record some aspects of our artistic expression for the purpose of sharing it with the group.

Playback became a form of group communion. During our sessions we routinely began by coming together as a group to introduce visitors and discuss the various art activities that we would be doing on that particular day. The group then broke down into different subgroups, or interest areas, to pursue artistic expression. Some people would also choose to work alone. After an hour or more of artistic activity we came back together again for the purpose of viewing the playback. The videotape became an important facilitator of group identity and cohesion: no matter how separate our individual activities were, the playback process would reinforce our group participation in that we all contributed to the more general artistic and interpersonal process that was unified through the playback. If one was working in a music or poetry subgroup it was most gratifying to be able to watch the dance, dramatic improvisation, or visual art activity of other group members who might be working in a completely separate room. Playback took on a particularly significant role in our larger groups of adult clients. Some sessions would involve twelve to thirteen clients, six to eight graduate student interns, the group leader, and a video technician. In these large groups; a video summary of the day's activity, using descriptions of group interaction as well as intimate close ups, helped to bring individuals in touch with each other, and the group as a whole, in a way that was not possible through discussion within a relatively limited amount of time.

The structure of our sessions resembled the classic myth cycle of separation, penetration, and return. Within this schema the playback was a rite of passage, which helped make the transition to closure and a return to group consciousness after individual artistic activities. In this way we were able to reinforce both individual and communal expression. We would usually discuss the playback experience and focus our attention on those situations where the videotape opened up feelings that needed further analysis and support. Often, however, and particularly with large groups, it was not even necessary to discuss the playback. The simple act of watching it as a group precipitated strong feelings of solidarity and community. During these silent playbacks we were visually and auditorily processing our group experience. There were times when talking about what we were viewing, or what we had done, would have taken away from the intensity of the feelings that were provoked by the playback. I also found the discussion could in certain cases fragment feelings of order and emotional clarity that were provoked by the playback, which was for us a "sacramental" and sensory sign of inner experience.

THE ART OF VIDEOTAPE

When using videotape within an expressive therapy context the varied scope of artistic expressions involving body movement, sound, visual imagery, poetic metaphor, and enactment necessitates that the videotaping process be pursued from an artistic perspective. Our work reinforces the dramatic and enactment qualities that this author believes are characteristic of all psychotherapy. When recording an expressive therapy session, the person with the camera is provoked by the aesthetic and dramatic action and must respond in a way that will absorb and transform this artistic emotion.

In his description of "the Gestalt theory of expression" Rudolf Arnheim defines expression "as the psychological counterpart of the dynamic processes that result in the organization of perceptual stimuli" (Arnheim, 1972). He feels that perceptual configurations are inherently dynamic and contain directed tensions. "By endowing the object or event with a perceivable form of behavior, these tensions give it 'character' and recall the similar character of other objects or events. This is what is meant by saying that these dynamic aspects of the percept 'express' its character" (Arnheim, 1972).

Applied to videotape, Arnheim's theory would maintain that the perceptual quality, dynamism, and clarity of the image will determine its expressive impact. We have repeatedly discovered in our clinical work that the poorly organized, fragmented, out of focus, and rambling videotape not only fails to hold attention but tends to precipitate unsettling and negative feelings in the viewer. The well organized, aesthetically pleasing, succinct, and emotionally coherent tape will stimulate a structurally parallel emotional response in most people, so long as the person is capable of perceiving order outside of the self. We have found that in many ways the videotape controls the emotions that are precipitated during the playback. Unequivocably our experience has shown that *the quality of the videotape will directly influence the quality of the response.* We define quality artistically in terms of aesthetic coherence, emotional honesty, and interpersonal relevance and not from the sole criteria of technical proficiency. In light of our findings we place a large emphasis on the value of skill and artistic resourcefulness in creating a videotape for playback.

Within expressive art therapy sessions we involve clients in the artistic process of creating videotape. When viewing the production of videotape as an art form, different styles of perception, varied interpretations, emotional interests, and emotional omissions of the person using the camera become manifest. As is any art form, videotape is a projection of the personality of the individual artist. This subjective element is often obscured by the presumption of "objectivity" that people associate with the videotape process. In creating a tape one person might focus exclusively on close-ups, another on distant shots, another on group activity and interactions, another on individual expressions, another on a combination of all these things, etc.

In light of the impact that the poorly produced videotape tends to have on a group, we will often view the playback privately with clients when they are learning how to operate the equipment. Clients tend to appreciate this private viewing in that they might not yet be emotionally ready to exhibit their first efforts at videotape recording to the group.

Many clients will first become engaged with the relatively simple activity of operating a camera fixed on a tripod and kept in constant focus on an individual person or a group activity. This stationary camera approach typifies much of conventional videotherapy. A more demanding and artistic orientation to the medium would involve the client in learning how to work with a portapak, framing images—both stationary and moving, changing focus, adjusting light, and constantly accommodating the equipment to changes in spatial position. When working with a portapak, in-camera editing and a more artistic approach to the *composition* of the tape are required. In my experience only a small percentage of our clients have gotten seriously involved in this more technically demanding dimension of videotape. The majority of clients appear to be more interested in self-confrontation and viewing their expression in various art modalities during playback.

Within an expressive therapy group of adult psychiatric patients conducted at the Addison Gallery of American Art, one of the participants became interested and quite adept in using the equipment. After nine months of participation in the group as a client he returned for three years as a volunteer. He would record sessions and help to demonstrate the use of the camera and other taping units to clients and graduate students who were participating as interns. This man, who was in his early thirties, became involved with video by first observing his rigid and virtually catatonic behavior during playback. In subsequent sessions he noted how he was able to become gradually more expressive and spontaneous during group activities. He complained of severe bodily pains, which restricted his movement. When he began to use the camera, he observed how the pains would subside and virtually disappear as he concentrated on operating the equipment. This relief, together with his aesthetic and intellectual curiosity about the hardware, drew him into a serious artistic relationship with videotape recording. Every week he worked at improving his skill and took great pride in his increasing technical competence. Over time the pains no longer bothered him, and he became one of our most sophisticated and expressive video artists.

TECHNICAL ISSUES

Videotape is not without its problematic features. One of the greatest drawbacks of the medium is the ever present possibility of equipment failure. Perhaps this precariousness also increases the drama of videotherapy in that we are never totally certain that everything will work correctly.

Within the Addison Gallery program we would always have at least two well-serviced portapaks and a video technician, and we would still have occasional technical mishaps. Because expectations tend to create a certain dependence on having a playback experience after the making of a tape, for both the camera operator and the people being recorded the failure of the equipment to produce this gratification can be disconcerting. All that can be done in this situation is to treat the disappointment as the subject matter of the therapeutic process. We have at times successfully "transvaluated" these difficulties into poignant discussions about other disappointments and broken expectations in our lives.

In working with severely disruptive children (ages 8 to 11) we have discovered that the playback experience has to be focused on the individual child if we are to hold their attention and use the viewing of the videotape as a means of controlling behavior. When we showed tapes of group activities to these children, they would continuously act out during playback. In the beginning of our work they could not relate to themselves as part of a group. We found sequential "portraits" of each child very effective in holding their interest. During playback they would study their own behavior as well as the individual mannerisms of the other children. We would at times have to resort to consciously showing the portraits of the most disruptive children at the end of the playback because the anticipation of seeing themselves was one of the only ways of keeping them from interfering with the playback experiences of their peers.

The video portrait was also very effective in a different way with adults. We found that the portraits helped the group to focus on individual members and differentiate them from the group as a whole. The portrait was extremely useful in allowing more withdrawn and silent members to communicate with the group. With a microphone clipped to their collars, and with their facial expressions being recorded in sensitive close-up shots, people who have never been truly *heard* and *seen* by the group were given the opportunity to enter into a close relationship with the group through videotape.

TECHNOLOGICAL SHAMANISM

Interestingly enough I have discovered that media as technologically advanced as videotape have a definite continuity with ancient shamanic healing practices. In *The Gates of the Dream*, Geza Roheim says that "the fundamental mechanism of the dream is the formation of a double, the dream image of the soul" (Roheim, 1979). Shamanism as a mode of healing grew from the enactment of dreams. Aboriginal communities believed that illness and emotional disturbances were caused by the estrangement of the soul from the body. During dream states the soul was perceived as leaving the body, wandering about as suggested by dream imagery, and returning again when the person awakes. If the soul did not return, personal difficulties would ensue, and the shaman was called upon to go in search of the person's soul. The standard shamanic procedure was the enactment of the person's dream, or source of conflict, with the shaman becoming involved in a state of ecstacy that became the route to the dream consciousness and domain of the spirits who were holding the person's soul.

I believe that much of the psychodynamic power of videotherapy, and particularly its more artistic and dramatic forms, comes from a latent continuity with shamanic practices. Like the dream, the videotape playback is the "double" of the person's art, spirit, behavior, or whatever terminology one wishes to describe the action that is recorded on the tape. Like shamanism and dreaming, the videotape process is characterized by feelings of surprise, wonder, and magic. The videotape is a reliving of life experience, an enactment process similar to that of the shaman, who dramatically recreates an experience to make it alive in the present for group members.

Both the shamanic enactment and the videotape playback function as a "bridge" between different spheres of consciousness, time, and space. They are intermediaries between present and past and link our waking experience with our dream space. The shamanic metaphor of the "intermediary" has maintained itself through all forms of psychotherapy where the therapist enters into a relationship with a client to assist that person in the process of integrating the conflicting dimensions of life.

The shamanic dimension is, in my opinion, the factor that separates the artistic and dramatic uses of video in the expressive therapies from more conventional approaches to videotherapy. The expressive therapies allow for the experiencing of intense emotions within the supportive structure of art. The work of art can in this respect provide boundaries for the individual's and the group's feelings while making them manifest.

Through videotape, expressive behavior can become more completely visible to the self. The playback experience allows the process of creation to emerge into clearer focus. As with the dream and dramatic enactment, videotape transforms the original experience and presents it from a new vantage point, in this case from the perspective of the person operating the camera. As a result of this transformation and its presentation within the sensible form of electronic patterns of light, the reliving of the experience, as with the dream and other art works, stimulates the person to compare perceptions of the videotape to memory traces of the event. The lack of complete correspondence, or what we might describe as perceptual dissonance, helps to create an energy-inducing tension, which accounts for the emotional arousal that we often feel when viewing videotape. The playback experience can in this way assist people in conducting a reality check with their self-images. Discomfort is usually experienced by people who are fearful of confronting their actual self-image and who are afraid that the videotape playback will destroy the wishful and idealized identities that they have constructed for themselves. The person who is truly open to self-observation and curious about the visual, aural, and kinesthetic configurations of his or her behavior, and that of others, tends to become emotionally aroused and excited by self-confrontation.

The classic shamanic conception of the body separating from the mind or soul can be applied to videotherapy. As with shamanism, videotherapy provides *imagery* of bodily action taking place within another temporal sphere. The observing mind then experiences videotaped expressions within the realm of the present. Because the human mind and feelings have remained remarkably consistent over thousands of years, we are still largely impressed by the "mystique" of television's transformation of time and space. In many ways its technical "magic and virtuosity" have replaced other modes for unifying time and space in our culture. I believe that this factor accounts for the continuous eagerness that clients show when it comes to viewing videotape playbacks of their behavior.

Like the dream and the shamanic enactment, the video playback can become a source of "empowerment" if the process of self-confrontation helps the person to renew a sense of personal spontaneity and a belief in the value of expression. The reverse can also happen if the videotape serves the purpose of providing continuous negative reinforcement and if it fails to validate the person's humanity.

The effectiveness of the videotape playback can be evaluated according to the same guidelines that one would use to assess the power of the shamanic enactment — dramatic coherence, emotional depth and honesty, aesthetic appeal, the ease with which the participant can identify with the action portrayed, and the extent to which the enactment parallels the emotional configuration of the conflict.

THE FUTURE

Videotape presently plays an essential role in helping both clients and therapists to understand the psychodynamics of creative action in therapy. As the expressive art therapies continue to grow and reunite psychotherapy with its shamanic beginnings, videotape will take on a continuously increasing importance because of its unique ability to let us relive the process of experience.

At the present time video is not only used in clinical practice and research but also as an essential component of supervisory and training programs for expressive therapists. Movement and dance therapists require videotapes of a person's work as part of the evaluation procedure for registration. Perhaps the other mental health professions will begin to show a similar sensitivity to the evaluation of a person's interpersonal skills in the licensing and registration procedures of psychotherapists.

As videotape becomes an increasingly familiar part of psychotherapeutic training and practice in all disciplines, increasing emphasis will be placed on the artistic and creative use of the medium. Once the basic properties of this form of communication are understood, the future lies in the exploration of its expressive capacities. Videotape is only a means to an end. It is valued in relation to its ability to further the humanistic goals of our work in the arts and therapy. The danger of videotape and other psychotherapeutic technology lies in losing this human perspective. Caution is advised in depending too much on technical tools as forms of therapeutic reinforcement and communication. Videotherapy, like television, can become addictive and might encourage the kind of passive responsiveness that characterizes over dependence on television viewing as a substitute for personal expression. As stated throughout this paper, the value of videotape in therapy resides in its ability to serve art, communication between people, and personal insight. To the extent its unique properties further these goals in psychotherapy, it cannot be ignored.

REFERENCES

Arnheim, R. *Toward a psychology of art.* Berkeley: University of California Press, 1972.

Condon, W. S., & Ogston, W. D. Sound and film analysis of normal and pathological behavior patterns. *Journal of Nervous and Mental Disorders*, 1966, *143*, 4.

McNiff, S. *The arts in psychotherapy.* Springfield, Il.: Charles C Thomas, Publisher, in press.

McNiff, S., & Cook, C. Video art therapy. *Art Psychotherapy*, 1975, *2*, 1.

Newsome, B., & Silver, A. (Eds.). *The art museum as educator.* Berkeley: University of California Press, 1978.

Part Two
Applications of Videotherapy

CHAPTER 4

PSYCHOLOGICAL APPLICATIONS OF VIDEO EQUIPMENT IN GROUP PROCESSES

FRED CUTTER

THE visual recording of behavior in groups enhances effectiveness of interventions in ways not fully antici-pated by standard training in the behavioral sciences. As with all new knowledge, there is a social lag in the assimilation or application of innovative techniques. This is especially true with the use of video playback methods on TV-conditioned subjects in group contexts. To achieve full advantage of this technological resource, professionally mature practitioners need to become aware of impediments to fuller use of video equipment, as well as clinical opportunities created by changing technology.

BACKGROUND

Anybody can be trained to turn on video equipment. Conse-quently, organizations will spend in excess of $30,000 for a color system but will be reluctant to provide one person to function as a video technician. When they do, the person is usually trained in radio/television programming rather than social science. Conversely, the idea of putting a mental health professional behind the camera seems both denigrating and a waste of professional training to all concerned. The philosophy here is that the judgment to select relevant and essential be-havior for recording can only be approximated by professional training in mental health. The camera person is more like a director in a documentary movie in what he/she chooses to record. Given this basic premise, it is far more appropriate to train a behavioral science professional to operate video equipment than to expect a radio/television technician to recognize important behavior for recording. This section will introduce the advanced professional to those ideas which help translate video recording into effective behavioral observation or intervention, and especially in group context.

When asked to deal with something new, most mature people fall back on analogous models. For video the models are sound recording or home movies. Sound recording for clinical practice with clients has been available for at least one generation. The usual technique is to turn the recorder on and ignore it. The machine records everything with equal emphasis while the professional goes about his or her business. Consequently, sound playbacks are tiresome and demand much pre-editing to select an appropriate interval for attention. Indeed, one behavior scientist known to the writer has selected two or three minute segments arbitrarily for transcription. Another fruitful alternative was to play back a segment a large number of times until every nuance was analyzed. The time demands of these options usually make the cost-benefit ratio prohibitive for regular clinical usage, although valuable for training. Over the years new professionals have learned to use sound recording expecially in group or individual therapy sessions for later supervision.

The 8mm movie is fun to make, but very limited to view, especially without the advantage of editing. It also assumes the photographer is a technician rather than the behavior therapist who must attend to clients while the photography goes on. Neither the 8mm nor the 16mm movies have been used extensively in clinical practice, although some outstanding examples of recording by participant observers are known who were unusually gifted scientists-photographers, such as Bateson and Meade (1942).

With the advent of movable video equipment and its ubiquitious appearance in behavioral science facilities, mental health professionals found themselves faced with expensive equipment and a presumption that operation would yield instant sound/ moving pictures of critical behavior. This premise has not been fulfilled. The potential available in video equipment has not been fully realized, although many exceptional behavior scientists have found innovative ways to use this equipment.

Some of these are described in this book and in the previous work of Fred Stoller (1969) and Harry Wilmer (1968).

Any mental health practitioner can derive a clinical value from video equipment if he or she becomes aware of the ideas presented in the balance of this chapter. These ideas were developed in group applications of video recording and playback since 1975 (Cutter, 1978).

RECORDING AND PHOTOGRAPHY

The human eyewitness always selects what is worthy of attention. The camera cannot select by itself. The image on the monitor is less interesting than what an eyewitness sees. The camera operator must preselect content that is important to the patients or behavior scientists who will be viewing the completed tapes. Selection occurs in every group session by leader attention to some behaviors and not others. The camera person has the burden of attempting to select for recording psychologically relevant action. The simplest procedure is to focus on the people the group leader is talking about, or who are speaking. To do this requires the camera person to point the camera and make a host of selections with respect to operation: focusing, aperture, switching cameras, moving camera. All of these operations yield an emphasis on the behavior and image recorded for later playback. Such emphasis preempts the viewers' ability to select as in the live encounter. The later audiences are dependent upon the choices made by the camera person, who has the psychological responsibility of emphasizing important and minimizing unimportant action—at least by the criteria of the group leader.

While acting on these criteria is difficult, it is no more so than the clinical problems of the co-therapist in complementing the effectiveness of the group leader's role. The clinical photographer need not be "right on" every time and, despite the preceding, can contribute significantly even if lacking the same perspective as the group leader. However, this person must avoid random photography. The choice for visual recording must reflect some clinical considerations and control of the equipment. Otherwise, the subsequent viewer is bombarded with noise: clinically irrelevant information. For this reason, viewers in playback situations are even more vulnerable to boredom than the ordinary TV fans. Viewer interest can be maintained by first employing selection. A viewer will always watch his or her own image, or a person with whom he or she shares an encounter, but not indefinitely.

An additional resource in recording is to introduce movement in playback by moving the camera. This is especially helpful when one person tends to hold a monologue. The ways to move the camera and what this camera work can do for the recording will be described below.

However, a word of assurance is necessary to the mental health professional who feels all thumbs when it comes to operating anything mechanical. Aggravating this self-doubt will be the awareness of what 16mm movie documentaries or educational TV can present. The reader should note that video recording is an instant version of 16mm moving images, better suited to produce *cinema verite* than the polished and carefully edited movie. Like scribbled notes, the object is information storage; the difference is that the camera person is more like a co-therapist whose feedback complements the work of the group leader.

Recording Methods

The video methods for recording relevant activities and the rationale for use by behavior scientists are described in this section.

Overall Framing of the Person in a Context

Usually these are long views. The value comes from orienting the viewer to person, place, time, and psychological context. These should occur frequently, often enough to help the viewer remember who is talking, who is listening, and what the meeting is intended to accomplish.

Panning

The camera rotates slowly over the entire scene, which is

primarily a surveillance function in the group. The camera is monitoring all behaviors in the group for an action worthy of special attention. The operator can combine this movement with a personal scanning in other directions, which attempts to anticipate new patient reactions. By noting facial changes or inhibited movement, the camera person can focus on the patient just before a more overt reaction. Additionally, such slight movements are clues to unspoken thought that the group can note in later feedback.

Zooming

This is a close-up picture of a person, body part, or detail. Its purpose is to observe an action closely and in doing so to emphasize its importance to the viewer and later the subject. Zooming is especially helpful in identifing affect through body language.

Focus Changes

These occur when zooming in or out. The net effect is to give the viewer a blurred image, which comes into sharp focus later. This sequence helps to stress the importance of the detail photographed. It is usually avoided by switching cameras in broadcast TV.

Trolley

The camera moves on its tripod or wheels to yield different angles in the photography. This is useful in shifting perspective or emphasizing some different aspect of an ongoing group member's participation. Trolley of the camera also helps to hold viewer interest by camera movement.

Camera Selector

When two cameras are in use, switching from one to another gives the viewer two different perspectives on the same process. The cameras should be placed so as to yield relevant and appropriate views. Camera changes allow a quick shift from one person to another. The camera selector also allows a "wipe in" or "out" of two scenes simultaneously and is helpful in relating the content of two views, for example as husband-wife, patient-staff, two peers. It may not always be needed or available. Its major value is to provide images that complement what the one operator can focus upon. It requires someone other than the group leader to switch cameras to prevent overload. Most often this will be the camera person, who may easily become overloaded also. There is a cost-benefit factor to consider in the use of two or more cameras.

Recording Rationale

The rationale for choice of camera work is largely a matter of professional judgment. What behavior does the psychologist wish to elicit at which time? What does the mental health viewer want to see? The clinical photographer must fall back on his or her own professional criteria to select action that is most relevant to diagnostic or psychological interventions. The following are more general principles that can guide a professional camera person in the operation of video equipment in a clinical context.

Since the vocal sound track is always available for continuity, the visual image can shift to those participants who are listening, interrupting, or not reacting. This provides the viewer with information about nonverbal participation. As such the video track will emphasize body-language kinds of interaction to the accompaniment of a manifest verbal dialogue. Action or movement will become more important than the spoken word in later feedbacks.

The camera operator should look for movement in the speaker or the listeners, since visual reactions to spoken words are more likely to yield clinically noteworthy behavior in the subsequent moments. Where a listener is changing posture, using hand gesture, turning head, or making a nervous gesture, there the photographer is most likely to encounter important behavior. Movement is often followed by speech or other interactions of interest to a clinician.

Reaction time of the photographer has to be fast. Shifting the focus from a speaker to a reactor calls for the same shift in gaze as a group leader might use. These shifts in camera focus should give a later viewer a sense of knowing what the participants are doing in relation to each other. The resultant camera changes are usually more abrupt than in TV photography, which is geared to entertainment rather than professional information.

Sequences are useful guides to orient the camera. The clinical photographer can start with a subject speaking, shift to those reacting, return to subject, and repeat as the process unfolds to yield some behavioral manifestations that are illustrative of a clinical problem. The operator should remember to follow through in the process of focusing the camera on a complete sequence. A movement signals the start; photograph this; do appropriate camera work to record additional behaviors; relate to context to give the viewer a complete perspective; look for a punctuation, some verbal or nonverbal signal that changes the subject.

The viewer needs frequent orienting information in the form of quick close-ups of speakers, overall views of the scene; clocks, calendars, names and symbolic people: guards, nurses, agency workers. These provide cues that are usually available in the live situation. Often they are noted subconsciously but are missed in video playback.

FEEDBACK OF VIDEO RECORDING

Recorded behavior permits extension of clinical observations through time and space. Scheduled activities for patients by one professional such as psychologist, physician, social worker, nursing, recreational, occupational, and other staff become available for direct observation by the psychotherapists or mental health team. Evening and weekend activity involving groups, families, or solitary behavior can be recorded and then reviewed by appropriate staff in optimal places and at convenient times. The review can be a simple playback of the total tape, preselected portions, or edited vignettes. Responsible staff can use this review to evaluate total programming or provide additional attention to individuals within the total context.

Clients can study tapes with a psychotherapist. The range of possiblities are total playback, random selections, predetermined portions; patient, professional, significant other; immediate, delayed, spontaneous, or scheduled; in private or in group. These possibilities are listed to raise the awareness of the reader to the range of choice and the consequent necessity to consider the needs of the client in arranging an optimal series of feedbacks. A short review of some rationales for each is offered.

Total Playback Versus Selections

Total playback takes the most time and is the most demanding mode on patience. However, it is appropriate to consider for the first session, where the patient simply needs to indulge narcissism or become familiar with video images of the self. A client can be encouraged to stop the recorder whenever he or she wishes to discuss a segment.

Selections for review can be made on the basis of professional judgment as relevant to defined behavioral goals. The simple choice is already a statement about the importance of the reviewed behavior for client growth. Less authoritarian professionals may prefer to ask the patient to choose the portion. This becomes a projection of need and resistance, both of which can be documented by noting the behavior on and off the tape.

The selections can also be randomized by choosing any place on the videotape. A combination approach is to play the first two or three minutes followed by a client choice, then a professional choice, and closing with the last two or three minutes.

All of these reviews presume a professional dialogue with one client or a group. A selected subgroup of staff, peers, or family is also a possibility for participants in feedback sessions.

Timing of Playback

As in all efforts to provide client care, the professional should have a rationale. During the course of a session a significant item of behavior may occur, usually during an encounter between two people, that is worthy of instant review; stopping the camera and playing back the segment is an instant confrontation with self and irrational motivations. The nature of these motivations can be confirmed by group consensus and softened by group support. After the review the video recording can be continued. In the absence of a compelling reason to give an immediate playback, it is preferable to wait for the next regular session of the group for a playback. This interval permits affective distancing through time and enhances the ability to "see oneself as others do."

Some Logistics

If video recording becomes a routine aspect of the group process, a smaller portion of group time, perhaps a five-minute segment at the start, can be used routinely for review. Another resource is to use four rotating cassettes so that events on three previous sessions can be recovered for comparisons. Since tapes cost about thirty dollars each, the number of storage cassettes committed to one group is a function of money. In principle, every cassette can be saved forever, limited only by space and money.

The logistics of saving tapes can be reduced by some arbitrary sampling such as the first five, the last five, and a middle five minutes, or less, from each cassette. This permits a sixty-minute session to be sampled by five to ten minutes of edited portions onto a storage tape (any 60-minute cassette), which can then accept four to ten sessions depending on length of samples. This sampling technique allows the professional to review the growth of a client over the entire course of psychotherapy and, incidentally, to help the client develop more prespective on the personal struggles to reduce problem behavior.

In groups it is probably a good principle to limit reviews of tapes to group sessions so that significant behavior is not lost to group awareness. Thus, individual study of group recording is not optimal. Two or three reviewers with the explicit consent of all the group can examine some special portion as an exercise but should report their experiences afterwards to the group.

Edited Vignettes

As implied in the discussion on storage, portions of recorded behavior can be stored on another tape by an editing function available on newer models of video equipment. This editing function allows the professional to create a vignette, perhaps ten minutes long, which samples behavior of an identified client prerecorded in different times and places. Thus, a program that routinely records behavior on one or more occasions per day can be used to document the week's changes of client, or the continuity of one activity. The vignette is ideal as an aid for staff decisions about patient care or programming and for a review of group sessions through time.

The Video Playback Itself

The use of the playback is limited only by the professional judgment of the group leader using the equipment. It represents a source of data that can be introduced or stopped at the discretion of the leader. Through distancing, resistive clients will begin to see and hear how others perceive them, and selected defensiveness can be reduced. Another advantage is the presence of TV conditioning or "set." People are highly reinforced in American civilization for paying attention to TV screens. They are almost never given a bad experience by the TV image, or can "turn it off' mechanically. As a result of such reinforcements, patients in psychiatric settings seem to pay more attention and are less defensive, or resistant, to video playbacks of their groups than to the real-life encounter! There is less talking, sleeping, yawning, shuffling off to the bathroom, or other distractions than occurs in the actual meeting. The tape can be replayed until some appropriate sequence occurs, and the professional stops the machine for comments or reactions. Sometimes gestures can be caught and frozen for reply. This process permits messages to reach otherwise inaccessible patients with more extreme defenses.

Manipulating the Equipment

For inhibited, nonverbal clients, or people who are especially sensitive to their visual image, the opportunity to manipulate the equipment becomes a behavioral intervention that permits growth. The simplest procedure is to activate the equipment in a closed circuit mode. The camera picks up an image for display on the montitor, but it is not recorded on the tape. This permits the client to interact with the image on the screen knowing that "permanent tape" is not being made. Another approach is to place the client behind the camera, and after some rudimentary instruction on zoom and focus, let the client select people for photography. The images recorded become projective choices for the client behind the camera, or conversely nonverbal statements about participants in the group. The leader can create a context by giving instructions: photograph the person who is "helping the most" (the least) the kindest, the nicest, etc.

The closed circuit mode can be used as a stage for psychodrama or role playing. It also has value for transitions in a resistive group that is being introduced to regular video recording.

GROUP APPLICATION

Just as group differs from individual psychotherapy, live encounters without recorded component differ from those with recordings. The presence of video equipment changes the group situation just as two or more patients compared with individual therapy alter what a psychotherapist can use in interventions. This section will review options in terms of more familiar group therapy ideas.

Group Consensus

Group Consensus is one of the common concepts used to reinforce a leader's interpretation. The sheer experience of its presence is far more influential than any one intervention possible by a professional. Skilled leaders seek to elicit agreement at critical moments. Video playback permits a second and more systematic effort to elicit consensus in the viewers than is possible in the ongoing group.

Thus with events recorded on videotape, the group therapist

can provide one or more playback sessions in which the identified patient observes a previous behavior and relates peer reactions to recorded events. The usual group consensus is enhanced by repetition.

In playbacks, as in any psychotherapy with fragile defenses, there is always the danger of overwhelming the client and producing a condition of too much anxiety. Video playbacks add a dimension of vividness that can be perceived with greater threat, and especially with a group consensus that is critical. The usual support and reduction of perceived threats should be used liberally if the professional becomes aware of excessive threat.

Resistance

Resistance is always present in every context and remains the universal grist for the psychotherapeutic mill. Resistance to group leaders' roles and interventions can be better recognized in playbacks, and the usual skills can be employed. However, a different form of resistance is reluctance to give consent for video recording. In some situations the resistance of one person can become contagious so that the entire video recording process is disrupted or prevented. This phenomenon is more likely to occur at the early occasions of recording than after it has become ongoing.

The user of video equipment should be heartened by the realization that going slow gives the patient group time to desensitize to the idea. The comfort of staff is also a nonverbal cue for patients to accept recording and represents a separate dimension affecting patient resistance.

While waiting for all members of a group to accept video recording, the group leader can agree to allow some members to avoid being recorded. In time, such members will desensitize, or the group will begin to interpret or resolve this resistance. For others, this pseudorational resistance may mark the presence of a defensiveness in other areas that preclude the patient's participation in any form of psychotherapy, for example sociopathy, alcoholism, or paranoia. In time, these patients will eliminate themselves from the group therapy whether or not video recording is present.

The psychotherapist seeking to use video recording in groups should not be deterred by one or more patients who vehemently object. Their rights of resistance can be respected or approached by allowing them to sit out of camera range. On subsequent sessions their less manifest motivation can be elicited and appropriate treatment decisions implemented. Regardless, the reluctance to be videotaped provides data that permit more accurate evaluations. Thus, resistance to videotaping can be used in professional care of all patients — even though actual recording may never occur for some.

Time Concepts in Group and Video Playbacks

Experienced time is always here and now as the leader and members participate in the existential encounter. Psychotherapy is attempted in the various efforts to reflect a perception of self back to the identified patient. The ability to assimilate these reflections is called insight, and the subsequent alteration of irrational behavior is the goal. The professional encounter is simply another event or experience with respect to time.

Video recording permits additional time variations. Experienced time is usually contrasted with measured or real time. In video recording the tape reflects elapsed time, which can be changed from real time by stopping and starting the equipment. In contrast to recorded time there is playback time, which is usually perceived as longer in the experienced time perspective of the viewer, expecially if elapsed time is equal to real time in the actual group session. Playbacks of real time tend to be more demanding because reduced stimuli in the monitor are not equal to the experience for the viewer.

The user of video equipment needs to be aware that time perceptions are different in playback sessions, expecially for nonrecorded participants. The usual feedback approach is to record the total encounter, rewind the tape to the beginning, and start a feedback session. This naive process burdens the viewers with the unfolding of elapsed time. Even highly involved participants will find the playback of elapsed time more tedious than the experience of the group session in real time.

These different time perspectives must be considered and compensations introduced to optimize playback sessions. Feedback from recordings of total encounters or sessions of ongoing groups should be preselected. The leader can make notes on a standard "use sheet" (*see* Appendix A) following the actual sessions, which will help subsequent viewers locate incidents for review. Once located, a significant incident can be played for group participants or staffs. The real time is rarely over five minutes for any one sequence. Participants can then use the bulk of the time to observe and discuss the events.

Another approach is to edit separate incidents into one short vignette, which collects events by person, pattern, or scheduled activities so as to show the patient or staff member data that span time and induce insight or document a clinical judgment.

Both approaches allow the mental health professional to use a time concept in selecting, juxtaposing, or recovering events for more careful examination. In this sense the psychotherapist can stop experienced time or recover past encounters by use of recordings. The video equipment becomes a time machine for the videotaped events.

The problem of tedium in playbacks is also approachable by the use of a clinical photographer. Here the camera can be operated so as to approximate the view clinicians seek. The camera work noted earlier are the basic tools for the photographer. A trained photographer will yield videotapes that are more interesting for psychotherapy.

Elapsed time will still be vulnerable to tedium in some degree. Several further suggestions are offered. Elapsed time can be shortened by turning the camera on and off at critical moments. This process occurs automatically when portable, hand-carried equipment is used, especially at events or assemblies. The more usual occasion of a group process will tend to use a stationary, larger camera with recording equipment that distracts the participants with on-off noises. The larger obstacle though is the difficulty of anticipating a significant encounter.

Thus, it is better to have elapsed time equal real time for any one group recording.

The perception of experienced time can be shortened from elapsed time by using smaller time intervals for orientation or long views, perhaps one or two seconds. A nearly tachistoscopic presentation is sufficient for most viewers especially if recurring during slow intervals.

Panning shots should never be hurried but by the same token should only be used when there are no encounters visible. Much group process is chaff. Outside of starting and stopping behavior that punctuates the whole session, the bulk of behavior is preliminary and defensive. However, these interpretations cannot be fully perceived until a behavior occurs that focuses on some clinical problem. While awaiting these incidents, the camera person should be scanning the group to record the usual or defensive behavior of all participants. During these moments the goal is to provide enough information so that the viewer can examine the whole person's demeanor or actions. Panning should yield about two to four seconds exposure for each participant.

Specialized Groups

Group approaches to problem behavior are probably as ubiquitous as psychotropic medications in psychiatric settings. Despite the unevenness of clinical applications in both modalities, one can generally applaud their availability while encouraging more careful study of applications and professional skills. The kinds of groups described next are relatively unknown and have a visual complementarity that make video recording expecially helpful. These are described here as illustrations of the kinds of enhancement video equipment can offer. The usual kinds of group procedures can also be complemented by video equipment.

Consensus Rorschach

This group approach to the ink blots was first reported in 1959 (Blanchard), received some renewed interest in 1968

(Cutter), and slowly become more widely known, but still rarely used. The essential process is one of asking two or more people in some recognized relationship to agree upon the definition of any one blot of the standard Rorschach series. These can be compared to individual protocols elicited earlier. The most typical relationship is husband-wife. While some practioners use only sound recording or no recording at all, the Consensus Rorschach encounter yields the most potential for applications in assessment and psychological interventions with participants when it is videotaped.

The recording process is more effective if two cameras are used with one focused on the ink blots and the hand behavior of clients. The other camera should be focused on the participants to catch body language and positions. A clinical photographer should operate all the equipment. After the direct recording, a psychologist should prepare a summary of individual and consensus responses plus the different discussions preceding achievement of consensus. These are called content-polarities, which group processes as content. Manifest content is not personal data, or even personality of the members, but rather dimensions of any group. A sample list follows to illustrate:

1. Time of starting groups
2. Time for stopping any one session
3. Total frequency of sessions
4. Leadership expectations
5. Membership expectations
6. Seating arrangements
7. Roles for participants
8. Rules for all members
9. Permission to record
10. Completion goals for the groups
11. Duties of a co-therapist
12. Interruptions, etc.

A group organized for the purpose of training group leaders is one that provides an optimal occasion for video recording by an operator. Indeed, it also provides a training opportunity for practice in clinical photography as well as playback. By designating one member as photographer on a rotating basis, the operator becomes a co-therapist. The co-therapist is limited to the nonverbal, i.e., visual interventions in the choice of what gets photographed and how. After a suitable session of twenty to thirty minutes, the co-therapist plays back the recording. This feedback can be judged by its enhancement or distraction of what participants experienced. They can review the whole sequence or focus on a segment that provided the highlight of the session. After suitable playback and repeats, the clinical photographer can be critiqued for his/her motives in selecting visual content (Cutter & Farberow, 1970). This outline-summary of the consensus process can then become a guide to staff review or clinical feedback of the Consensus Rorschach encounter. The videotape for each blot can be played one or more times and, if appropriate, scheduled for ten sessions, one for each blot discussion.

This kind of psychotherapy can be identified as video-assisted guidance with communication problems in which content will be limited to "nonpersonal" ideas. This presentation will often resolve resistance, while permitting a psychologist-therapist to intervene with more resource information than usual.

The same procedure can be repeated through time with a different ink blot series or perhaps only using three to five of the standard blots for each encounter. (More information is available in Cutter & Farberow.)

Group on Groups

Mental health professionals are expected to and often do lead psychotherapy groups. Unless they have received group therapy themselves or group process instruction, they will bring very little preparation for the skills needed. Their knowledge of pathology is a prerequisite but never really sufficient for effective leadership. Reading and didactic courses are also a prerequisite but again never sufficient to yield group leadership skills. The mode most often available is to observe a more seasoned practitioner, usually as a co-therapist. Alternatively the novice group therapist reports experiences to a supervisor, either orally or by means of sound recording. Video recording is becoming more available than in the past, and trainee group therapists are increasingly making use of this equipment.

The group on groups (Cutter, 1978) approach is an experiential group in which potential leaders become members of an ongoing group.

Patient Government Meetings

Patient government meetings in any inpatient service can be modeled after all ward staff meetings. Optimally this should draw upon the ideas of therapeutic communities described by Maxwell Jones or Harry Wilmer. However, it is sufficient to have a patient government format whatever the philosophy the professional staff employs. In services not modelled after the therapeutic community philosophy, patient governments are usually oriented to minimal tasks such as election of officers, following parliamentary procedures, solving problems such as buying and making coffee or clean-up duties for common areas, recreation, and occasional management of difficult problems. Staff members function as resource people, and patients exercise choice in a social context that is familiar and in which they can play normal social roles such as citizen, chair, member, or secretary.

The video equipment should be turned on before the meeting begins and run a few minutes after it ends for spontaneous behavior. Sessions are usually less than one hour. The camera person scans the assembled patients, focusing on those whose body language expresses some affect, especially if responsive to a speaker. The principle of photographic selection is to look for clinically relevant behavior such as any mental health professional might do in observing the group. All patients are asked to sign a consent form that releases use of voice and image for playback to staff, patients, and trainees. Patients refusing to give consent sit in an out-of-range position. General resistance will dissipate over time with most people wanting to "see themselves." Ongoing resistance usually comes from sociopathically defended or substance abuse patients and will become transitory.

Toastmasters

Patient government officials provide leadership in electing a toastmaster and topic master and alternate with pairs of five-minute, three-minute, and thirty-second speakers. The format is the standard toastmaster presentation. This occurs on an occasion separate from government meetings, usually evenings with visitors present. It lasts about forty-five minutes, with a nonpatient selected as discussant. The toastmaster program provides confidence-building experiences and also allows the staff members to judge the social competence of each patient, especially when compared to performance of daily patient government sessions. Videotaping in this format is basically the same clinical problem as with patient government. The clinical photographer maintains the social role of a technician and selects people and events for recording as unobtrusively as he/she can. The photographer's movements should be smooth and relatively slow. Jerky or fast movement attracts attention. The monitor should face away from participants for the same reason. Audience reactions are relatively more important since the verbal content is usually not affectively charged or overdetermined. Patients' movements, as in chatting, being restless, coming and going, reflect their social competence, attention span, and degree of anxiety and provides useful behavioral cues to subsequent viewers.

Movement Therapy

Movement/dance therapy is not universally available as an intervention approach to the mentally ill. Where it is available, the physical motion of the participants is recordable by video equipment. The following comments are intended to orient the unfamiliar mental health professional to the activity and to point out some applications of video equipment.

Movement therapy is a form of psychotherapy in which the therapist uses movement interaction as the primary means of accomplishing therapeutic goals. It is a process therapy that is concerned with how an individual transforms an ongoing flow of energy to overt body movement, to imagery, and to verbalization. Movement therapists, concerned with this transformation process, believe that it is possible for a therapist sensitized to a range of human movement experience to actually see the ways in which a person blocks the expression of his/her needs; to see what it costs the person to give up old movement patterns and explore new ones; to see how experienced blocks in a person's movement process may be worked through and integrated by him/her (Pesso, 1969; Needham-Costonis, 1978).

In helping the disturbed patient to elaborate on his/her own movement, elements of time, space, energy, direction, weight, flow, and repetition are examined. The movement therapist uses these as expressive choices. The client is helped to transform action into optimal movement behavior. Changed patterns are related to tension states (Bernstein, 1972).

Each participant is recorded on videotape during expressive movement sessions two hours per week. A previous videotape session is played as part of the regular movement session one hour per week. The videotape unit and technician are perceived by participants as a valuable part of video-movement session.

Video feedback provides direct information about eccentric habits and movements of disturbed individuals. It also visually captures the disparity between one's inner perception of body posture and the reality of the image of one's posture. Video provides the means to reexamine a movement session. It has many advantages over recall ability and handwritten recording, which the movement practitioner uses as a directive and diagnostic tool.

All-Ward Playbacks

During the normal conduct of patient government, toastmaster, or movement sessions, it is difficult to make fully effective interventions or interpretations. The focus is on problem solving for the common cause or the task at hand. In the playback session, the tape can be stopped and discussion encouraged. Feedback and subsequent consensus allow optimal peer interpretation. The elapsed time, one or more days, also allows some affective distance to develop.

Daily playback sessions can be scheduled using one or more

previously recorded patient government, toastmaster, or movement therapy sessions. A psychologist turns on the equipment and activates the pause button when an appropriate sequence is viewed. In effect, this is a group discussion led by a group therapist, using a review of previous behavior. The rationale for comments is that both patient government and toastmaster formats are opportunities to practice socially familiar roles that are positive and normal. Individual differences provide examples that document mental health or illness. Playback of movement sessions has different goals and requires the technical competence of a movement/dance therapist. These playbacks are better integrated in movement sessions. However, on a selective basis group movement, comparisons for individual differences, can be played back for the whole patient/ staff assembly. Comparisons can be made of the same patterns manifesting in patient government, toastmaster, or other activities.

Suicide Prevention Classes

These prophylactic sessions present six principles of suicide prevention to high risk patients — those between suicide attempts (Cutter, 1977). Acutely psychotic, depressed, or self-injurious patients are excluded until improved. The groups are more structured, and discussions are focused on helping high risk people develop their own suicide prevention plans in anticipation of future self-injury behavior.

Videotaping these sessions provides orientation material to new patients which desensitizes the stigma of being suicidal while enhancing self-help potentials, including peer support or intervention. Playbacks for the same patients permit more influence that enhances the live encounters, especially in relating self-injury methods to overdetermining psychological factors. The latter demonstrate the compulsive and irrational clinical elements in the motivations of the self-injurious person.

EQUIPMENT COORDINATION

Routine operation of video equipment is facilitated if a total system (camera, recorder, monitor, and sound components) is available, preconnected by patchcords. If stored on a movable cart arrangement, a clinical photographer can move the equipment to a new location and activate the equipment in five to ten minutes. The return process is even shorter.

Record keeping is facilitated by a "use sheet" for each recording session. An example is attached as Appendix A. These provide documentation for annual records and when the tape is used again.

A patient consent form overprinted on a regular Release of Information Request form provides a general wording that five years experience has confirmed as optimal. Additional wording is illustrated for training uses (*see* Appendix B).

CONCLUDING REMARKS

Inpatient facilities are a subculture unto themselves. Efforts to introduce video equipment represent a metagroup process that typically encounters resistances which are rationally expressed, i.e. invasion of privacy, protection of patient right to refuse. While these are valid issues, an underlying and less rational motive is patient or staff anxiety focused on "seeing themselves" on TV or movies. Sometimes it is simply fear of the new.

The writer has approached different groups with different rationales. Psychology interns were confronted with the video experience in a group on groups context. Anger levels were high. Fifteen minutes into the session, the writer rewound the tape asking the rhetorical question, "Would anybody mind if I erase that tape?" The feelings shifted 180 degrees but with equal anger. They wanted very much to see the playback. The irrationality of their particular objections became more apparent, and usage during the balance of the academic year was uneventful.

Colleagues could not be approached in this manner, but inviting their help to draft appropriate wording for consents, and the time lag for corrections, helped achieve a greater willingness to allow "others" to be videotaped. Most group or individual therapists have minimal resistance to videotaping once the initial obstacles are resolved.

Patients as individuals will look to their primary therapists for cues in their initial or continuing resistance. Responses to groups or patient government meetings are influenced by the culture or atmosphere on the living unit.

The writer would recommend raising group consciousness about videotaping a session before the equipment is first scheduled. This can by done in terms of obtaining consents or perhaps showing a prerecorded tape of patient activities elsewhere. Another option is to demonstrate the equipment and to feed the narcissism of one or more patients in leadership roles. Any or all of these will be partially successful. However, there will always by one or more clients who resist the process. They can sit out of range, keep quiet, or agree to voice recording only. In time, the patient will give up the objection or leave the unit.

The professional seeking to introduce video equipment should be pleasantly surprised if no reactions occur. If they do, he or she should first join the resistance by accepting manifested objections and conceding whatever it takes to gain acceptance. In far less time than initial negativism might suggest, the clinical photographer will be able to implement video equipment usage. The reward will be enhanced effectiveness in the process of gaining behavior change for clients.

REFERENCES

Bateson, G. *Why the otter didn't play.* 16mm sound film, San Francisco, Fleischacker Zoo, 1950.

Bateson, G. & Meade, Margaret. *Balinese character: A photographic analysis.* Special Publications of the New York Academy of Sciences, vol. 2. New York, NY Academy of Sciences, 1942.

Bernstein, P. L. *Theory & methods in dance-movement therapy.* Dubuque, Iowa, Kendall/Hunt, 1972.

Blanchard, William. The group process in gang rape. *Journal of Social Psychology, 49*:259-266, 1959.

Cutter, F. Role complements and changes in consensus Rorschachs. *Journal of Projective Techniques & Personality Assessment, 32(4)*:338-347,1968.

———. *Coming to terms with death.* Chicago, Nelson Hall Co., 1974, 1977, 1979 (paperback).

———. *Suicide prevention classes with high risk patients.* Paper presented at American Association for Suicidology, Boston, Massachusetts, May 18, 1977.

———. *Manual for psychology students.* Fresno, CA, Fresno VAMC, 1978.

———. *Clinical applications of video equipment manual.* Fresno, CA, Fresno VAMC, 1978.

Cutter, F. & Farberow, N. L. Consensus Rorschach theory & clinical applications. In B. Klopfer and M. Meyer (Eds), *New developments in the Rorschach, vol. III.* New York, Harcourt Brace & World, Inc., 1970.

Needham-Costonis, Maurene. *Therapy in motion.* Urbana, University of Illinois Press, 1978.

Pesso, Albert. *Movement in psychotherapy.* New York, New York University Press, 1969.

Stoller, Frederick H. Video tape feedback in group setting. *Journal of Nervous and Mental Disease, 148(4):*457-466, 1969.

Wilmer, Harry. Innovative uses of video tape on a psychiatric ward. *Hospital and Community Psychiatry, 19(5):*21-25, May, 1968.

Appendix A

VIDEO CASSETTE USE SHEET

<u>RECORDING</u>

ACTIVITY:
TIME:
DATE:
PLACE:
EQUIPMENT:
TECHNICIAN:
STAFF:
PATIENTS (CONSENTS): Use additional space on back.

<u>CONTENT NOTES</u>

1ST QUARTER (0-200):

2ND QUARTER (200-400):

3RD QUARTER (400-600):

4TH QUARTER (600-800):

<u>PLAYBACK</u>

STAFF:
TIME:
DATE:
PLACE:
PATIENTS: Use additional space on back.

TAPE DISPOSITION: REUSE _____ SAVE ALL _____
                                   DATE   DATE

_____

STORE NUMBERS _____

_____

Appendix B

REQUEST FOR AND CONSENT TO RELEASE OF INFORMATION FROM CLAIMANT'S RECORDS

NOTE: The execution of this form does not authorize the release of information other than that specifically described below. The information requested on this form is solicited under Title 38, United States Code, and will authorize release of the information you specify. This information may also be disclosed outside the VA as permitted by law or as stated in the "Notices of Systems of VA Records" published in the Federal Register in accordance with the Privacy Act of 1971. Disclosure is voluntary. However, if the information is not furnished, we may not be able to comply with your request.

TO: Veterans Administration Hospital
2615 E. Clinton Avenue
Fresno, CA 93703

NAME OF VETERAN (Type or print)

VA FILE NO.
(Include profile)

SOCIAL SECURITY NO.

Name and Address of Organization, Agency, or Individual to Whom Information is to be Released

VETERAN'S REQUEST

I hereby request and authorize the Veterans Administration to release the following information, from the records identified above to the organization, agency, or individual named hereon:

INFORMATION REQUESTED (Number each item requested and give the dates or approximate dates—period from and to—covered by each.)

I voluntarily agree to the recording and playback of my voice and image while participating in scheduled programs of care provided by the VA Hospital staff. I understand all tapes will be erased electronically when the purposes shown below have been accomplished. To protect my privacy tapes will be stored and shown by authorized VA Hospital employees only, to myself, other participants and trainees.

PURPOSES FOR WHICH THE INFORMATION IS TO BE USED

All tapes will be used to facilitate direct care, evaluate progress, and provide training for selected VA personnel.

NOTE: Additional items of information desired may be listed on the reverse hereof.

DATE

Signature and Address of Claimant, or Judiciary, if Claimant is Incompetent

CHAPTER 5

VIDEO AS ADJUNCT TO PSYCHODRAMA AND ROLE PLAYING

RICHARD H. LEE

IN this chapter, some ideas and examples are given that can best be understood and used by a reader who shares certain assumptions and definitions. These will be presented as a few fundamental rules or bounds that facilitate the functioning of a psychodramatically oriented group with video recording and playback capabilities. Their purpose is to create a setting that will support maximum freedom and spontaneity for each member.

ASSUMPTIONS

Psychodrama

Right to Pass

The most fundamental contract between any group member and the rest of the group is the right to "pass" or say "no, I'm not ready" in response to any question, proposal, or request. Thus, each person in the room is regarded as the sole expert on his/her readiness to explore any area of his/her own life and on the means of exploration that best meets the needs of the moment. It is the obligation of the director (therapist, group leader) to protect any potential protagonist (a client or patient whose personal life is the subject of exploration) from pressure to do anything for which he declares himself unready.

No Physical Violence

Each member agrees that there will be no physical violence displayed in the group. At appropriate times, the director may instruct group members in techniques designed to portray violence in dramatic form and/or to release violent feelings in a safe manner, using pillows and other props as necessary.

Sharing

Following any role-playing exploration of a protagonist's life, the director calls for a period of "sharing" in which other group members speak only about the experiences they had in the room during the dramatization and associated experiences they have had in their lives. The director intervenes to minimize the giving of advice and psychological analysis and asks instead for self-disclosure from members willing to "share."

This bounded form of sharing, combined with the rules for readiness and against violence, develops a democracy of perception in which people share their inner lives from an equal position: personal associations stirred by one another and the psychodramatic action. The addition of video recording and playback offers a further democracy. The protagonist may now become an equally empowered bystander to his own actions, during the playback (*see* Hollander and Moore, 1972). This additional element of democracy softens the distinction between professional training and personal therapy since the availability of videotape playback allows study of the therapeutic process by the protagonist as well as other group members and the director.

Role Reversal

The fundamental transformation within psychodrama is role reversal (*see* Moreno and Moreno, 1975). A special quality of understanding is achieved when a protagonist willingly puts himself into another person's position, wears the other's history, assumes his posture, speaks in his idiom, and is responded to by others as the person whom he is playing. This experience is very different from talking about another person, no matter how well we think we understand him.

Role reversal can be used in many different situations. A protagonist may portray some important person in his life who is absent or dead, seeking to understand more about the person's inner life and feelings. Role reversal may also be used by two group members seeking to encounter each other in a new way. Each is asked to switch places physically with the other and then to speak and/or think aloud about the relationship with himself as the other.

The only conditions necessary for such an encounter to be productive are that each player be willing and able to portray the other authentically. Complete accuracy is unnecessary. Authenticity of portrayal, and the ability of a director to predict it in a given situation, come with practice. The other bounds described above must be in force, and the desire for new understanding must exceed the desire to prove a point—for both players and for the director.

DOUBLING: A very powerful and widely useful variant of role reversal is called *doubling*. In this form, a protagonist portrays himself and another group member is also asked to portray the protagonist, establishing identity with him, moving, acting, and behaving as the protagonist might behave. The "double" may be encouraged to speak what he imagines the protagonist may be feeling but not saying. In general, it is the "double's" task to aid the protagonist in his attempt at self-expression.

Whether the director or another group member becomes a double to the protagonist of the moment, three general rules should be observed:

1. The potential double should seek permission to assume the role — "may I double for you?"

2. The double speaks in the first person as though he were the protagonist.

3. The protagonist has the final word — he will be encouraged by the director to put into his own words whatever the double said that was right and to change what was wrongly represented by the double.

Video

Minimum equipment assumed is one video camera; one microphone; one videotape recorder/playback deck; one monitor for picture and sound playback. Various additions are possible, and each setting will have particular special needs. Consultation is desirable before purchase of equipment, since there are many variables: tape format (EIAJ-1, 3/4" cassette, etc.); lens range depending on room shape; lighting; audio quality, acoustic isolation of room; editing capabilities; broadcast or closed circuit uses; security for equipment and tapes.

In general it is best to position equipment permanently within a room that is secured from intrusion. With proper wiring in place, it should be possible for an authorized user to open the room with a key, throw a switch or two, and begin a session with full facilities operating. Once the equipment is in place, and a session has begun, it is important that the equipment be operable by as many group members as possible, one at a time. When someone wishes to be out of the action for a while, offering him/her control of the camera is an ideal move. A special quality of "cool" observation is frequently reported by such pro tem camera operators. Frequently, too, a moment is captured by the operator that can be shown to the group after the formal "sharing" and that may lead to a new round of exploration and/or dramatization. Ideally, the camera operator should be able to see a digital tape counter and to note the location on the tape of scenes for possible playback.

Special Equipment Configuration

Further democracy may be supported by a particular equipment design in which no one need leave his place in the group to go behind the camera. In this design, the camera is mounted atop the monitor and is fitted with a remotely controlled pan and tilt mechanism and a remotely controlled zoom lens. The control mechanisms for pan (left, right), tilt (up, down), zoom (in, out), and focus (near, far) may be wired to a small box, which can be passed from hand to hand within the group. Such a box may be safely handled by young children and protects the delicate camera from shock and fingerprints.

Permission

Before any recording is begun, each person in the room must

be asked permission for a recording to be made, and the director must take responsibility for enforcing whatever agreements are made in the group about the disposition of the tapes once recorded. In general, it is best to obtain minimal permission in advance of recording, since no one knows for sure what will happen in the session before it starts. If everyone present agrees to recording during the session, the director may promise to erase the tape at the end if anyone asks or to limit the audience for playback to people present in the room during recording. He/she may also propose a date on which the tape will be erased.

The director should specifically encourage the development of a group climate in which calls for playback of any portions of a tape may be made by any group member. If action is in progress, the director or cameraman should note the tape counter number at the point requested for playback, and delay the playback until an appropriate time.

How the tape will be stored and who will be responsible for its security and ultimate erasure should be made clear before the machine is started. In some circumstances, tape will be recorded and erased immediately following a meeting. On other occasions, it will be saved for a single viewing within a month or so. Only rarely will permission to show a tape outside the group be requested, and then usually for showing to a specific few persons (family, consultants, trainees). Ideally, the original group should be invited to all such playbacks.

Permission for the tape to be shown to anyone not present during the recording should be unanimously given after the recording is made. Ideally, a full viewing of those portions of the tape to be shown outside the group should be arranged in advance for the whole group, and any member should have veto power. Written clearance from every group member should be required if the tape will be shown outside the group. The written clearance should clearly limit the prospective audience and duration of permission. Group members should be paid a fee if others will profit financially from showing the tape.

The most difficult general issue around clearance for the use of tapes with public audiences is the question of "informed consent." Most people have had too little experience sharing their personal lives via television to know in advance or with confidence what the effects will be on themselves and their families, and on people who may be described or portrayed on the tape. Thus, very serious thinking and consultation should precede any project involving broadcast or public use of video-tapes of the kind described in this chapter.

If tapes will be shown on a regular basis to people not present during the recording and visible to those recorded, an attorney should be consulted in advance. He should be asked to prepare an adequate contract for permission to use recordings made. Laws vary widely from state to state. A good source of referral to an appropriate attorney is the bar association of the state in which the recording will be made and/or shown (*see* Berger, 1978).

Group

It is assumed that there exists an explicit contract between the director (representing the facility) and the one or more members of the group who will do psychodrama or role playing for whatever purpose (therapy, training, research, etc.). In addition to those bounds already outlined under *Psycho-drama,* and *Video,* there must be rules governing how members may enter and leave the group, fees if any, and scheduling of meetings.

Several other factors warrant attention in advance of the meeting: (1) Does this group (or subgroups within it) have a prior history? (2) Do they expect to have a common future as a group? Groups of people who live and/or work regularly to-gether will function differently from a group of strangers who meet for a weekend workshop. Groups of married couples will behave differently from groups of co-workers. A group made up of members of one extended family, where entry is only by marriage, birth, or adoption and exit only by death or divorce, is a special case.

Although most psychodrama and role playing are done in groups less tightly bounded in space and time, many examples and illustrations in this chapter come from family therapy applications. This reflects the author's major professional orientation and experience. These examples may be useful to others who see clients apart from their families, particularly in settings where intragroup relationships are well established (groups of co-workers, long-term ongoing therapy groups, groups in residential treatment settings).

Bystander

It is principally to allow flexible exchanges of role between "actor" and "bystander" that video is useful in psychodrama and role playing. Extensive treatment of the question of role flexibility and the value of the "bystander" is undertaken by Kantor and Lehr (1975). They argue that "the bystander function is the ultimate carrier of error information." "Error information" here means two things: (1) information about discrepancies between the intentions and the effects of each member's behavior, and (2) information about the system's overall operation — what to do more or less of to maintain itself in good functioning.

In any roleplay, one or both of these domains of meaning may be observed. The addition of video playback will enroll the players themselves as bystanders to their own actions.

Director's Choices for Playback

While as a general rule any group member may request playback of any event at an appropriate time following completion of the action phase, there are certain events that a director should especially look for and call for replay. The most important class of such events is that in which a protagonist or couple or family behaves in new ways that succeed in overcoming old obstacles in their relationships. In general, such moments begin with anxiety and end with relief and celebration. They may be played back immediately to enhance the celebration and generally require little or no introduction or comment.

Very early in treatment, when the therapist/director sees something he likes and appreciates in the behavior of one or more group members, he can profitably replay such a sequence with appropriate introduction and comment. This will serve to enhance the therapeutic relationship and to increase the frequency of such recognized and appreciated sequences.

Care should be taken not to play back behavior that the therapist wishes to reduce in frequency. It will be tempting from time to time to use the camera as a weapon to highlight pathology. This nearly always fails to achieve the intended effect. It generally results in a deterioration of the therapeutic alliance and increased client vigilance about the therapist's critical negative judgment. It may suppress the targeted behavior in the sessions but will likely have little effect when the clients go home. Such pointing out of negative sequences will reduce spontaneity in the sessions and may result instead in a sense of hopelessness.

When a client calls for playback of a "bad" event, care should be taken to discourage his use of that playback as a weapon in an attack on himself or against another group member. Once an adequate relationship has been established, however, playback of a client's own errors when he/she asks to see what he did wrong can be helpful. This should be followed immediately by an enactment, recording, and playback of an improved version by the same client.

In general, whatever behavior is singled out and given special attention by a videotape playback will occur more frequently in the future.

Some other events to be considered for playback are the following:

1. Physical action, where slow motion and repeated viewing offer a dramatically different visual perspective. Such events are particularly useful in working with children, perhaps because children seem to use physical action to express and explore their inner lives more freely and frequently than adults do.

2. Facial close-ups revealing deep or competing emotions.

3. Emotionally successful role reversals and doubling.

4. Meetings with members of extended family who cannot regularly be present. Such tapes may be replayed in their entirety over several subsequent sessions, with adequate pauses for discussion of the feelings stirred.

5. Structured exercises such as those described later in this chapter.

Doubling Playback

Following any psychodramatic or role-play exercise, a playback may be viewed and responded to in a number of ways. Here is a particularly liberating set of instructions that seems to offer optimal degrees of safety and improvisational freedom. The exact wording presented here is intended to suggest a set of themes. It is generally better to paraphrase from this text rather than to repeat it verbatim.

Instructions

1. "I will start the playback and let it run until someone watching starts to speak."
2. "When someone speaks, I will stop the tape. The speaker should then say 'As myself' or 'As Gertrude (for example)' and then, speaking in the first person, say what he or she may be feeling but perhaps not saying on the tape."
3. "If one person speaks for another, the person spoken for may use what was said for him, changing it or putting it into his own words."
4. "After each doubling comment during the playback, each person doubled should be given a chance to respond before someone else speaks."
5. Begin playback, stopping for comments, taking your time. Mark or note how far you get in a given session. Some rewinding after major stops will help "rewarm" the viewers when the tape is restarted — showing a running start from old to new viewing.
6. Before the tape has run more than one minute, if no one else has spoken, the therapist/interviewer should stop the tape and speak, modeling the doubling. The therapist may say something like (a) "as myself, here, 'I'm wondering whether or not to comment on my anxiousness — in this scene I am feeling frightened of something, but I don't know what it is exactly.'" or (b) "As Gertrude, 'I'm sad and angry about my

father — sad that he seems to have so little freedom, and angry that he imprisoned me within his bars.' "

Preparation

If an initial interview, or several, assures the director that members will speak their own feelings and inquire about others', no preparation is necessary beyond the "right to pass," video permission, and the above instructions for doubling playback. A more complex task confronts the interviewer when one or more group members say or seem to feel things such as "I know you want to hurt me" or "You're just doing (saying) that because you intend to. . . ." In this circumstance some preliminary work is required, which must be tailored to fit the individual clinical situation. The goal of this work is to prepare the group members for an expectant, curious, wondering frame of mind about each others' inner lives, without so much need to express certainty about other members' intentions and motives.

Special Case: One-To-One Therapy

Individual therapy with video requires some other special cautions. Particularly to be avoided is videotaping an individual interview with a person who might be diagnosed as borderline psychotic. Such interviews present problems in several ways:

1. Clients must be adequately prepared for the experience — can this one be trusted to say no if he is not ready for the experience?

2. All bounds must be understood as intended. This is very difficult to confirm with someone who may be thought disordered around boundary issues.

3. Structured activities (such as those presented later in this chapter) must be provided, and sometimes this is difficult when the therapist is the only available other player.

In the absence of these special attentions, a one-to-one interview with such a client may have unpredictable negative consequences, perhaps decompensation a few days after playback.

Two General Precautions

1. Use video with people you don't know well only in groups and with clear pass rule and introduction.

2. If in doubt, see your client in a meeting with at least one significant other person in his/her life while using video. Focus playback on the relationship during a structured exercise and away from intrapsychic issues.

WARM-UPS AND THERAPEUTIC EXERCISES

Warm-Up

The benefits of role play and video playback that can grow and flourish in a properly bounded group may be postponed or obstructed by early experiences of self-consciousness and inhibition in some group members. This will be lessened by increased duration of exposure.

More active steps may be taken to improve the quality of the "warm-up" and thereby reduce self-consciousness and increase spontaneity.

The general theory of group warm up centers around a paradox: we are least free when we fear we are too free; we are most free when we feel best held. "Best held" here means free from concerns that what we might do or say or reveal about ourselves will be inappropriate or premature.

As an example, imagine the early minutes of the first meeting of a group of strangers in which no suggestions are offered by the director, or in which people are told to stand up in the middle of the group and do whatever they want to do. It is likely that most members will sit quietly terrified, concerned that they might make fools of themselves in front of all these people.

By contrast, imagine a new group beginning with the director asking each person in turn to say a name by which he/she would like to by called and giving people the right to pass if they do not yet feel ready to speak. In this second example, each person can be sure that when he participates, his contribution will be seen as entirely appropriate — risking nothing. He is "held" by the warm-up instructions and is safe from what he may fear he might do if he acted without a clear sense of what is appropriate and acceptable to the group at that moment.

A collection of exercises is presented here, beginning with one in which the behavior called for is very circumscribed and proceeding to others in which greater freedom of action is encouraged. Experience as a director will build intuition about how much freedom a group can best use at a particular moment. If too little structure is offered, there will be tension, silence, and stereotyped behavior from group members — people will appear stuck, helpless, bored. If too much structure (too narrow instructions) is provided, the members will stretch the rules and improvise upon them. It is better, therefore, to propose a little too much structure and be flexible as the group stretches and improvises upon it.

Blindfolded Block-Stacking

This procedure, first devised by Rosen and D'Andrade (1959) to show the development of achievement motivation in children, has proven very fruitful in a different context. In has been used over the past seven years as an early warm-up focused on helping and helplessness, mutual dependence and independence. These are important issues early in the development of any group. They are also issues central to many couples and families entering therapy. The only "props" required are a box or bag of children's wooden blocks, two or more blindfolds, and a clock or watch with a second hand.

Instructions

1. Pour the blocks into a pile in the center of the floor.
2. Point to and look at two spots on the floor where players may sit facing each other with the blocks between them, each player showing a profile to the camera.
3. "Are there two volunteers to play a brief game in front of the camera? Playing and some instructions and discussion will take about ten minutes altogether."

4. Use whatever truths about the situation may serve to warm up the group sufficiently that two volunteers emerge and seat themselves.

5. "Is each of you right-handed?"

6. If "yes" from both, proceed as follows. If one or both are left handed, substitute "your more skillful hand" for "your right hand" throughout. If one or more are ambidexterous, inquire about writing, sports, or guitar playing, then substitute "more skillful" and let the player decide.

7. "The object of this game is to build a stack of blocks as many blocks high as you can and to leave it standing at the end of two minutes. We will count how many blocks are on top of one another in a column. You may use several blocks in a horizontal row if you wish, but we will count only how many blocks high your stack is."

8. Show some examples of towers and count aloud the number of blocks in each tower.

9. "Is all this clear?"

10. Answer questions and generally assure yourself that the instructions are understood. Learn to sense puzzlement, however disguised.

11. "To make the game more interesting (produce blindfolds) I'd like you to wear these. The camera will see how it goes, and we will be able to watch it at the end of the play."

12. Adjust blindfolds.

13. "Now, please put your right hand behind you and wait for me to tell you to begin."

14. Check watch, camera, reset tape counter or note its reading.

15. "You may begin."

16. The two players, working from a common pile of blocks in the center, will be constructing two towers, one on either side of the pile. Focus camera on the whole event, including at least both towers.

17. At the end of two minutes, "Your time is up, you may remove your blindfolds."

18. Count the number of blocks in each tower.

19. You may wish to discuss this event, or simply move on to the next two rounds — postponing discussion until the end of

three rounds.

20. "Would you be willing to do this again, a little differently? This time I would like one of you to do the same thing as before: to build a tower of blocks as many blocks high as you can and leave it standing at the end of two minutes, and to do this blindfolded and with your right hand behind you. The difference this time is that the other player will not stack blocks, but will be available to help the stacker. This help may be in the form of conversation. The helper may not touch the stacker or the blocks. Is this all clear?"

21. Ascertain clarity.

22. "Which of you would like to stack and which to help?"

23. Silently note the process of decision. Confirm or modify your impressions during the later playback.

24. When the decision has been made, signal to proceed.

25. "Are you both ready? You may begin."

26. Two minutes of play. Focus camera on the tower and the helper's face.

27. "Your time is up. Remove your blindfold please."

28. Count tower.

29. "Would you be willing now to reverse roles? You will now be helper, and you the stacker, okay?"

30. "Are you both ready? You may begin."

31. Two minutes of tower building showing tower and helper's face.

32. "Your time is up. Please remove your blindfold."

33. "What did this feel like to each of you as you did it?"

34. "Which was your favorite of the three rounds? Which did you like least?"

35. "How did it feel to help and be helped?"

36. "Did any of this experience remind you of anything else in your life?"

37. Open to general discussion including nonplayers as you rewind the tape to the start of round one for playback.

Variations

You may have more than two players. In the second and

subsequent rounds, each player gets to choose a partner and a role — he/she may be helper or stacker with one or more partners. This is very useful in families.

You may have several triads formed within a large group to repeat the exercise among themselves — two players and a director in each triad. They may rotate.

Playback

After rewind, at an appropriate point in the conversation, propose playback, with the understanding that anyone may stop the tape to comment or replay a segment. If the tape viewing is not finished in this meeting, another opportunity should be offered.

The Letter

This technique, described by Sacks (1974), acts as a warm-up by setting bounds that protect the protagonists from interruption. Further, by establishing the convention of an exchange of dicated letters, each player is relieved of having to process visual cues and is given time to consider and compose expressions of his own thoughts and feelings. Further, whose turn it is to dictate and be listened to is prescribed, relieving the players of many of the difficulties of free-form discussion.

Instructions

1. Help arrange floor space, cushions, or chairs so that people may sit back to back or at least be out of each other's sight.
2. "If you are willing, we will dramatize an exchange of letters. Whichever of you speaks first will say 'Dear . . .' and then a person's name. You may say the name of a person in this room, or the name of some other person in your life, past or current. Then you will dictate a message, however long or short you wish; when you have finished, you will close your letter and sign your name."
3. "As soon as a writer feels ready, he or she should say

'Dear . . .' and then someone's name. It's probably better not to try to compose the whole letter all at once, but just to start with 'Dear . . .' and see what comes after that."

4. Protagonist A begins "Dear . . ." and finishes "Sincerely, A."

5. At this point the director or a group member may add a single "P.S." to the letter, speaking in the first person as protagonist A (doubling).

6. Protagonist A adds a "P.P.S.," putting the "P.S." straight: changing what is wrong, and putting into A's own words what is right.

7. If this letter (A1) is addressed to group member B, the next letter will be a reply (B1).

8. If protagonist A wrote to his mother (not present in the group), B may be encouraged to write as A's mother in reply if B knows A and/or his mother. If not, A may be asked to write a reply as his own mother. Then B will write to A about the experience of hearing the exchange of letters with his mother.

9. Continue to listen to the group generate letters until a possible dramatic piece emerges.

Other Applications

This technique may be used later in a group's development to aid unaggressive members who may have a hard time fighting for the floor. It may also be used to minimize vagueness and abstraction, since it tends to focus on highly concrete and specific experience. It may be used in the sharing phase of a session, or at any other time when a director wishes to foster the dramatic reality that a person addressed is really listening.

USE WITH WARRING PROTAGONISTS. Whether in marital therapy or consultation to an organization, clinicians and others have the frequent experience of trying to help two or more people who are enraged beyond their ability to act quietly and appropriately on their own behalf. Use of The Letter in such situations is greatly enhanced by videotape recording and playback. The protagonists have an opportunity to hear and see themselves speaking in turn, reflectively, and without defensiveness against interruption. Frequently, they will see a solution emerge into a calm resolution. This has resulted in later spontaneous use of The Letter.

LETTER TO STILL PHOTOGRAPH. A variant that may be used in one-to-one therapy, after the appropriate precautions, is a proposal to the client to write a letter to the person on the screen. A single-frame still picture or a short slow motion sequence should be chosen, held on the screen, and addressed and signed "Dear . . . Sincerely . . ." The interviewer may then add a "P.S."

LETTER TO BLANK SCREEN. While recording a client's face and voice, if the interviewer feels that a letter to an important absent person is potentially fruitful, the monitor screen may be turned off. The client is invited to imagine the face of the important other person on the screen and to write him/her a letter aloud. Effectiveness of this technique is enhanced by placing the camera as close to (on top of) the monitor as possible so that eye contact with the screen during recording will result in the illusion of eye contact with the viewer during playback.

Sculpture

This collection of techniques has been described by Duhl, Duhl, and Kantor (1973) and Papp (1976). Two versions are described here.

Boundary Sculpture

This technique is particularly effective when working with people whose interpersonal relationships are impaired by too close adherence to the Golden Rule: "Do unto others as you would have them do unto you." By "too close adherence" is meant the unexamined assumption that my personal space is shaped the same as yours and that my rules for access to my personal space are the same as your rules for access to your personal space. The exercise offers a powerful demonstration of individual differences in personal emotional space through exploration in the metaphorically equivalent realm of physical space.

Many variations are possible to fit varied situations. The instructions presented here are intended as an example from which to improvise.

Instructions

1. Assure that adequate camera work is possible. Either appoint an experienced member to start as camera operator or use a remote control device with which you are thoroughly familiar. A great deal of camera work will be required.

2. "I wonder if one or more of you would be willing to try an experiment? It involves using the physical space in this room to stand for the personal space that each of us carries around with us. Perhaps you can recall times when people have stood too close to your face while talking to you, or too far away, and how that feels: invading or too distant. You may have noticed that being close to some people feels warmer or cooler than being close to others. You may remember people who have come too close to you too fast, or who have failed to 'knock' before they opened your 'door.' You may also have known people who prefer to be surrounded by one color or another. All of these experiences suggest that each of us might fruitfully explore and share some exploration of our personal emotional spaces as though they were physical containers of some kind around us."

3. "Is one of you willing to try this experiment with me?"

4. If not, inquire about people's current feelings and associations stirred by the subject. If so, proceed.

5. "Please stand comfortably and face me, trying to allow your body as much freedom as possible to express its sense of my closeness or distance from you. I will walk away from you until we both have the sense that I am 'out of your space,' that is that you don't seem aware of my presence in your space except as I speak."

6. Walk away, out of the door of the room if necessary. Keep the camera focused on the subject.

7. Walk back toward the subject, facing him/her, and stop at the point that you feel he/she shows awareness of your presence

in his space — a hand movement, nervous smile, change in posture, shift in weight, raised shoulder, whatever. Experiment here with backing up a little, moving forward a little to establish the perimeter.

8. Continue to approach the subject until it is clear that you are too close. If you feel you are too close but have not seen any outward signal to that effect from the subject, you might say:

9. "I feel that I'm too close for comfort, but I have not seen a signal from you. I wonder what will happen if I move even closer."

10. Continue to approach until you receive a definitive signal to stop. Keep moving even if the subject begins to back away from you or lets you push him backwards. Silently ask yourself "Do I feel as though I could walk right through this person?"

11. Repeat this exercise, approaching from the subject's right side, left side, and behind, noting which approaches yield signals and at what distances from the subject. Characteristically, you will experience the space around a healthy right-handed subject as bulging outward on the left (his weaker side), inward on the right. Some subjects will let you closest from the rear, others need a lot of space behind. Explore without comment, reserving comment for playback, later.

12. "I wonder if you'd be willing to take a walk with me here in the center of the room, just to get a feeling for the space? As we walk, I'd like you to notice the shape of your space, where it's bigger or smaller. Also, where are the doors through which other people may enter or leave? What are the walls made of? How high are they? Are they warm, cold, do they have colors? Are there windows through which you may look out? May others look in? How must I approach and ring or knock to request entry? What if I fail to observe the proper protocol?"

13. Throughout the verbal questioning, try out the various approaches — pantomime showing the doors, walls, etc. Get a "feel" for this subject's personal space.

14. Repeat with other willing group members. Use variations:

    a. Have one member do your job and another be the subject.

    b. Have two people build a shared space, another person try

to get in and out by the rules and breaking the rules.
c. Follow intuitive leads.

15. Sharing, after or during playback, with and without doubling; focus on individual differences, explicitness of signals.

Family Sculpture

This technique has goals similar to Boundary Sculpture. It addresses a family or ongoing group at a systems level, however, rather than at the individual level.

Instructions

1. "You've all likely spent a lot of time talking about how you'd like this family to be, and how you see it now. Talk, however, can be limited in helping us share each other's visions of how things might be and how they are. I wonder if people here would be willing to experiment with ways of showing rather than telling each other about their views of the family?"

2. "One way to do that would be to take turns being 'sculptor' using the other people and furniture and things here as though they were clay. Whoever is sculptor at a particular moment might ask the others to strike a different pose, put a particular expression on his or her face, stand in a particular place in the group."

3. "I wonder if there is someone here who is willing to volunteer to be the first sculptor?

4. If not, process current feelings and partial understandings. If so, proceed.

5. The sculptor, with support from the director, places each person to show an "ideal" picture of the family — how he/she would most like it to be.

6. The same sculptor, with support, shows how he sees the family "as it really is."

7. Another person becomes sculptor and does two parallel sculptures.

8. Each person is offered a turn. Those who pass are offered another turn at the end.

9. Playback with or without doubling.

10. Sharing.

Transgenerational Themes

Several theorists have argued that our current lives are directly influenced by our multigenerational family pasts. Notable among these are Berne (1970, 1977), Boszormenyi-Nagy and Spark (1973), and Paul and Paul (1975).

In work with families, using psychodrama and video, my colleagues, Richard Chasin, Jody Scheier, and I have come to develop a general hypothesis in this realm, which is shared here in hopes that others may expand upon and refine it.

Hypothesis

Each person who has children will be particularly sensitive to those aspects of his children's behavior which remind him of unfinished business he has with his own parents. Thus, he is likely to respond with intense feeling and a special quality of attention to some aspects of his child's behavior. This behavior is likely to increase in frequency in response to the special attention. Thus, children are covertly "enrolled" as their own grandparents, particularly in those aspects of their grandparent's lives in which the middle generation (parents) have felt most "stuck" around issues of loyalty.

True Clinical Case Reporting vs. Illustrative Examples

To offer a reader something more than a theoretical presentation of a potentially useful idea, a writer may present anecdotes from his/her clinical experience. Such anecdotes may be arrayed along a continuum at one end of which is a detailed case presentation, including the process of the interviews and the growing evolution of clinical hypotheses and interventions, interspersed with the distractions, misleading and wrong moves, and colorful idiosyncratic details of a particular family's life. At the other end of this continuum is the wholly fictional illustrative tale, more like a fable than a process recording. The fable can teach a truth about life distilled from many experiences, is much easier to read, but is misleading in its own ways — things are never as simple in "real" life.

Each extreme end of the continuum presents serious problems in a chapter such as this. The detailed case presentation must be changed in several ways before publication. Names and other uniquely identifying data must be altered to protect the clients. Much material must be omitted to make the case illustrative of the single hypothesis to be illustrated. Conclusions must be drawn which are oversimple given the real-life complexities in the particular case. Finally, short of publishing verbatim transcripts of all the interviews, the author's selection of particular moments and his interpretive biases will make the resulting report more story telling than hard data.

The "fable" extreme works well only when the "truth" to be illustrated is commonly known and believed. It has the advantage, however, of being honest about itself — it does not pretend to be literally true in detail, and it offers the reader or listener a chance to assess its fundamental rightness through its fictionalized simplification.

What follows is a case illustration that should be read as somewhere between detailed case example and fable. It is distilled from real-life clinical experience but written to be read as a fable, judged by intuition for its rightness and forgiven for being simpler and easier than real life.

Fable-Case

A woman brings in her six-year-old son because she is afraid he is depressed. Indeed, he spends a lot of time staring out the window or at a spot on the wall, apparently withdrawn from communication with others in the room. This behavior has been noticed in school, and this notice has given the necessary added impetus to an already concerned mother to seek consultation.

The child is checked out by competent physicians, who find no medical problems. An extensive developmental history is taken, which reveals nothing extraordinary in the child's early life except that he has progressively spent more time withdrawn and staring and less time in active contact with those around him. Everyone is puzzled.

On the general premise in family therapy that a larger part of the family system should be involved when a problem resists solution in a smaller subsystem, the child's aunt (mother's sister) is invited to a meeting with the family. The topic of this interview turns to the child's grandparents. His aunt reports that her father was quite depressed in his later life and used to stare out the window much of his free time. She further reports that her younger sister (child's mother) was very active in trying to cheer up their father and to engage him in interesting and pleasurable activities. Sometimes, she reports, this was briefly successful but had no sustained effect, and the father had died quite depressed.

It was proposed at this point that a brief role-played reenactment be performed and videotaped. The child was shown how to operate the camera's remote control and asked to take pictures of the play. Mother was asked to play father, sitting in his favorite chair, staring out the window. Aunt was asked to play mother (father's younger daughter) and to try cheering up her father. She tried joking, asking advice, tickling, telling important personal secrets, asking for help with homework, bringing gifts. Each attempt worked briefly, but then father (played by child's mother) relapsed into staring out the window.

The boy watched attentively and performed his task of camera operator extremely well throughout the play, except toward the end. In this final sequence, as Mother (played by the boy's aunt) made her last several tries at distracting and cheering up her father, the boy focused the camera away from the action, toward the part of the room where the wall meets the ceiling. Then he put down the controls and stared at the TV monitor showing this picture.

It was not until the playback of the tape was well underway that mother realized the significance of this role play. While doubling herself as she was playing father, she saw a smile flicker across her face as her sister (playing the boy's mother as a child) tried to cheer her (as father). She noticed the smile appear and then quickly fade, and she said (as double for father) "This feels good. Look at all the attention I'm getting. But if I give up my depression, will I have to give up my daughter too?"

Then she began to cry, and her son went over to her and sat on her lap. After a brief silence, his aunt asked that the tape be rewound a few seconds and replayed. When this was done, she talked of her envy of her sister's closeness to their father and her sense of exclusion from their private world. Mother then reported her former husband's irritation and struggles with her over how to handle their son.

The boy had moved to the other end of the office and was playing happily with some puppets. We three adults moved down, picked up some puppets and started to play with him. He showed us a puppet lying on the floor and said "He's dead now, but he's alive now too. You can talk to him and he can hear."

Aunt picked up this cue and had her puppet address the dead/alive one, saying "I miss you, Daddy, but in a way you will always be with me."

Mother followed and said through her puppet "I miss you too. The times we spent together were really special."

The boy asked to leave the room to go to the bathroom. While he was out, his mother and aunt and I discussed ways that Aunt might help Mother to play with her son when he was happy and active and to leave him alone when he seemed to need to be alone with his thoughts.

Mother and son moved out of state shortly after this meeting. An accidental meeting with Mother occurred about three months later. At that time she reported that her sister had been very helpful in taking care of the boy and helping her to follow up on the meeting. The boy seemed to be adjusting well to his new school situation.

Video-Integrated Communities

Once video equipment is in place and easy to turn on and use, the room in which it is located may be used in free time by groups of staff, colleagues, board members, and friends. Frequently, after people have gotten over their initial hesitation and self-consciousness, the camera becomes a special kind of friend to the informal gatherings that may occur. So long as care is taken not to allow its use to hurt anyone by pointing out faults or documenting grievances, and so long as everyone in front of the camera is invited to participate in any viewing of and reflection on his/her behavior, a special sense of community may be anticipated.

Video so extends our flexibility in role taking that it is a pity when its benefits are narrowly limited to professional therapeutic interventions and formal supervision and training.

REFERENCES

Berger, M. (Ed.). *Videotape techniques in psychiatric training and treatment*, 2nd ed. New York: Brunner-Mazel, 1978.

Berne, E. *Sex in human loving*. New York: Simon and Schuster, 1970.

————. *What do you say after you say hello*. New York: Grove Press, 1977.

Boszormenyi-Nagy, I., & Spark, G. *Invisible loyalties: reciprocity in intergenerational family therapy*. Hagerstown: Harper and Row, 1973.

Duhl, F., Duhl, B., & Kantor, D. Learning, Space and Action in Family Therapy: A Primer of Sculpture. In Bloch, D. (Ed.), *Techniques of family psychotherapy, a primer*. New York: Grune and Stratton, 1973.

Hollander, C., & Moore, C. Rationale and guidelines for the combined use of psychodrama and videotape self-confrontation. *Group Psychotherapy and Psychodrama, 25* (3), 1972.

Kantor, D., & Lehr, W. *Inside the family: toward a theory of family process*. San Francisco: Jossey-Bass, 1975.

Moreno, J. L., & Moreno, Z. T. *Psychodrama, third volume, action therapy and principles of practice (Vol. 3):* Beacon, N.Y.: Beacon House, 1975.

Papp, P. Family Choreography. In Guerin, P. (Ed.), *Family therapy: theory and practice*. New York: Gardner Press, 1976.

Paul, N., & Paul, B. *A marital puzzle: transgenerational analysis in marriage counseling*. New York: W. W. Norton, 1975.

Rosen, B., & D'Andrade, R. The psychosocial origins of achievement motivation. *Sociometry, 22* (3), 1959.

Sacks, J. The Letter. *Group Psychotherapy and Psychodrama, 27* (1-4), 1974.

CHAPTER 6

STIMULUS/MODELING (SM) VIDEOTAPE FORMATS IN CLINICAL PRACTICE AND RESEARCH

Nazneen Sada Mayadas and Wayne D. Duehn

THE use of videotherapeutic strategies for clinical problems is receiving increased attention both in practice and in research. By and large the primary emphasis of this literature has focused on video's confrontational capacity through instant and delayed replay. The therapeutic benefits underlying confrontation rest on the assumption that knowledge gained through videotape presentation of self—alone or in interaction with others—results in desired behavior change. As such, problematic behavioral deficits or excesses have become focal points of video interventions, leaving skill acquisitions to clinical interventions other than videotherapy. The aim of this chapter is to extend videotherapy into formats that include behavioral alterations through use of stimulus-modeling procedures. For purposes of clarification the following definitions are offered: video stimulus formats are presentations of cues designed to elicit specific kinds of observer reactions. Video modeling formats are more comprehensive in that they not only include stimulus cues but also a range of behavioral responses to those cues, as well as resulting consequences of those respective responses. Reviewed will be the theoretical underpinnings of stimulus/modeling formats, their current applications and status in practice, together with suggestions for future videotherapeutic usages and research designs.

STIMULUS CUEING

The basis for using stimulus-modeling videotherapeutic

146

procedures relies heavily upon concepts of stimulus cueing and modeling from social learning theory (Bandura, 1977). Social learning suggests that environmental events such as instructions, examples, and various sensory inputs affect behavior. These events may either act as prompts or inhibitors of any behavior or behavioral set. Such external factors influence overt behavior only when that behavior has been previously reinforced. Depending on past experience (reinforcement), these external events serve to cue or instruct the individual of the likelihood that reinforcement will follow the behavioral response. In the absence of experience, instructional sets that connect external events with behaviors are nonexistent.

During clinical assessments it is not uncommon to hear patients validate the social learning premise. For instance, a closed elevator may serve as a cueing stimulus for an anxiety attack for a person who was once trapped in an enclosed area. Similarly, when interacting with an authoritarian figure, one individual may characteristically respond with assertive behavior, another with compliance and resignation, while a third may not attend to the emitted authoritative stimuli—all based on their diverse past experiences. In other words, stimulus cueing is highly situation and person specific, based on past learning. This principle of stimulus cueing is put to its maximum advantage in videotherapy since it provides a methodology through which environmental events can be directly controlled within the context of ongoing therapeutic interactions. Clinical objectives are either to extinguish, build, or alter the relationship between selected behaviors and stimuli in the patient's own environment. Thus, the clinician is frequently faced with problems that in part stem from (1) failure of environmental events to trigger appropriate behavior, (2) environmental events inhibiting a desired response, (3) environmental events with behavioral excesses, and (4) indiscriminate stimulus cueing of behaviors. Videotaping of these environmental events, or their simulated approximations, brings the stimulus cueing processes under the systematic and more direct management of the therapist.

A prerequisite for effective use of stimulus cueing in videotherapy includes operationalizing problematic behaviors. Requisites for video presentations of relevant stimulus cues likewise require identification and operationalization of discreet environmental events. Information relative to these may be collected using traditional or standardized clinical procedures, for example assessment interviews, schedules, checklists, questionnaires, and *in vivo* assignments.

A second requisite for cueing is to ensure that patients attend to stimuli. To accomplish this end in videotherapy, content must be brief, authentic, and possess high visual and auditory impact. This is supported by Katz (1975), who states that such tapes are reactive in the sense that they are designed to elicit an affective as well as cognitive response from observers. Given that videotape presentations are accurate, intensified portrayals of environment, the therapist can differentially and systematically present these tapes for desired cueing. For example, repeated replays of the stimulus may be useful to desensitize individuals to particular stressful events, such as phobias, sexual dysfunctions, and anxiety reactions, and in value clarifications and cognitive restructuring. Conversely, repeated playback of stimulus tapes may be systematically presented as a means of sensitizing patients to their affective, cognitive, and behavioral excesses or deficits in selective problematic situations, e.g. assertiveness training, communication and social skills training, consciousness raising techniques, etc. A third usage, central to the definition of stimulus cueing, is that stimulus tape presentations may serve as actual cues in constructing, increasing, decreasing, or extinguishing behavioral repertoires.

MODELING

Findings of both laboratory and clinic settings demonstrate that modeling is an effective, reliable, and (relative to other learning procedures) rapid technique for instituting new behaviors and strengthening or weakening previously acquired responses. Modeling is effective in teaching a diverse range of overt and cognitive behaviors (Thelen, Fry, Fehrenbach, and Frautschi, 1979). In modeling, persons view multiple appropriate interactional behaviors relative to demands of the situation under study. Much social learning is fostered by exposure to real-life models who perform, intentionally or unwittingly, patterns of behavior that may be emulated by others. Once learners have developed an adequate conceptual set, increased reliance is placed on the use of verbal or pictorial symbolic models. A modeled performance provides substantially more relevant cues with greater clarity than can be conveyed by a mere verbal description. The establishment of complex social repertoires is generally achieved through a gradual process in which individuals must pass through an orderly learning sequence that guides them in progressive steps toward the final form of the desired behavior. Consequently, the efficacy of modeling procedures will depend to a large extent on the care with which the modeled performance is programmed (Ullman and Krasner, 1965).

A combination of verbal and demonstrational procedures is most effective in transmitting new patterns of behavior. Bandura's (1969) extensive research highlights factors that increase the efficacy of vicarious learning. Behavioral performances are more likely to occur when there is full, accurate, discriminative attention directed at the intended modeled behaviors; when modeled behavior is vivid, novel, and multiple; when the model is perceived as having high prestige, expertise, and demographic similarity to the observer; when the model is rewarded for engaging in the depicted behavior; when the model is seen as having interpersonal attractiveness; when the observer has received a specific instructional set; when conflicting, competing, or nonrelevant stimuli are minimized; and when the observer is given feedback and is rewarded for modeling.

Given these conditions, vicarious learning or modeling, as well as its procedural implementations, is easily achieved through videotherapy. Modeling through videotapes has great potential for use by clinicians in that the array of complex interpersonal and social skills can be identified, portrayed, systematically presented, and subsequently imitated by patients, thus eliminating trial and error learning inefficiencies so characteristic of many therapy modalities. Thelen, Fry, Fehrenbach, and Frautschi (1979) suggest that incorporation of video modeling promotes therapeutic control, convenient use of multiple models, repeated observations of the same model, use of the modeling tape with numerous clients, and the potential for self-administered treatment sessions.

STIMULUS CUEING AND
MODELING PROCEDURES IN VIDEOTHERAPY

Despite evidence that points to the efficacy of using video stimulus modeling procedures in clinical settings, therapists have been reticent to use these formats, limiting video application primarily to confrontational feedback. Central to the focus of concern here is the prevalent lack of reliable modeling stimuli that depict actual and measurable behaviors. While the need for development of stimulus-modeling (SM) tapes for clinical practice and education has received increased attention, little systematic effort has been put forth in this direction (Thelen, et al., 1979; Ivey and Authier, 1978; Kagan, 1975). This may be due, in part, to a lack of manpower and economic resources, technical "know-how," and clinicians' indifference regarding the incorporation of new technology and knowledge into practice skills. However, reports are now appearing substantiating direct clinical application of stimulus-modeling video methodologies (Fryrear and Werner, 1970; Duehn and Mayadas, 1977; Mann, 1972; Muzekari and Kamis, 1973; Persons and Persons, 1973; Sarason and Ganzer, 1973; Hartman and Fithian, 1974; Renick, 1973; LoPiccolo and Miller, 1972). In keeping with this more recent videotherapy focus, the approach discussed here combines stimulus-modeling videotapes with behavioral rehearsals and the more traditional videotape feedback procedures. These stimulus-modeling videotape formats are developed from clinical experience, reviews of literature, and problems presented by specific patients in treatment. Consistent with the conceptual distinction between video stimulus and modeling formats, stimulus cueing content is presented in video format apart from the modeled responses. This results in a product that allows the clinician to use the tape selectively either as a stimulus cue, such as in assessments, sensitization, and desensitization procedures, or as a means for presenting the entire cueing and modeled response sequence when treatment objectives dictate specific behavioral change, for example assertiveness training, social skill acquisition, decision making, etc. Thus their application within the treatment context is determined by threapeutic objectives, treatment phase, clinician's theoretical orientation and skills, and specific contextual demands.

STIMULUS-MODELING (SM) TAPE DEVELOPMENT

Content Identification

Recurring problem themes presented by specific patient groups determine the substantive content for stimulus-modeling (SM) videotape development. The rationale for starting with problematic responses in videotape development is that this approach provides beginning guidelines or directions as to how a specific video presentation can be focused and narrowed to ensure patients' attention to the stimulus cues and models. Each video presentation must be restricted to the affective and immediate relevant areas of concern. It is essential for stimulus usages to identify specific environmental antecedent events, which cue or do not cue problematic behaviors. For example, with information collected from nonassertive women, Rathus (1973) extracted seven frequently experienced problematic areas and developed assertive video models for each specific nonassertive situation. Similarly, Duehn and Mayadas (1977), from clinical extrapolation and case content analysis, focused on assertive responses to social ridicule, self-disclosure, and interpersonal decision making with homosexuals. In another study, selected problematic communicational patterns of marital dyads were used as a basis for developing nineteen modeled video vignettes (Mayadas and Duehn, 1977).

An important point in content identification is that video portrayals should include graduated stimulus cueing and sequental proximations of the modeled behavior. This is based on clinical work of Bandura (1969), who found that if models behave in a manner too far ahead of subjects' competence, it may inhibit subjects and subsequently promote their withdrawal from the actual interactional situation. The implication of these findings suggests the need for models to portray both behavioral approximations as well as the desired performance under several and diverse conditions.

Content Operationalization

Once problem areas and typologies have been identified, operational means are necessary for their incorporation into stimulus-modeling video formats. The first and probably most frequently used method relies on studio simulations. Here the clinician scripts a problematic vignette and engages coached actors and actresses to enact the given situation. The degree of improvisation varies from total scripting to brief instructional sets. The advantages of simulations lie in the clinician's ability to control factors that increase stimulus cueing and modeling efficacy. For example, scripts can be deliberately written to (1) relate common concern and/or elicit emotional responses and (2) capture the centrality of modeled behavior. Actors can be chosen who match physical and demographic characteristics of patient populations and who can accurately portray the behaviors under scrutiny. Through use of multiple cameras, zoom lenses, special effects generators, and editing devices, stimulus cueing and modeled performances are made vivid, discreet, explicit, while extraneous stimuli are diminished or minimized. Need for this is reinforced by Thelen, Fry, Fehrenbach, and Frautschi (1979), who point out that in modeling complex behavior and contexts it is necessary to both simplify and amplify the responses to be learned so as to avoid overwhelming the learner.

This studio-based operation may result in production of stimulus-modeling tapes of commercial quality, which can be marketed and shared with clinicians and educators in that particular area of practice. Drawbacks of this approach include limited access to studio facilities, high production costs, and time restriction beyond those of the average clinician. Some of these costs may be lowered by using relatively less expensive video equipment such as single camera black/white portable units.

A second approach involves taping actual stimulus situations and model performances as they occur in the natural environment. Authenticity is the primary advantage of this method. However, given limited hardware available to the practicing clinician, technical quality is frequently sacrificed through *in vivo* productions. Also, the videotaping procedures, which include the additional presence of a camera person, camera, lighting, microphones, etc., may have a reactivity effect on the situation and behaviors under focus. In addition, extraneous and competing stimuli may intrude on the video presentation and result in costly and time-consuming editing procedures.

A third procedure for developing stimulus-modeling tapes is to use patients' own behavior as stimuli and models for future responses. The rationale for this method assumes that a major source of stimulus modeling events in a person's environment is his/her own productivity (Bandura, 1969). Put another way, information that an individual has about himself/herself and the knowledge of the consequences of his/her activities serve as models for repeated performances. Operationally, tapes can be made of patient's approximations and complete performance of the desired behavior either *in vivo* or simulations. Through content analysis of the patient's tapes and editing procedures, the desired behavior can be isolated and presented apart from extraneous and competing stimuli. Although its potential efficacy is suggested in theory, the "self-as-model" has had little, if any, direct and systematic usage in videotherapy. While Stoller's (1968) concept of focused feedback considers predetermined behavioral categories, the total or sequential segments of the interactional process are reviewed with confrontational intent.

Content Rating and Reliability

It is imperative that content for tapes, whether scripted, extemporaneous, or *in vivo* be consensually validated and reliable; that is, is there agreement among observers over time that the tape displays the behavior, interaction, and/or situation it purports to portray? Thus, criterion levels for any given modeled performance must be predetermined. Videotaping may need to be repeated until this established criterion level has been reached. *In vivo* displays of those behaviors falling below criterion level are eliminated through editing procedures. Criterion levels are established by adherence to conventional conceptual rules of correspondence and by reliable consensual validations obtained through statistical rating procedures (Mayadas and Duehn, 1977; Duehn and Mayadas, 1978).

CLINICAL APPLICATIONS OF STIMULUS-MODELING VIDEOTAPES

In treatment, the stimulus-modeling tapes may be combined with behavioral rehearsals, videotape feedback, and home assignments and presented to the patient in the following order:

1. ASSESSMENT: This includes taking an inventory of the problem areas, problem selection, behavioral specifications, contracting, commitment to cooperate, assessment of frequency, duration, and controlling contingencies of behaviors (Gambrill, Thomas, and Carter, 1971). It is important to determine during this step what behaviors the patient specifically wants to acquire, delete, or alter.

2. VERBAL INSTRUCTIONS: Bandura's (1969) research provides consistent and decisive evidence that subject's attention is a necessary precondition for learning. Further, such instructions are more likely to facilitate modeling when they both activate a person to respond and describe the relevancy and ordering of responses. To insure attention to instructional sets, the therapist verbally provides relevant information on the specific skill to be practiced, concurrent with the stimulus cueing and various modeled presentations.

3. STIMULUS-MODELING TAPE PRESENTATIONS: Both the stimulus portion and the approximate and multiple responses to the stimulus are presented to the patient, relative to the therapeutic objective.

4. ATTENTION ASSESSMENT: The therapist discusses with the patient the latter's cognitive and affective reactions to the tape. It is essential that the patient be taught to recognize stimuli that elicited the video model's response. This is achieved through a series of questions in which the patient is asked to identify the specifics of each situation that led the models to behave "as they did," "when they did," and "why they did."

5. **Focused Feedback:** The stimulus-modeling tape is stopped at predetermined selected intervals to emphasize specific cueing and behavioral components. Approximations of skills are hierarchically ordered based on the patient's current performance level and the complexity of the skill to be learned. In other words, when the skill to be learned is multidimensional, the replay must be slowed and various components partialized to manageable size and practiced in an ascending order of complexity.

6. **Behavioral Rehearsal:** Patient and therapist role play the specific behavior relative to patient situation and treatment objective. These behavioral rehearsals are videotaped for playback, critique, and subsequent practice.

7. **Performance Feedback:** After behavioral rehearsals are taped, focused feedback procedures are used to provide the patient with information on the quality of his/her performance (learning theory suggests that reinforcement be given for achievement before making suggestions for improvement). During replay, therapist again stops tape to focus on selected aspects of pre-determined behaviors of concern. The patient is asked to comment on his/her own performance, make statements of relevancy of behavior in question and on quality of the response in terms of the appropriate criterion and specific situations. The therapist also gives suggestions as to how patient responses could be improved.

When modeling procedures are coupled with videotape feedback, the impact on self-viewing and monitoring of selected behaviors is considerably enhanced. Videotape feedback is a virtually undistorted reproduction of the situation under observation and acts as a self-corrective device for behavior change. This unique combination of viewing a stimulus-modeling tape and immediate playback of enacted behavior for critique provides patients with a mechanism for verification of their actual interactional pattern and opportunities for behavior change (Duehn and Mayadas, 1975). Use of videotape feedback not only aids in correcting dysfunctional behaviors but acts as a potent reinforcer for desired behaviors already in the social repertoire of patients. Because the initial experiences of viewing oneself on video may be anxiety producing, patients should be given an opportunity to view themselves on videotape prior to treatment.

Within treatment, steps two through seven are repeated until behavior reaches the criterion level of mutual satisfaction for both patient and therapist. Thelen, et al. (1979) note a lack of empirical evidence related to the duration of viewing and number of presentations required for learning retention. For example, in the authors' experience one modeled presentation and subsequent feedback on performance may be insufficient for learning. Moreover, it can have deleterious effects in that the procedures may be confusing, resulting in the patient experiencing frustration when expectational goals are not immediately met. Noting these affective reactions as well as temporary performance setback, Sarason and Ganzer (1973) suggest the continuous need for the therapist to provide realistic expectational set and numerous opportunities for model presentations and performance feedback.

8. HOME ASSIGNMENTS: Finally, specific behavioral rehearsals and assignments are given which are to be carried out through covert and actual role enactments. Projected reactions of self and others are discussed. In order to facilitate generalizability as well as to insure change maintenance it is necessary to arrange opportunities for practice in the patient's own social environment as close in time as feasible to when the skill was learned.

The stimlus-modeling procedures outlined above are illustrated through a case study which has been previously reported (Duehn and Mayadas, 1977).

CASE ILLUSTRATIONS

The videotape "Coming Out: Assertive Training for Living" was developed through consultation with members of the North Texas Gay Task Force and AURA, Fort Worth, Texas. Content for the tape was derived from commonly occurring problematic interpersonal situations actually encountered by homosexuals and a range of behavioral responses to these situations by assertive members of the gay community.

A twenty-six-year-old male accepting his homosexual orientation sought help with social and interpersonal problems incurred in his decision to "come out." During the initial assessment interviews, he identified skill deficits in the following impinging situations: (1) informing family and friends of homosexual life-style; (2) handling stereotypic reactions (ridicule, ostracism, spectator curiosity, etc.); (3) ambiguity regarding extent of self-disclosure ("Whom to tell and how much?"); and (4) repercussions of self-disclosure (possible job loss, severance of friendships, etc.). Baseline data relevant to specific problem situations were collected, and pretest measures of assertion were taken over a period of two-and-one-half weeks (five sessions).

Following the assessment phase, the patient was seen for six one-hour weekly sessions. Assertive skills related to "coming out" were depicted in a variety of independent interpersonal situations.

Phase I — Assessment; Pretreatment:

Sessions 1 to 5:

Assessment interviews. As part of the assessment package, the patient's responses to the stimulus portion of the SM were videotaped (i.e., both the multiple and approximate responses to the various stimulus segments to the tape vignette were withheld). Ratings of this tape served as one pretreatment measure of assertiveness (Gottman, McFall and Barnett, 1972).

Phase II — Treatment

Session 6:

SM tape: cocktail party. Various assertive verbal and nonverbal responses to social ridicule are presented. Home assignments are given consistent with treatment session focus.

Session 7:

Report back; if home assignments are successfully completed, present SM tape depicting multiple assertive behaviors in disclosing gay orientation to close friend.

Session 8:

Report back; if home assignments are successfully completed, present SM tape of those assertive models where sexual orientation is disclosed to a family member.

Session 9:

Report back; if home assignments are successfully com-

pleted, proceed to next SM tape of various assertive
responses to turning down sexual overtures in a gay bar.

Session 10:.

Report back; if home assignments are successfully completed, present SM tape in which gay friend is introduced to a heterosexual acquaintance.

Session 11:

Report back; review of home assignments, and final role
enactment of cumulative assertive behaviors.

Home assignments (which included covert and overt behavioral rehearsals and actual behavioral performances) consistent
with the treatment session focus were prescribed throughout
Phase II.

Phase III — Evaluation: Posttreatment

Sessions 12-16:

Pretreatment measures of responses to the stimulus portion of the SM tape are recorded (same procedure as
pretest, *see* Sessions 1-5, Phase I). Data on the six measures listed below were collected following treatment
Phase II. Specifically, posttreatment measures were taken
one week, two weeks, one month, three months, and six
months following the last treatment session (Session 11,
Phase II).

Pre- and posttreatment responses to the stimulus tapes were
rated on six behavioral components of assertiveness adapted
from Hersen, Eisler, and Miller (1973), with one modification.
In keeping with Fensterheim and Baer's (1975) observations
that the verbal behavior of the sexual variant is usually defensive rather than offensive, a measure (5 point scale) of the
client's defensive-offensive verbal behaviors was included in the
investigation.

Means were computed on all six measures from ratings of
two independent judges. Using an interrupted time-series,
single-subject design, multiple t tests were applied to determine
differences between pre- and post- treatment measures (Gottman, McFall, and Barnett, 1972). Suitability of t test application for single-subject, interrupted time-series analysis was
indicated by the stability of baseline data on all six criterion

measures during the five pretreatment sessions.

The results were as follows: duration of looking, t (4) = 2.38, $p < .05$; duration of reply, t (4) = .38, p n.s.; loudness of speech, t (4) = 2.18, $p < .05$; defensive-offensive, t (4) = 2.86, $p < .05$; affect, t (4) = .65, p n.s.; and overall assertiveness, t (4) = 3.42, $p < .05$. These results indicate that the patient showed significant improvement on four selected assertive measures. The patient's subjective assessment of therapeutic gain was consistent with other independent ratings. Content analysis of "report back" revealed that the patient was able to disclose his homosexual orientation to friends and family and effectively (assertively) deal with others' and his own reactions. He indicated a lessening of anxiety in selected social situations where homosexual overtures were made and when specific derogatory comments were directed toward him.

ISSUES AND IMPLICATIONS

The effectiveness of video stimulus-modeling procedures in treatment appears to be promising, although substantial empirical evidence is yet scarce. Bailey and Sowder's (1970), Griffith's (1974); and Thelen, Fry, Fehrenbach and Frautschi's (1979) reviews of the scientific validity of video procedures conclude that there is relatively little evidence from carefully controlled studies to support use of these procedures, or to justify the concurrent enthusiasm that has accompanied their applications. Primarily the limitations have been absence of control groups, undetermined reliable assessment measures, and lack of evidence for behavior change generalization and maintenance. This current lack of research seems inexcusable and rather paradoxical in that inherent in video methodology are numerous opportunities for collection, storage, and later, evaluation of raw data. Unfortunately, those who have advanced the cause of videotherapy have viewed themselves essentially as clinicians and have not subjected their clinical practice to the scrutiny of systematic empirical investigation. Little is known, for example, of the individual and separate effects employed in the format, the components of these techniques, and their interactions with patient characteristics on outcome measures. With regard to the last (patient characteristic), there is need for studies employing videotherapy with a variety of clinical populations and problem typologies in which treatment components are systematically varied. Particularly needed are stimulus-modeling formats that address themselves to frequent problems encountered by clinicians in the public sector: problems of anxiety and depression in mental health, social and vocational skills training for public welfare recipients, and parenting skills for child welfare settings, to name but a few.

Research is also needed to determine optimum number and length of model presentations consistent with parient's information-processing capacity. Likewise, ordering and timing of exposure to stimulus and modeled behaviors, verbal instructions, practice performance, and other format components need to be further specified to ensure maximum learning.

In conclusion, the video methodology explicated here needs to be incorporated into clinical practice. Specifically needed are technological skills for developing stimulus-modeling tapes, the employment of these materials in explicitly designed treatment formats, and assessment of their efforts on clinical outcomes.

REFERENCES

Bailey, K. G., & Sowder, W. T. Audiotape and videotape self-confrontation in psychotherapy. *Psychological Bulletin, 74*:217-137, 1970.

Bandura, A. *Principles of behavior modification.* New York: Holt, Rinehart and Winston, 1969.

———. *Social learning theory.* Englewood Cliffs, New Jersey: Prentice-Hall, 1977.

Duehn, W. D., & Mayadas, N. S. *Assertive training for marital therapy.* Paper presented at the 36th Annual Meeing of the American Association of Marriage and Family Counselors. Houston, Texas, October, 1978.

———. The Use of stimulus/modeling videotapes in assertive training. In Fischer, J., and Gochros, W. L., (Eds.), *Handbook of behavior therapy with sexual problems* (Vol. 2). New York: Pergamon, 1977, pp 431-438.

———. The use of videotape feedback and operant learning (OIL) in marital counseling with groups. *Group Psychotherapy, 28*:156-163, 1975.

Fensterheim, H., & Baer, J. *Don't say yes when you want to say no.* New

York: McKay, 1975.

Fryrear, J. L., & Werner, S. Treatment of a phobia by use of a videotaped modeling procedure: A case study. *Behavior Therapy, 1*:391-394, 1970.

Gambrill, E. D., Thomas, E. J., & Carter, R. D. Procedure for socio-behavioral practice in open settings. *Social Work, 16*:51-62, 1971.

Gottman, J. M., McFall, R. M., & Barnett, J. T. Design and analysis of research using time series. *Journal of Clinical Psychology, 39*:273-281, 1972.

Griffith, R. D. P. Videotape feedback as a therapeutic technique: Retrospect and prospect. *Behaviour Research and Therapy, 12*:1-8, 1974.

Hersen, M., Eisler, R. M., & Miller, P. M. Development of assertive responses: Clinical measures and research. *Behaviour Research and Therapy, 11*:505-521, 1973.

Hartman, W. E., & Fithian, M. A. *Treatment of sexual dysfunction: A bio-psycho-social-approach.* New York: Brunner/Mazel, 1974.

Ivey, A. E., & Authier, J. *Microcounseling: Innovations in interviewing, counseling, psychotherapy, and psychoeducation.* Springfield, Il.: Thomas, 1978.

Kagen, N. *Influencing human interaction.* Washington, D. C.: American Personnel and Guidance Association, 1975.

Katz, D. Videotape programming for social agencies. *Social Casework, 56*:44-51, 1975.

LoPiccolo, J., & Miller, V. H. A program for enhancing the sexual relationship of normal couples. *Counseling Psychology, 5*:41-45, 1972.

Mann, J.: Vicarious desensitization of test anxiety through observation of videotaped treatment. *Journal of Counseling Psychology, 9*:1-7, 1972.

Mayadas, N. S., & Duehn, W. D. A stimulus modeling videotape for marital counseling: Method and application. *Journal of Marriage and Family Counseling, 3*:35-42, 1977.

Muzekari, L. H., & Kamis, E. The effects of videotape feedback and modeling on the behavior of chronic schizophrenics. *Journal of Clinical Psychology, 29*:313-316, 1973.

Persons, R. W., & Persons, M. K. Psychotherapy through media. *Psychotherapy: Theory, Research and Practice, 10*:234-235, 1973.

Rathus, S. A. Instigation of assertive behavior through videotape-mediated assertive models and directed practice. *Behavior Research and Therapy, 11*:57-65, 1973.

Renick, J. T. *The Use of Films and Videotapes in the Treatment of Sexual Dysfunction.* Paper presented at the 81st Annual Convention of the American Psychological Association, Montreal, 1973.

Sarason, I. G., & Ganzer, V. J. Modeling and group discussion in the rehabilitation of juvenile delinquents. *Journal of Counseling Psychology, 20*:442-449, 1973.

Stoller, F. H. Focused feedback with videotape: Extending the group's functions. In Gazda, G. M. (Ed.), *Innovations to group therapy and counseling.* Springfield, Il.: Thomas, 1968.

Thelen, M. H., Fry, R. A., Fehrenbach, P. A., & Frautschi, N. M. Therapeutic videotape and film modeling: A Review. *Psychological Bulletin, 86*:701-720, 1979.

Ullman, L. P., & Krasner, L. *Case studies in behavior modification.* New York: Holt, Rinehart and Winston, 1965.

CHAPTER 7

VIDEO IN SEX THERAPY

Jack S. Annon and Craig H. Robinson

THE use of videotherapy in the treatment of sexual problems obviously implies that behaviors and attitudes may be modified or learned by observing some form of sexual stimuli. Therefore, as a starting point we will briefly examine what effects such sexual stimuli, e.g. pornography, may have on behavior when observed in nontherapeutic settings.

PORNOGRAPHY

Exhaustive and detailed accounts of some behavior changes occurring as a result of observing sexually explicit material, presented both live and in symbolic fashion, have been described by a number of researchers in the area (Mann, Sidman, & Starr, 1971; Mosher, 1971; Kutschinsky, 1971; Robinson, 1974b). The findings from these studies, and others, seem to warrant the following conclusions:

1. No study has convincingly shown any long-term effects of pornography on sexual behavior and attitudes.
2. Attitudes regarding various sexual behaviors appear to be quite stable, despite exposure to erotic visual material.
3. Many males and females exposed to erotic films frequently report various degrees of short-term sexual arousal.
4. There tends to be increases in the frequency of coital activity (if the activity already exists in the individual's behavior repertoire) within twenty-four hours after viewing pornography; however there still is no significant increase in the overall rates of intercourse.
5. It is relatively rare that novel sexual activities are tried, or low-frequency sexual behaviors are increased, following exposure to erotica. The most reliable behavioral effect is an increase in masturbation during the twenty-four hours

following exposure.

6. The majority of individuals who increase masturbation following exposure tend to be individuals with already established masturbatory patterns.

7. Viewing pornography often results in a temporary increase in sexual fantasy, dreams, and conversation about sex during the first twenty-four hour period following exposure.

While there are numerous other tentative conclusions that may be drawn from the available literature, the preceding seem to have the most potential relevance for the present chapter. That there are so many consistent "minimal" effects when pornography is viewed under natural or laboratory conditions would appear to justify the hypothesis that, given an appropriate therapeutic setting, coupled with therapeutic instructions, the minimal or nonexistent behavior and attitudinal changes currently displayed following exposure to sexually explicit stimuli might be greatly enhanced or instigated.

SEXUAL PROBLEMS

Considering the demonstrated effectiveness of vicarious learning procedures, i.e. videotherapy, described throughout, it is interesting to note that the extension of these procedures to the treatment of sexual problems has been relatively limited to a few clinical reports, with evaluative research being almost nonexistent. Wincze (1971) attempted to compare the effects of systematic desensitization with "vicarious extinction" in treating a twenty-nine-year-old woman who had no interest in sex and whose marriage was on the verge of a complete breakdown because of this. He first used a typical systematic desensitization approach, followed by vicarious extinction procedures where he had the woman observe films involving heterosexual petting and intercourse. This was then followed by reinstatement of systematic desensitization procedures. Improvement was only noted during the systematic desensitization procedures, and Wincze suggested that perhaps the films were too fear provoking and inappropriate to the particular patient's experiences. In a subsequent study involving twenty-one females complaining of sexual frigidity, Wincze and Caird (1973) compared the relative effectiveness of systematic desensitization and "video desensitization" to an untreated control condition. Both groups showed significant decreases in heterosexual anxiety immediately after treatment. However, in follow-up the video-treated group showed more overall positive changes than the group exposed to standard desensitization procedures. McMullan (1976) demonstrated the efficacy of some "automated" vicarious learning procedures for treating females concerned about lack of orgasm. A further report of evaluative research in this area (Robinson, 1974b) will be described in greater detail later.

Clinical reports are obviously more common than research studies. Hartman and Fithian (1972) provide client couples with visual materials such as films and still shots of couples in different coital positions or videotapes of research couples using nondemand coital techniques. For working with nonorgasmic women, they also use an audio tape of a woman who describes how she became orgasmic and how she taught other women to function well sexually. This is later followed with a videotape of intercourse showing this formerly nonorgasmic woman, as well as a videotape of the woman that she emulated, becoming orgasmic.

A number of others have reported equal success in following the Hartman and Fithian approach to treatment. For example, More (1973) describes using videotapes and films in a similar fashion by showing the client couple videotapes of research couples engaging in the various activities in which the clients have been asked to engage. More stresses the importance of showing the couple the videotapes *after* the client couple have first engaged in the activity on their own so as not to induce "performance anxiety." On the other hand, Renick (1973) reports using very similar procedures except that he suggests showing the client couple the videotapes of research couples *before* the clients have engaged in a particular activity so as to provide a possible "model" for them. Both clinicians report equal success, and only systematic research will be able to evaluate which procedure might be most effective for what particular client with what presenting problem.

Serber (1974) reports using videotapes in treatment in a somewhat different manner. Couples are given homework assignments of sexual activity along with instructions on how to use a videotape recorder. The couples then make a video-taped recording of their homework assignment and subsequently bring the tape in with them to their interviews with the therapist, where all three view the tape and mutually discuss what they observe, followed by feedback and further directions from the therapist.

In addition to these approaches with videotapes, others have reported using vicarious learning that employs a variety of audiovisual materials. For example, Lehman (1974) describes using slides in helping orgasmically dysfunctional women. Sayner and Durrell (1975), to reduce anxiety-related sexual functioning, ask couples to sit through hours of pornographic movies, or to read sexually explicit books together. Ellis (1975) uses a wide variety of materials such as pamphlets, books, readings, films, talks, and workshops in his "psychoeducative" procedures to help clients disabuse themselves of irrational ideas about sex. LoPiccolo and Miller (1975) incorporate some vicarious procedures into their program for enhancing the sexual relationship of normal couples by having couples view a movie showing a wide variety of foreplay and intercourse techniques from which they can later select and enjoy some experimentation in sexual activity, free of pressure for any particular result.

The Sex Advisory and Counseling Unit of the Human Sexuality Program at the University of California Medical Center in San Francisco (Vandervoort & Blank, 1975) provides a broad range of educational and counseling services that, among other techniques, uses audiovisual and written materials, as well as charts and programmed home assignments. As part of their approach to the group treatment of preorgasmic women, they show a female masturbation movie to help "demystify" the process of orgasm, followed by an assignment to go home and masturbate, but not to the point of orgasm (Barbach, 1974). Mann (1975) further reported that the unit is also in the process of carrying out a controlled study of vicarious group counseling of preorgasmic women. This combination of clinical treatment and research is certainly needed to evaluate the affectiveness of the wide variety of audio and visual materials now becoming available for use in the sexual area (*see* the catalogs of EDCOA Productions, Inc.; Focus International; Multi Media Resource Center, Inc.; etc.). It is interesting to note that very few clinicians have appeared to take advantage of the powerful modeling effects that might be achieved by having the client view a "model" who successfully "learns" the desired behavior, rather than viewing a model who already possesses the desired behavior.

The extension of vicarious learning procedures to the treatment of sexual problems seems to be a potentially powerful therapeutic strategy. However, the delineation of those conditions under which such procedures might be expected to be most therapeutically effective can only be discovered by research and not clinical intuition alone. To illustrate one approach to vicarious learning research in the sexual area, a brief description of one research project that investigated the "successful learner" concept follows.

RESEARCH

The genesis of this particular treatment research program came following numerous discussions by the authors speculating about the probable therapeutic efficacy of showing clients with sexual concerns various sexually explicit visual materials. With the proliferation of visual "aids," produced by reputable companies for educational and treatment purposes, the authors began wondering just what specific effects, if any, such materials might have on clients' sexual behavior and attitudes. Therefore, a treatment program that attempted to rely as exclusively as possible on vicarious or observational learning (via videotape) as the therapeutic medium was designed and implemented (for a complete description of the investigation see Robinson, 1974b).

The main purpose of the research was to assess the effects of a specially developed videotape treatment program on the sexual behaviors and attitudes of orgasmically dysfunctional women. The following experimental hypotheses were tested: Compared to untreated control subjects, subjects exposed to a

series of videotapes, i.e. vicarious learning, would experience
(1) an increase in certain sexual behaviors, e.g. self-stimulation,
discussed and/or modeled on the videotapes, (2) more favorable
attitudes toward certain sexual activities presented on the videotapes, and (3) the occurrence of, or an increased frequency of,
orgasm. The study further investigated, relative to each other
and to an untreated control group, two variations of the videotape treatment program. Both segments of the brief therapy
program consisted of three cassette videotapes ranging in
length from twenty-nine to fifty-four minutes. The first three
tapes comprised the "A" (or "Attitudinal") series, i.e. A_1, A_2,
and A_3), and were considered analogous to the "Permission"
and "Information" giving levels of the treatment model, discussed later. The remaining three tapes constituted the "Specific Suggestions" (or, Behavior") portion or "B" series, i.e. B_1,
B_2, and B_3. The basic format for all of the tapes involved a
male therapist talking to a role-playing couple ("successful
learners") who had sought help for the female's difficulty in
experiencing orgasm. In the A-series the therapist presented a
wide range of sexually related information to the modeling
couple. In the B-series, however, most of the information presented was limited to the area of self-stimulation and was accompanied by very specific suggestions given by the therapist
to the female of the couple. No suggestions were ever given to
clients to follow what was modeled on the tapes. They were
merely asked to just "view the videotapes."

Results indicated that a variety of sexual behaviors could be
acquired and/or increased in frequency by such observational
learning procedures. Of particular importance was the finding
that both videotape treatment conditions were highly effective
in enabling client subjects to learn various methods of self-
stimulation for the purpose of enhancing sexual arousal. Of
the six who initially stated that they had never, or were not sure
whether they had ever, masturbated, five began using self-
stimulation after merely viewing the videotapes. Of the ten who
at the outset stated they did not currently use self-stimulation
for sexual arousal, nine subsequently began engaging in masturbatory activities. Of the fifteen who were exposed to either of
the treatment group conditions, fourteen increased their frequency of masturbation. Results further suggested that both

videotape conditions, i.e. A + B, or B only, were highly effective in promoting more positive attitudes toward self-stimulation activities as compared to the "A only" condition. Although the data strongly supported the first two experimental hypotheses, hypothesis 3 was only partially supported in that the frequency of orgasm most reliably increased for just those client subjects who had experienced orgasm before. Only one client subject who had never experienced orgasm under any conditions was able to experience orgasm solely as a result of viewing the videotapes.

It should be remembered that the program was designed to see what effects, if any, a therapeutic program based almost solely on vicarious learning would have on certain sexual behaviors and attitudes of females concerned with sexual arousal and orgasm. The therapeutic package was never considered to be necessarily sufficient in and of itself to enable all client subjects to reach their individual goals. The treatment approach did, however, prove to be a major first step for most client subjects in establishing a foundation and later momentum for attaining their various goals concerning increased sexual responsiveness. In all but one case, individual treatment following the research program involved relatively few sessions and typically consisted of merely giving a few more specific suggestions logically following those that appeared on the videotapes. Furthermore, in each case except one, every female either eventually reported the occurrence of orgasm or markedly increased the frequency and conditions in which orgasm was experienced. The obvious financial and therapeutic benefits most client subjects received by being first exposed to this supplementary vicarious therapeutic approach certainly warrants further research attention.

Given the "success" of the program and considering the rigid conditions under which it was presented, it seems likely that there are several ways in which the effects of vicarious learning might be enhanced, such as providing clear pretherapy instructions, providing the material in incremental order, using models who resemble the observer, viewing positive affective consequences accruing to the model, and observing models who provide verbalized guidance and reinforcement.

The data also suggest that the frequent assumption that clients with sexual concerns must first develop more general positive sexual attitudes before significantly changing their sexual behaviors is questionable. The study indicates that the more global attitude changes client subjects showed following exposure to approximately three hours of videotaped material (A-series) regarding a wide range of sexual topics had little if any relationship to subsequent behavior change in specific self-stimulation practices. Significant behavior changes only occurred following exposure to the B-series, which involved "limited" information and specific suggestions directly related to the client subject's problem area.

A CONCEPTUAL SCHEME FOR THE
USE OF VIDEO IN SEX THERAPY

From the previous discussion it can be seen that a number of promising results have been obtained by the use of video in sex therapy. However, there are still some questions that need to be considered, such as what form of videotherapy learning will be most helpful for what specific problems presented by what type of client to which therapist from within which orientation? Should the therapist use slides, films, videotapes, or pictures for each problem? Indiscriminate use of particular video just because it is available is not obviously therapeutically justified.

What is needed is a conceptual scheme that can be adapted to many settings, whatever the client or therapist time that is available, that can be used by a wide variety of people in the helping professions, that allows for a range of treatment choices geared to the level of competence of the individual therapist, and one that would ideally provide a framework for screening out and treating those problems which will be responsive to brief therapy approaches and those which may require intensive therapy, and, finally, one that would also provide guidelines for the therapist on when to refer.

After devising and testing a number of approaches in different settings with a variety of people with diverse problems, a model was developed and shared, refined, and then taught to others, and has subsequently been used by a wide range of clinicians in the helping professions. This scheme has been described extensively elsewhere (Annon, 1975, 1976a, 1976b; Annon & Robinson, 1977, 1978). However, a brief overview of the model with particular emphasis on its application to the use of video in sex therapy will be offered.

The PLISSIT Model

As an aid to memory, this model is referred to as the PLISSIT model or, more accurately, P-LI-SS-IT. It provides for four levels of treatment, and each letter or pair of letters designates a suggested method for the use of video to handle presenting sexual concerns. The four levels are *P*ermission, *L*imited *I*nformation, *S*pecific *S*uggestions, and *I*ntensive *T*herapy. Theoretically, each descending level of approach requires increasing degrees of knowledge, training, and skill on the part of the therapist and thus allows individuals to gear this approach to their own particular level of competence. How many levels clinicians will feel comfortable in using will depend upon the amount of interest and time that they are willing to devote to expanding their knowledge, professional training, and skill at each level. The remainder of this section will be devoted to very brief suggestions on how to apply these levels of assistance.

Permission

Sometimes all that people may want to know is that they are "normal," that they are "okay," that they are not "perverted," "deviated," or "abnormal," and that there is nothing wrong with them. Often they are not bothered by the specific behavior that they are engaging in, but they are bothered by the thought that there may be something "wrong" or "bad" with what they are doing. The clinician may be just a sounding board for them checking out their concerns or the therapist may be able to let them know that they are not alone or unusual in their concerns and that many people share them. Such permission giving may be supplemented, or replaced, by the use of video such as appropriate films, videotapes, slides, or pictures that are directly relevant to their particular concern, such as thoughts, fantasies, dreams, feelings, or overt behaviors. (For a more detailed discussion of the application of Permission to each of these areas, see Annon, 1976a.)

Permission giving is most appropriate and helpful when it is used in direct relation to the client's goals, which will make it easier for the therapist to decide what form of permission giving, if any, will be most beneficial for a particular problem.

It may appear that the basic assumption underlying this level of treatment is that the therapist may sanction whatever sexual thought, fantasy, or behavior in which a consenting adult wishes to privately engage; however, there are some definite limitations to such an assumption. It is very important that the client is making an *informed* choice. The authors strongly feel that it is the therapist's responsibility to inform the unaware client of any possible adverse consequences that may result from engaging in certain thoughts, fantasies, or behaviors that the therapist knows may ultimately have negative or harmful consequences.

Further limitations are obviously set by legal considerations, e.g. rape, sexual activity with children, as well as by the therapist's breadth of knowledge in the area, the theoretical orientation of the therapist, and the therapist's value system.

Certainly this level of approach will not solve all sexual concerns or perhaps even many; however it may resolve some concerns for some people. If permission giving does not resolve the client's concerns, and the therapist is not in the appropriate setting or does not have enough time, relevant knowledge, skills, or resources, then this is the time to refer the client elsewhere. On the other hand, if the therapist does have the appropriate setting, knowledge, and skills, then he or she can combine permission giving with the second level of treatment.

Limited Information

In contrast to the previous level, which is basically letting the clients know that it is all right to continue to do what they have been doing, or *not do* what they do not wish to do, limited information is seen as providing clients with specific factual information directly relevant to their particular sexual concern. This may result in their continuing to do what they have been doing, or it may result in their doing something different. For example, providing specific information for a young man concerned that his penis may be somewhat smaller than average may be all that is necessary to resolve this concern (e.g. the foreshortening effect of viewing his own penis, no correlation between flaccid and erect penis size, that the average length of the female vagina is usually three to four inches and that there are very few nerve endings inside the vagina, etc.). A few minutes of such relevant information may change the client's viewpoint about his situation and lead to more confidence and different behaviors.

While these first two levels of treatment may be conceptually viewed as separate levels, there obviously may be considerable overlap. Furthermore, both may also be used in conjuction with the remaining two levels. In general, each preceding level enhances the effectiveness of the following level. However, because each descending level of treatment usually requires more time, knowledge, experience, and skill on the part of the therapist for its most effective applications, each level is presented and discussed separately.

It should also be pointed out that it is important to provide "limited" information directly relevant to the client's concern. Robinson's research (1974a, 1974b), described earlier, indicated that even presenting three hours of a broad range of sexual "information" has little direct influence on changing a client's attitude or behavior associated with a specific problem. Presenting "limited information" directly related to the client's concern does.

There are numerous areas at this level where video therapy may be most helpful in treating sexual concerns. For example, women who may be overly concerned about their breasts or genitals may view pictorial books, slides, films or videotapes of other women that illustrate the broad range of breast and genital shape, size, and configuration that is commonly found among women. For others concerned about their first pelvic or breast examination, viewing films or videotapes of women going through such procedures may be very effective. These are only a few examples of where providing limited information through videotherapy may be most helpful; however, it is not within the scope of this chapter to provide extensive information for each of the many other possible areas of application. For those interested, further readings are available elsewhere (Annon, 1976a; Annon & Robinson, 1978).

The limitations that applied to the first level apply here equally as well. Furthermore, the application of this level of treatment may resolve some problems that could not be handled by the application of the first level alone. On the other hand, if giving limited information is not sufficient to assist the client, then the therapist has two options available. He or she may either refer the client for treatment elsewhere or, if the appropriate setting, knowledge, skills, experience, and video resources are available, may proceed to the third level of treatment.

Specific Suggestions

In contrast to permission and limited information giving, which generally do not require people to take any active steps to change their behavior unless they choose to do so, specific suggestions are direct attempts to assist them in changing their behavior to reach their stated goals. This is done from within a brief therapy framework, which means that the approach is time and problem limited.

Before therapists can give specific suggestions to clients, they must first also obtain certain relevant information about their clients and their unique set of circumstances. If they were to immediately launch into a number of suggestions after only hearing clients label their problems, they may not only waste the client's time by offering suggestions that have already been tried, but they may further compound the problem with inappropriate suggestions. What is needed is a Sexual *Problem* History—not to be confused with a more detailed Sexual History. If this third level of treatment is not successful to help the client, *then* a complete sexual history may be a necessary step for the last level of intensive therapy. Guidelines for taking a sexual problem history that are deemed necessary for a brief therapy approach to treatment are as follows:

1. Description of current problem.
2. Onset and course of problem.
   a. Onset. (Age, gradual or sudden, precipitating events, contingencies)
   b. Course. (Changes over time: Increase, decrease, or fluctuate in severity, frequency, or intensity; functional relationships with other variables)
3. Client's concept of cause and maintenance of the problem.
4. Past treatment and outcome:
   a. Medical evaluation. (Specialty, date, form of treatment, results, currently on any medication for any reason)
   b. Professional help. (Specialty, date, form of treatment, results)
   c. Self-treatment. (Type and results)
5. Current expectancies and goals of treatment. (Concrete or ideal)

The taking of such a problem history will necessarily have to be adapted to the therapist's setting and the amount of time available. The proposed problem history is easily adapted to five minutes or five hours.

This level of treatment is seen as providing clients with specific suggestions directly relevant to their particular sexual problems and designed to help them achieve their stated goals. This level is especially effective for dealing with those problems that are concerned with arousal, erection, ejaculation, orgasm, or painful intercourse. The specific suggestions given (e.g. graded sexual response; redirection of attention; sensate focus techniques; dating sessions; alternate sessions; interrupted stimulation; squeeze technique; vaginal muscle training), and the method used (e.g. pictures, slides, films, videotapes), will of course depend upon the information obtained in the sexual problem history.

As mentioned earlier, there are now available a wide variety of films and videotapes for use in the sexual area (*see* the catalogs of EDCOA Productions, Inc.; Multi Media Resource Center, etc.). However, it is interesting to note that few therapists have appeared to take advantage of the powerful modeling effects that might be achieved by having the client view a "model" who successfully "learns" the desired behavior, rather than viewing a model who already possesses the desired behavior (*see* the Sensate Focus series of EDCOA Productions, Inc.).

It is not within the scope of this chapter to offer extensive specific suggestions covering all possible sexual problems. For the interested clinician a detailed description of the application of such suggestions to the more prevalent heterosexual problems encountered by males and females is available elsewhere (Annon, 1976a). However, it is within this level of treatment where many vicarious learning methods can be most advantageously used in videotherapy. Efficient use of this level of treatment will largely depend upon the therapists' breadth of knowledge in the behavioral and sexual area, their skill and experience, and their awareness of relevant therapeutic suggestions and video resources. The limitations discussed previously apply here equally as well.

This level of approach concludes the presentation of what is called the brief therapy portion of the P-LI-SS-IT model. As stated previously a number of sexual concerns may be successfully treated by this brief therapy approach; but, on the other hand, a number of problems that cannot be solved by this approach will also filter through. This is the point at which therapists may refer clients for appropriate treatment elsewhere, or if they have the requisite time, knowledge, experience, skills, and video resources, they may apply the fourth level of treatment.

Intensive Therapy

In the model proposed here, intensive therapy does not mean an extended, expensive, standardized program of treatment. In the P-LI-SS-IT model, intensive therapy is seen as highly individualized treatment that is necessary because a standardized treatment was *not* successful in helping the client to reach his or her goals.

For readers who have already received training within a particular discipline and a framework for intensive therapy, this is the appropriate time to initiate such treatment. For therapists who are interested in a psychological learning approach to the intensive treatment of such sexual problems, refer to Annon (1971, 1975).

CONCLUSION

The use of videotherapy in the treatment of sexual concerns has been a relatively recent event. A number of promising results have been obtained, which suggests that this may be a potentially powerful therapeutic approach to such treatment. However, the delineation of those conditions under which such procedures might be expected to be most therapeutically effective can only be discovered by research and not clinical intuition alone. There is a clear need for a planned systematic approach to treatment and research if the conditions of most effectiveness are to be discovered and used on a scale. This chapter has attempted to provide a tentative scheme for such treatment and research.

Therapists will naturally have to adapt their use of the model to their particular setting, the amount of time that they have available, their particular level of competence, and the videotherapy materials available to them. It is also important to emphasize that while the brief therapy part of the model is not intended to resolve all sexual concerns, it may handle many. It is the authors' firm opinion, based on an ever increasing amount of clinical and research evidence, that it is now unethical to involve clients in an expensive, long-term treatment program of any type without first trying to resolve their problems from within a brief therapy approach. There will be times when the specific suggestions that work for many others will not be effective for a particular client's problem whether the therapist has provided one or a dozen. There will also be times when interpersonal conflict may prevent many of the suggestions from being carried through. When this happens, and when the therapists feels that they have done as much as they can from within the brief therapy approach, *then* it is time for intensive therapy. This then means that a careful initial assessment of the client's special situation and experiences is necessary to devise a tailor-made therapeutic program that is unique to the particular individual and to his or her life circumstances. This is especially important, because what is available to the client beyond the fourth level of treatment?

REFERENCES

Annon, J. S. The extension of learning principles to the analysis and treatment of sexual problems (Doctoral dissertation, University of Hawaii, 1971). *Dissertation Abstracts International,* 1971, *32* (6-B), 3627. (University Microfilms No. 72-290, 570).

————. *The behavioral treatment of sexual problems: intensive therapy.* Honolulu: Enabling Systems, Inc., P. O. Box 2813, Honolulu, 96803, 1975.

————. *The behavioral treatment of sexual problems: brief therapy.* New York: Harper & Row, 1976a.

————. The PLISSIT model: A proposed conceptual scheme for the behavioral treatment of sexual problems. *Journal of Sex Education and Therapy,* 1976b, *2* (1), 1-15. (Also in J. Fisher & H. L. Gochrose (Eds.), *A handbook of behavior therapy with sexual problems, Vol. 1. general procedures.* New York: Pergamon Press, 1977).

Annon, J. S., & Robinson, C. H. *The PLISSIT approach to sex therapy.* Tape cassette E-7 AASECT, 5010 Wisconsin Ave., N.W., Washington, D.C. 20016, 1977.

————. The use of vicarious learning in the treatment of sexual concerns. In J. LoPiccolo & L. LoPiccolo (Eds.), *Handbook of sex therapy.* New York: Plenum Press, 1978.

Barbach, L. S. Group treatment of preorgasmic women. *Journal of Sex and Marital Therapy,* 1974, *1,* 139-145.

EDCOA Productions, Inc., 310 Cedar Lane, Teaneck, New Jersey, 07666.

Ellis, A. The rational-emotive approach to sex therapy. *The Counseling Psychologist,* 1975, *5,* 14-21.

FOCUS INTERNATIONAL, INC. 505 West End Avenue, New York, New York.

Hartman, W. E., & Fithian, M. A. *Treatment of sexual dysfunction.* Long Beach: Center for Marital and Sexual Studies, 5199 East Pacific Coast Highway, 90804, 1972.

Kutchinsky, B. The effects of pornography: A pilot experiment on perception, behavior, and attitudes. *Technical Reports of the Commission on Obscenity and Pornography,* Vol. VIII. Washington, D.C.: U.S. Government Printing Office, 1971.

Lehman, R. E. The disinhibiting effects of visual material in treating orgasmically dysfunctional women. *Behavioral Engineering,* 1974, *1,* 1-3.

LoPiccolo, J., & Miller, V. H. A program for enhancing the sexual relationship of normal couples. *The Counseling Psychologist*, 1975, *5*, 41-45.

Mann, J. Is sex counseling here to stay? *The Counseling Psychologist*, 1975, *5*, 60-63.

Mann, J., Sidman, J., & Starr, S. Effects of erotic films on sexual behavior of married couples. *Technical Reports of the Commission on Obscenity and Pornography*, Vol. VIII. Washington, D.C.: U.S. Government Printing Office, 1971.

McMullan S. *Automated procedures for treatment of primary orgasmic dysfunction.* Unpublished doctoral dissertation, Rutgers University, 1976.

More, J. The use of videotape and film in sexual therapy. Paper presented at the 81st Annual Convention of the American Psychological Association, Montreal, 1973.

Mosher, D. L. Sex callousness toward women. *Technical Reports of the Commission on Obscenity and Pornography*, Vol. VIII. Washington, D.C.: U.S. Government Printing Office, 1971.

Multi Media Resource Center, 1525 Franklin Street, San Francisco, California, 94109.

Renick, J. T. The use of films and videotapes in the treatment of sexual dysfunction. Paper presented at the 81st Annual Convention of the American Psychological Association, Montreal, 1973.

Robinson, C. H. The effects of observational learning on the masturbation patterns of preorgasmic females. Paper presented at the annual meeting of the Society for the Scientific Study of Sex, Las Vegas, November, 1974a.

———. The effects of observational learning on sexual behaviors and attitudes in orgasmic dysfuntional women. (Doctoral dissertation, University of Hawaii, 1974b). *Dissertation Abstracts International*, 1975, *35* (9-B). (University Microfilms No. 75-5040, 221.)

Sayner, R., & Durrell, D. Multiple behavior therapy techniques in the treatment of sexual dysfunction. *The Counseling Psychologist*, 1975, *5*, 38-41.

Serber, M. Videotape feedback in the treatment of couples with sexual dysfunction. *Archives of Sexual Behavior*, 1974, *3*, 377-380.

Vandervoort, H. E., & Blank, J. E. A sex counseling program in a university medical center. *The Counseling Psychologist*, 1975, *5*, 64-67.

Wincze, J. P. A comparison of systematic desensitization and "vicarious extinction" in a case of frigidity. *Journal of Behavior Therapy and Experimental Psychiatry*, 1971, *2*, 285-289.

Wincze, J. P., & Caird, W. K. A comparison of systematic desensitization and video desensitization in the treatment of sexual frigidity. Paper presented at the meeting of the Association for the Advancement of Behavior Therapy, Miami, December, 1973.

CHAPTER 8

BEHAVIOR REHEARSAL TO VIDEOTAPE SIMULATIONS: APPLICATIONS, TECHNIQUES, AND OUTCOMES

PATRICK H. DOYLE

APPLICATION TO POLICE CADET TRAINING: BASIC TECHNIQUES AND OUTCOMES

$\mathbf{A}$ HOUSTON Police Department male cadet receives a call on his patrol vehicle radio informing him of a family disturbance at a certain address. On reaching the address the cadet is greeted by an insulting, agitated, thirtyish female who is hardly able to respond to the cadet's questions for wanting to discredit her husband's son as being a habitual criminal. During the course of fact gathering by the cadet, the son appears and is quite angry towards the female for calling what he terms the "pigs." He appears approximately seventeen years of age. Like the female, he is quite irritated and even potentially violent, so the cadet seats both and continues obtaining facts. However, the young man contemptuously maintains "I don't have to tell you s————."

Meanwhile a female cadet has answered a call concerning the armed robbery of a convenience store and has apprehended a suspect matching the description of the perpetrator. He is burly and menacing looking, appearing in his early twenties. She is taking him into custody at gunpoint, ordering him to lower his raised hands one at a time onto the hood of the patrol car. The suspect has been glowering at her from the beginning of the arrest and at one point asks her how long she'll last "jacking" people around. She continues, though, with the suspect ultimately being handcuffed; she then recites his legal rights to him.

At the same time yet another male cadet has viewed a

disturbance and approached a scene where approximately fifteen people are huddled together on a porch. As the male cadet nears the scene, two men in their early twenties attempt to avoid the officer by leaving; he directs them to rejoin the crowd, however, and asks them what happened, as all three are now walking toward the frightened looking collection of people. Obviously quite excited, the two respond at the same time, making it difficult to understand. After instructing just one to speak, the cadet learns someone was shot and the guy who did it ran away about half an hour ago. By this time the officer has reached the group. A gray-haired woman in her late forties is kneeling over a young man of approximately sixteen years of age and sobbing as she rocks back and forth. The young man's chest is smeared with blood. On seeing the cadet she shrieks in utter desperation, "Oh help me, my son's dying, help, oh help me, please," and is overcome with sobs. The cadet has already begun a call on his hand-carried radio for medical assistance, but an onlooker exclaims, "He's stopped breathing!" At this point the mother collapses onto the porch and sobs while the surrounding people start to press in to view the body more closely. The cadet takes charge by directing a woman who had been consoling the mother to take her into the house and stay with her; shortly thereafter he identifies an eyewitness of the shooting from the crowd.

Finally, concurrently with the previous three cadets, a female cadet had received a call while riding in a patrol car with a male partner. On arriving at the location of a reported disturbance, they are met by a fiftyish, stout woman who strides towards the cadet and her partner with a scowl. Deliberately and scornfully snubbing the female cadet, she attempts to register her complaint with the male officer. He does not permit this, however, immediately indicating that the female cadet is conducting the investigation and the complainant will have to give her the information. At this point the complainant turns with a sneer to the female cadet and, shaking her finger as if to chastise, says "If you women would stay where you belong the world wouldn't be in this shape." As the complainant attempts to continue a denunciation of women holding jobs, the female cadet interrupts by saying "I can see you feel strongly about this, but right now we need to conduct an investigation—did you call about a disturbance?" The complainant then replies very sarcastically, "Yeah, I called. It's the same problem next door (pointing to a neighboring house). The mother is never at home and the kids run wild." Continuing, the complainant says "The kids play music so loud a decent person can't think."

Apparently as a result of the presence of the police and the pointing towards their house, three teenagers have come out of the neighboring residence to offer their side of the story. They are quite surly and immediately become verbally abusive towards the older woman. The female cadet quickly intervenes, sending the teenagers back to their house to avoid trouble; though her action is effective in controlling the situation, one of the teenagers makes a sexually suggestive remark to the female cadet as they are leaving, and the other two snicker gleefully.

As each of the preceding cadets completes the assignments, a videotape projector is turned off by an instructor from The Houston Police Academy faculty and the persons with whom the cadet has been interacting fade into a white screen. The four cadets had not left The Houston Police Academy during these episodes; each had been engaging in behavior rehearsal to videotaped figures projected onto a large (2.33m diagonal) screen rather than live people. The Houston Police Department now has four sets of video projectors with screens and a total of twelve videotaped scenarios averaging four minutes in length available for practice by cadets. Thus the cadets were simultaneously rehearsing confrontation management and emotional self-control to videotape simulations that represent the pressurized circumstances police officers regularly encounter. As observed by Menninger (1965), society places superhuman demands on police officers. He pointed out that the vicious tendencies we all share must be curbed by officers while acting in a self-restrained manner themselves. The resulting stress has led to high rates of divorce, suicide, and emotional illness among officers (Kroes, 1976), leading to their identification as victims of society.

Videotape simulations as illustrated in those used by police cadets are prepared via a number of unorthodox techniques. Chief among them is the subjective camera technique whereby the camera view represents the perspective of a participant rather than an onlooker. Thus in the finished product the figures, or correspondents, on the screen act toward the viewer, who in turn responds to them. As a consequence, scripts used in this sort of videotaping require the camera to faithfully convey the scene as a participant would see it; this contrasts with ordinary camera directions, which would call for a sequence of varying camera angles and distances to add interest and drama. Scripts must similarly provide acting directions that allow for realistic participation by the client. Hence the dramatic acting must be performed to a large extent to the silent camera lens representing the client rather than to another actor. In the earlier examples of a youth contemptuous towards the police officer, a threatening robbery suspect, and so forth, the actors played the respective parts as if addressing and responding to a person, though actually relating to a silent camera.

In videotaping a simulation, particular attention must be given to the timing of the silent periods in the videotape production, which would permit the client to make a response. In the actual behavior rehearsal the flow of the respective responses by the screen figures and the client must be effectively timed or else the realism of the simulation will be seriously eroded. If the resistive young man in the first example above tended to respond in a clairvoyant fashion to the cadet before he had time to express himself, the result would be confusion and loss of the sense of an actual interaction. During the videotaping of a simulation, the determination of the length of the silent sections is accomplished by the director silently mouthing or articulating the client's lines at the appropriate points in the script. For best effect, the director or an assistant takes a position at eye level with the camera lens. This is usually achievable by placing a chair close to the tripod of the camera so when seated the director's eyes and mouth are virtually adjoining the camera lens. With this arrangement the actors may maintain eye contact with the camera lens and, using peripheral vision, be aware of the signals of the director, who may prefer more or less to play the role of the client, albeit silently, to encourage more involvement from the actors. Of course, in the instance of the use of a portable camera, as when the walking of the client would be simulated, the director will need to be standing to achieve the same relative position to the camera lens.

This latter technique has proven to be amazingly effective. As a rule, such timing of the silent sections will result in client-screen figure interchanges occurring quite realistically. Even in the cases where a client has an exceptional rate of speech, either much faster or slower than the director's delivery, the scenario will usually be of considerable value. When a response is finished one, two, or even three seconds ahead of the screen figure's response, the client spends the remainder of the time rehearsing maintainance of eye contact rather than succumbing to the need to speak further. Thus the client gains practice in an often bothersome situation. The slower speaking client may have to complete the last few words of his response with the screen figure interrupting. As long as the meaning of the slower speaker's response was communicated before the attempt to break in, so that the screen figure's reply could reasonably be based on what was being said, such interruptions offer particularly valuable practice. The clinet can practice finishing statements despite others breaking in. For many clients, such practice is important. Of course it is realistic to have hiatuses and overlaps in conversation, as in real life people's remarks are rarely perfectly synchronized. Actually a large proportion of the scripts developed by this writer have purposely included interruptions, lags, and simultaneous initiations of remarks to permit rehearsal of appropriate responses in such commonplace circumstances.

To summarize, behavior rehearsal to videotape simulations generally consists of clients interacting with videotaped figures enlarged to life size by projection onto a screen. A script provides the client with responses, at least initially, so during the first few practice trials the client is reading all his/her lines as written to apply to the situation. As the client practices a scenario, dependence on the script reduces until he/she can easily complete the scenario without needing to refer to the script; at this point the client will have memorized a pattern of behavior, which presumably will result in more effective coping than was previously the case. In addition, having the pattern memorized and rehearsed in the realistic circumstances afforded by the life-size, color simulations would seem to enhance external validity or generalization.

While the client interacts with the screen figures, a therapist or trainer monitors the effectiveness of the client's behavior and periodically provides feedback. Thus the treatment package basically consists of overt rehearsal and coaching. As summarized by Galassi and Galassi (1978), the research literature tends to support the efficacy of such approaches, although their review did not include any instance of rehearsal to videotape simulations.

Figure 1 indicates the general layout during therapy or training with interactive videotape simulations.

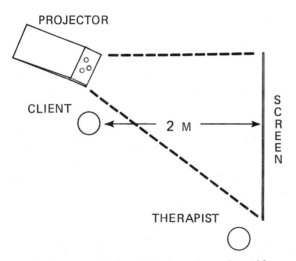

Figure 1. Physical layout during behavior rehearsal to videotape simulation.

It should be noticed that in the diagram the projector is shown positioned at an oblique angle rather than perpendicular to the screen. Although the projector would normally be placed directly in front of the screen, the arrangment shown is achievable with minimal adverse effect to the screen display, if the angle of the projector is not too severe. There will be some distortion on the sides of the screen display, but this is generally not noticeable. Also, the brightness of the picture does not seem to suffer perceptibly with this arrangement, although with some projection systems available this might prove a problem. The advantage is that the client may then assume a position directly to the front of the display so the screen figures accurately look at and make responses to him or her rather than slightly to the side.* The distance from client to screen is usually approximately 2m; being much closer to the screen will tend to interfere with the projection beam and significantly reduce the clarity of the screen images.

The therapist, as pictured in the diagram, is located near the screen and facing the client. This positioning has a number of advantages. Most obvious is the full view of clients' facial and gestural responses it offers for feedback purposes. Of considerable importance as well, though, is the proximity to the screen figures of a live person who is looking at the client. While the screen figures are compelling in themselves, the presence of the live person, especially positioned where more screen figures might appear if the screen were wider, further contributes to the realistic impact of the therapy. Also, as the client progresses, such positioning easily and naturally affords the opportunity for an occasional scenario in which correspondent parts are played by both the screen figures *and* the therapist. Thus the client could alternate his/her responses from screen figures to a live individual; responses to the latter should readily be accomplished with the same aplomb the client presumably has previously developed in relating to strict videotape

---

*There are of course rear projection systems available, but these are cumbersome, as considerable space must be available behind the screen to arrange the projector. Also, except for extremely expensive models, there is a substantial reduction in the brightness of the display. A more recent development is the mirror-projection system, which places the projector under the screen and, using a mirror, reflects the image back onto it. This approach may prove the most effective eventually; however, at this point the screen in such systems tens to be elevated considerably to accommodate the projector, which sits beneath it. This results in the screen display being unable to accommodate simulations involving sitting figures, who should be eye level with a sitting client. Due to the elevation of the screen, sitting figures would loom above such a client, resulting in an awkward and unrealistic simulation. Hence this system seems limited at present.

simulations. However, this would seem to be the sort of technique that should be used guardedly, perhaps as a means of innervating a client who demonstrated some resistance or lassitude. More than occasional use of this approach, though, would controvert a basic tenet of behavior rehearsal to videotape simulations.

The basic tenet is that automation of correspondents in the form of screen figures makes possible the large number of behavior rehearsals necessary for change. Whereas normally the therapist must enact a role for each instance of behavior rehearsal, which is quite an exhausting process, the use of videotape simulations only requires operation of a videotape player to provide similar practice. Meanwhile the therapist is free to observe, draw inferences, and provide feedback on the client's performance. In brief, behavior rehearsal to videotape simulations makes it convenient for a therapist to provide ample active practice to clients, practice considered critical to the success of treatment. Consequently, deviations in the direction of formats making active practice less convenient are to be avoided as a rule.

During the therapy, ambient illumination is usually reduced to enhance the brightness of the projected material as well as to minimize extraneous cues. In the early stages of learning a scenario, lighting naturally needs to be sufficient for the client to read his/her lines easily. However, with the verbal responses memorized, the client lays aside the script, and emphasis may be given to nonverbal gestures, now that the arms and hands are free.

Through interactive videotape simulations, police officers are given the opportunity to encounter stressful situations, which permits officers to develop effective coping behavior without risking harm either to themselves or civilians. The following outlines the technique used in developing appropriate scenarios for the videotape simulations used in police cadet training. Scenarios were developed by the author and a number of psychology graduate students in conjunction with veteran police officers. The first guideline was to identify situations that officers generally felt posed high levels of threat or potential for mishandling and were sufficiently frequent to warrant inclusion as the subject of a simulation. A poll of officers resulted in the identification and subsequent videotape simulations of the following situations.

1. Arresting a belligerent drunk in a bar
2. Issuing a citation to an especially sarcastic motorist
3. Intervening in a confrontation involving harassment of homosexuals
4. Preserving the scene of a homicide when fellow officers and news reporters are intent on gaining entrance to it
5. Apprehending an armed robbery suspect
6. Responding to provocations from adolescents while visiting a high school
7. Intervening in a volatile family disturbance
8. Obtaining emergency medical care for a young man suffering mortal gunshot wounds and then securing witnesses to the shooting
9. Investigating a theft in a minority neighborhood hostile to police as symbols of the status quo
10. Controlling onlookers and a hysterical mother at the scene of a hit-and-run accident of a young girl
11. Issuing a citation to a sexually manipulative traffic violator
12. (A scenario especially prepared for female officers) Managing patronizing males, sexually suggestive adolescents, and a vituperative anti-feminist female complainant.

By interacting with the foregoing simulations, the officers were exposed to abundant sarcasm, uncooperativeness, physical threats, and general contempt. Maintaining a firm and fluent voice under such circumstances was an especial emphasis of the behavior rehearsal, but the choice of phraseology was considered equally important. Patrol officers were canvassed at daily roll call to obtain phraseology they had found effective in defusing volatile situations or mitigating the hostile resistance normally encountered in police-civilian contacts such as issuing traffic citations. In turn this material was included in the responses to be given by the cadet. As an example, one scenario involves ordering a troublesome crowd at a hit-and-run accident to step back on the curbs. One member of the crowd refuses to comply and taunts the cadet, saying sarcastically, "I

live here! I belong here! You gonna hit me if I don't move?"
Rather than countering this with his/her own belligerence,
particularly by threatening force, the response of the cadet, as
indicated in the script, is to say firmly, "Everyone move back to
the curb, including you (the young man), so we can help the
injured girl." This verbal response is considered defusing in
that it sets a compelling frame of reference for cooperation
from the person without emphasizing the potential use of physical force. The initial portion of the cadet's response, "Everyone move back to the curb, *including you . . . .*", is very clear
and indicates the person resisting the officer is not to be treated
as a special "character" — what others have to do, he must also
do. The remainder of the cadet's response is designed to be
similarly effective. The order is to move back, "so we can help
the injured girl." This latter phraseology relates the order to
the welfare of the child, which provides a cogent reason for
complying, again without resorting to threat of force. Thus the
cadets are rehearsing specific means of gaining compliance that
minimize the dangers to both officers and civilians. At the same
time, though, it is hoped that making a substantial number of
such responses would to some extent result in a generally defusing approach to police work.

In an effort to determine the outcome of this training with
police cadets, an entire cadet class numbering fifty-six persons
was divided into two equal sized experimental and control
groups, which were matched on age, sex, race, educational
attainment, and previous law enforcement experience. The
experimental group received nine half-hour sessions of training
during a two-week period as well as the customary academy
training, while the control group only received the latter. Thus
the magnitude of training was considerable by the standard of
most social skills studies (Doyle and Klinge, 1977) with each
experimental group cadet receiving a half hour of group orientation followed by four hours of rehearsal. During a typical
half-hour rehearsal session the cadet would practice six simulations and receive feedback after each from an academy faculty
person.

At posttest a paper and pencil measure agreed with a behavioral one that the experimental group members were signifi-

cantly more likely than members of the control group to act in a calming manner rather than belligerently, and similarly less likely to either over- or underreact to stressful situations (Doyle and Hall, 1978). In addition to the posttest immediately after training, an eight-month follow-up test was administered. Though the effects of the training had attenuated, the experimental group still surpassed the control one on both measures and was significantly better on the behavioral scale.

Given the strain inherent in the role of a police officer, the use of behavior rehearsal to videotape simulations to develop emotional self-control and confrontation management skills seems to be one of the most important applications of this approach. In addition to providing the opportunity for the officer to learn coping skills, the emphasis on nonviolent alternatives in the context of a general concern for interpersonal effectiveness should help safeguard the citizenry from unnecessary physical trauma.

APPLICATIONS TO RE-ENTRY WOMEN'S ASSERTIVENESS TRAINING: MORE TECHNIQUES AND OUTCOMES

Another application of behavior rehearsal to videotape simulations was its use in developing assertiveness among reentry female college students (Doyle, Smith, Bishop, and Miller, 1980). The thirteen subjects primarily consisted of women who had interrupted their education to engage in child rearing. Nine interactive simulations were prepared for this study including such subjects as refusing requests and speaking as a member of a class or audience. In this latter simulation, the camera was positioned to provide the perspective of a member of a class seated near the back of the classroom. Thus the client has a view of rows of the backs of people's heads and a podium at the very front of the room. As the scenario begins the instructor has not yet arrived, so some individuals are talking while others are sitting quietly or looking around. Then as the instructor steps to the podium, the class focuses attention on him. His opening remarks are too softly spoken to be clearly audible to the client, however. In accordance with the script, the client raises her hand, gains recognition, and indicates the problem. Meanwhile a number of students have turned to look at her. In response to the client's request, the instructor nods his head in assent and talks more loudly as he proceeds. Somewhat later in the scenario the client again raises her hand and, after being recognized, "I have two questions. The first is . . . and the second is . . . ." The client has held the floor for a sufficient duration to ask two questions rather than just one. To this point, the client has made two responses in the simulated classroom; one involved bringing the instructor's low volume delivery to his attention while the other concerned asking two questions. The scenario continues similarly for a total of six such responses by the client.

As indicated in the above descriptions of the two responses directed to the instructor, the client was able to rehearse assertive responses in rich circumstances. The realistic setting, including back views of fellow students' heads until asking a question, when many turn to see her, would seem a priori to favor generalization of the rehearsed behavior to the actual world. Further, in taking the floor and requesting that the teacher speak more loudly, she was practicing the exercise of her rights under circumstances that meant interrupting a sizeable number of people. Many nonassertive individuals would feel they would be resented for interrupting an entire class in the interest of their own needs. Hence, the looks from the class would likely be a source of stress for the client and as such offer the opportunity to rehearse more adaptive reponses to such situations. In this case such richness is made feasible by videotape simulations. In the customary consulting office, in contrast, behavior rehearsal or role playing takes place between therapist and client and, as a consequence, is limited in recreating such circumstances. It is true that in certain group therapies the members could enact such a circumstance, but it would naturally require most of the group to subordinate their interests to the person playing the assertive role. This would not be practical as a means of providing extensive behavior rehearsal. In the second response she asked two questions, each of which required the instructor's time to answer under similar circumstances. Thus she was practicing fluency and feeling comfortable in making a more demanding assertive response.

This illustrates the use of the successive approximation principle in the design of interactive simulations. In this instance the client was first required to make a brief request, the granting of which required no loss of time to the class. Then she had to hold the floor longer with this being further followed by the instructor addressing the issues raised by her.

The therapy was divided into three one-hour sessions per week for each client. The first and second hour session consisted of group discussion and live role play. Because of the automated format of this therapy, it was possible to use peer counseling effectively in the behavior rehearsal sessions. During the first half hour one client interacted with the screen presentation while the other observed and provided feedback. After a half hour they exchanged roles, so each received the same amount of practice. To monitor this system, a therapist regularly visited the sessions. In addition, feedback on the procedure was obtained at the weekly group meeting at which all clients were present. Rehearsal of and feedback on five scenarios averaging five minutes in length were typical of a client's half hour of behavior rehearsal. The therapy was continued for six weeks for a total of eighteen sessions for each client; again this magnitude of treatment, a total of eighteen hours, including both the time in active practice and providing feedback, is quite substantial in comparison to most social skills studies. The difference, at least in part, would seem to stem from the automated format of behavior rehearsal to videotape simulations, which makes relatively sizeable amounts of treatment convenient.

In a within-subjects design, four measures were taken pre- and posttreatment. These were the Conflict Resolution Inventory (McFall and Lillesand, 1971), Rathus Assertiveness Scale (Rathus, 1973), Semantic Differential (Osgood, Suci, and Tannenbaum, 1957), and Personality Dominance Inventory (Doyle and Shafritz, 1977). Highly significant pre-post differences were obtained for each measure, strongly suggesting that the treatment was effective. Again because of the magnitude of training possible with the videotape simulations, which never fatigue, become ill, etc., stronger results seem more likely than when other systems are used, which are subject to the foregoing limitations. Thus, as in the case of the police study, behavior rehearsal to videotape simulations produced significant outcomes.

APPLICATION TO SUCCESS-FEARING INDIVIDUALS: PREPARING APPROPRIATE VIDEOTAPE SIMULATIONS

Applying the interactive videotape simulation approach to increase assertiveness in returning females led to the development of scenarios to help individuals become more successful. Although transactional analysis (Berne, 1972) has popularized the concepts of winners and losers, the work of Horner (1970, 1972) focusing on women has initiated systematic investigation into the success/failure or winner/loser dimension of behavior patterns. Fear of success, according to Horner, was attributable to the concern that too direct or vigorous pursuit of success (e.g. high academic achievement, professional status, athletic triumphs), especially by women, would lead to social rejection and loss of affiliative relationships. While particularly applicable to women, the fear of success has also been studied in men (Hoffman, 1974). Thus simulations were prepared for clients of either sex, which offered practice in the role of a *winner* and promised to make the person feel at ease in such previously forbidding circumstances.

With respect to the principles to be observed in developing these scenarios, several possibilities were evident. One could rely on a naturalistic approach in the Lewin-Barker mold (Willems, 1968), which would dictate unobtrusive observation in the real world of people exhibiting winning and losing behavior. The simulations would then be designed to enhance the responses characteristic of winners and minimize or extinguish those typical of losers. In this approach the key would be to find what distinguishes the two types in the real world rather than according to a particular theory. Another possibility would be to select a theory such as transactional analysis or perhaps Adler's individual psychology, which explicitly addresses these phenomena, and to derive therapeutic scenarios of client-screen figure interactions. Thus in transational analysis one would be designed to offset tendencies to play "games" stemming from the life position of *I'm not OK, you're OK*. In distinction to the two preceding means of developing scenarios, one is also able to conceptualize winners and losers in terms of learning theory, which, though not addressing these phenomena directly, offers understanding in highly empirical terms and straightforward treatment implications as well.

Other possibilities will be apparent to readers, based on their own training and biases as well as ingenuity; the basic technique, though, is one of determining a model for devising an interactive videotape simulation to enhance adjustment. Hence, one would, as illustrated, start with the adjustment problem and proceed to consider theoretical or conceptual frameworks that might be helpful. Behavior rehearsal to videotape simulations then, at least in concept, could be a vehicle for many theoretical approaches.

The approach largely adopted by this author was to conduct naturalistic observations of competitive situations but to attempt for the most part to understand the winning and losing behavior of the participants in learning theory terms. The observations did indeed seem to reveal that some persons tended to avoid winning, preferring to lose. Consider a professional tennis contest as an example. One player acquired what seemed to be an insurmountable advantage; however, with success close at hand he seemed to lose heart or become despondent and played with lackluster until he eventually lost the match. In terms of learning theory, in becoming depressed the person behaved as though the response of winning had been associated with deprivation. The work of Horner seemed applicable: based on his behavior the player could well have anticipated social rejection accompanied by loss of affiliative relationships.

In observing another tennis contestant, I noticed that he exhibited strong tendencies to discount his performance, seemingly taking every opportunity to discredit his achievements and praise those of his opponent. This strenuous self-denial seemed to suggest a psychoanalytic mechanism like reaction formation; perhaps the player was fending off strong arrogance inclinations by enacting an ingratiating role. Release of such impulses would, of course, tend to result in social ostracism. In learning theory terms the behavior could be construed less mystically: arrogant responses had been punished, resulting in a secondary drive of anxiety, which is allayed through ingratiating responses.

In both of the preceding cases, it did appear the social censure, as a result of winning, was the critical element. In the first case the despondency when on the verge of winning would seem to indicate a history of loss of social relations in such circumstances; in the second case the persistent discrediting seemed to be a classic reaction formation to less desirable social patterns. These data, while admittedly quite limited, suggested some exciting possibilities for videotape simulations. Using a portable camera it was possible to enact the last stages of a win in tennis and thus offer the appropriate clients the opportunity to rehearse more adequate responses. The following is the first segment of the resulting script, with annotations.

Scene: The final stages of a tennis match between two players; it is daytime. The client has just won a game and needs to win one more to take the match. If he/she loses the game, the match would be tied. This situation is the culmination of approximately two hours of play as shown in the appearance of the opponent. (*Cl:* client; *Op:* opponent)

Segment 1

Op: (Is approaching the baseline, having walked from one side of the court to the other.)
Six-five. Sets are even.

Note: The opponent is indicating the situation in which the client is on the verge of winning.

Cl: (Serves the ball to opponent — each hit of the ball by the client is mimed in slow motion; no actual racquets or balls are used.)

Op: (Hits served ball back)

Cl: (Hits ball strongly and accurately)

Op: (Mis-hits ball into net; reacts angrily then retrieves ball and throws it wide of server, who as a consequence must also retrieve it.)

Note: Client is proceeding to win, encountering anger

and annoyance on part of opponent; such circumstances formerly would have been associated with a shift to losing rather than continuing to irk the opponent. As shown in following lines, though, client continues to perform well, again serving the ball accurately.

Cl: (Obtains inaccurately thrown ball; serves ball to backhand side of opponent.)

Op: (Has begun glaring across net and refrains from speaking; mis-hits ball into net again; retrieves ball and this time just drops it across net.)

Cl: (Must come 3 meters toward the net to retrieve ball; obtains ball slowly to register annoyance at having to recover balls out of play, which are returned by opponent.)

End of Segment 1

In this segment of the simulation, as indicated by the script, the client is primarily experiencing the role and perspective of a winner rather than rehearsing behavioral responses. The slow motion, mimed racquet serves are intended only to resemble actual tennis strokes. Likewise, the client only suggests movement around the court; taking a half step in a direction while the camera actually covers the distance gives the client the perspective of engaging fully in the physical movement. The client also has no spoken lines in this segment, thus practicing a winning perspective on events more than large motor or verbal behaviors. As a first step in changing a pattern of losing behavior, this would seem propitious; it would be a case of faciliating a change in attitude, which should favor the acquisition of more active winning responses. As long as the client could only see himself/herself in an inferior role, he/she would feel embarrassed or awkward in rehearsing very ascendant responses with the therapist looking on; managing the resistance under such circumstances could prove a problem.

In addition to developing perspective, or expectations if you will, extinction of other responses is also occurring thus far in this simulation. The individual mentioned earlier who felt the need to be ingratiating is rehearsing winning *without discounting* it. Similarly the person observed to seem to forego success rather than risk loss of affiliative relationships would be continuing to play the role of a winner despite strong indications of disapproval from the opponent. On one hand, rehearsal of a perspective is making the client more comfortable in a predominant role, while on the other hand, extinction of the self-defeating behaviors is occurring.

The complete scenario contains a total of three segments. The next segment continues the pattern of miming strokes and winning points until the match has been taken by the client; the verbal responses associated with a winner's role are introduced, however. The final segment addresses the aftermath of the success; the client who perhaps has previously experienced alienation on account of a derisive manner following success rehearses a nonsolicitous but gracious deportment. Similarly, the client who feared loss of interpersonal relations finds that his/her winning results in social approval as the opponent invites the client for a soft drink.

One benefit of dividing a lengthy simulation into segments is that such structure suggests analysis of the client's performance in reference to the various parts. In behavior rehearsal, for example, the client may exhibit little tenseness in the first two segments of the preceding interactive simulation but find it quite difficult to relate to the loser without being scornful. Based on such observations, understanding of the client would be enhanced and further rehearsal to a particular segment, probably the third one in the above instance, would be quite convenient. It should be noted, though, that such analysis and selected rehearsal would be just as possible with a nonsegmented scenario. In the latter case, it would simply be a matter of viewing the simulation in the light of these possibilities, as indeed it ought to be if maximum benefit is to be gained. This would entail monitoring the progress of the videotape as indicated on the recording unit counter during behavior rehearsal. When the client evidences blockage or otherwise performs ineffectively, the point on the counter is noted. These points allow inferences to be drawn regarding the nature of the problem, as well as delineating sections of scenarios likely to be rehearsed profitably. To be most effective, therapists using either segmented or nonsegmented simulations should use the counter for diagnostic purposes during the early stages of therapy and then from time to time thereafter.

In addition to competitive sports, another area that seemed to offer fertile examples of winning and losing behavior patterns was that of formal groups. During the selection of leaders of such groups, as a case in point, the author found that on being nominated for chairperson or a similar leadership role, some of the people immediately declined to stand for the office. It was as if they had been ridiculed or otherwise aversively conditioned in the past when considering such a possibility. As a consequence, these persons apparently could not see themselves in such an ascendant role. Hence, rather than suffer anxiety or humiliation stemming from awkwardness, they were restricting themselves to a secondary or follower role.

The application of behavior rehearsal to video simulations for the purpose of overcoming disinclinations toward personal success in formal groups was generally straightforward. The entire process of selection of a leader was designed into a simulation — from nominations, through nominees making statements supporting their candidacies, to balloting and the determination of a winner (the client). As in the competitive sports scenario, immediately following the success the client experiences enhanced rather than diminished affiliative relationships. With the announcement of the client's election, the meeting adjourns and the previous chairperson invites the new leader to have lunch the next day. Behavior rehearsal of success followed by social approval, in this case from an authority figure, is a technique for helping to overcome client fears of alienating individuals as a result of being perceived as exhibitionistic, snobbish, etc., or, in the case of a woman, perhaps unfeminine. With repeated behavior rehearsal to this and similar videotape simulations, it would seem reasonable to expect that the client would begin standing for office, making effective supporting statements, feeling comfortable when successful, and finding more approval from others than he/she would have previously expected. Unlike the previous applications, the Houston police cadet program and the reentry women's assertiveness training, no outcome data have been collected to evaluate the influence of these simulations on the success/failure dimension of essentially competitive behaviors.

APPLICATION TO ALCOHOLICS:
USE OF STANDARD SIZE VIEWING MONITORS

The avoidance of responses associated with success in favor of ones that are self-defeating is certainly exemplified in the alcoholics. Though probably the result of multiple causes, including biological and sociocultural as well as personality factors, alcoholism has been associated with a distinct cluster of the latter. The cluster includes "a negative self-image and feelings of inadequacy, isolation, and depression" (Coleman, 1976). Hence it seemed natural to extend the application of videotape simulations in alleviating failure tendencies to treatment of alcoholics. The population to be treated was selected from the inpatients with a primary diagnosis of alcoholism in a United States Public Health Service Hospital devoted to serving United States Navy veterans. Rather than naturalistic observations to determine the failure patterns of behavior, an informal poll was taken to determine the clinical impression of the professional staff at the hospital. It was agreed that alcoholics tended to be self-depreciating but also immature in their relations with others.

The next step would have been to derive scenarios that would offer corrective practice for the specific problem behaviors. On this occasion, however, the life-size screen projection system was not available, only the standard viewing monitors with screens measuring approximately half a meter diagonally. The technique in this case was to develop a simulation in which only the face and neck of one figure would be shown on the screen; in these close-ups the key features of another person would approach life size.

The first scenario addressed the self-depreciatory tendency; it was simple in design. The client was only required to talk about himself/herself in positive terms to the single figure on the screen. In the interest of maintaining motivation, three forms of increasing length were videotaped. The first form required approximately thirty seconds of relating appropriately positive information regarding oneself; the second form, a minute; and the third, two minutes. The video presentation begins with a distant shot of a female approximately twenty-six years of age. This initial perspective enables the client to view the screen figure in her entirety before moving to the tight shot of the head and neck. While being quite limited in scope, really only effectively able to present the uppermost portion of one screen figure, the use of a standard viewing monitor instead of a projector system permits the client to be positioned somewhat nearer the simulation. This proximity to the display compensates to some extent for its smallness. Also, at the closer distances the resolution or clarity of a conventional monitor picture is better than that of a projection screen display.

In the initial distant shot the screen figure is walking towards the client. Careful to make the effect appear natural and at the same time hasten the transition from the distant to tight shot, the camera had zoomed in slowly to augment the increase in size resulting from walking towards the lens. Once the tight shot is achieved, the client exchanges greetings with the person on the screen and follows with suitable positive self-disclosure; the script directs the client to do this by relating a personal incident. Meanwhile the therapist observes the client and provides feedback, especially pointing out any self-derogation but also noting voice control, fluency, and emotional tone. As the success-oriented response of the client becomes stronger, he or she is shaped by rehearsing the longer forms of the simulation.

The second scenario dealt with the immature interpersonal pattern earlier identified. It focused on initiating social contact with another patient by asking him to play "dominoes." Again the opening shot was a distant one showing the entire screen figure, who in this instance was leaning against a wall perusing a magazine. This time the client was to walk towards the screen figure; thus the camera slowly zooms in on a side view of the screen figure as if the client is approaching him. In the actual behavior rehearsal to the videotape simulation, the client walks towards the monitor from a distance of approximately 2 meters to a point 1 meter or so from it. Then the conversation is initiated and the screen figure of whom little more than the head is visible turns to look directly at the client, who is saying "How about some dominoes?" "I wouldn't mind playing."

The emphasis in this scenario, as shown in the preceding line, is on the ability to relate in a self-controlled or self-possessed manner. Rather than overemphasize the importance of the domino game or seem overly eager for his or her own personal goals, the client was learning to relate in a more self-restrained manner. Relative to the success/failure dimension, the immature, selfish behavior would equate to a failure pattern. The person exhibiting such behavior presumably feels very uncomfortable playing more generally approved roles. Rehearsing to the simulation, however, should reverse the situation, though to an undetermined extent. While clinical impressions point to treatment gains as a result of using behavior rehearsal to videotape simulations with alcoholic disorders, controlled research in this area is obviously needed. At the same time it appears that insofar as one works within the limitations of the conventional monitor display, considerable use may be made of this commonly available equipment to present interpersonal simulations.

The application of interactive videotape simulations to the success/failure dimension of human behavior has been accomplished in sports, formal group behavior, and treatment of a clinical disorder, i.e. alcoholism. This line of work stemmed from the previously mentioned study of the reentry female as well as the work of Horner.

APPLICATION TO SOCIAL SKILLS TRAINING:
NONVERBAL AND VERBAL BEHAVIORS

Another very important application of interactive videotape simulations has been the subarea of behavior therapy termed *social skills*. As indicated by Phillips (1978), "Defining social skills is not easy, except in an immediate common sense way." For the purpose of this paper though, *social skills are behavioral, affective, or cognitive responses that reflect competence and thus provide a basis for self-esteem or that satisfy other emotional needs in a particular interpersonal context.* This is a broad definition and, hence, includes a wide range of behaviors, depending on the context. A person may reflect social skills by expertly relating a humorous anecdote at a partly, demonstrating a strong will in bargaining for a worker group, adroitly counter-propagandizing the opponent in a political contest, or self-disclosing deep feeling to an intimate friend. While the foregoing definition admittedly lacks specificity, it serves in this case to provide a measure of coherence to the term *social skills* as used in this chapter.

Among the most intriguing applications of behavior rehearsal to video simulations in the social skills area has been the development of nonverbal behavior patterns. While verbal responses are frequently of obvious significance, nonverbal ones may not be assigned proper importance. In one scenario the opening scene has a burly man in his early thirties standing before a table on which are resting a number of quart-sized glass containers. He grasps one container and seems to become annoyed that it is not possible to carry all of them. The man then turns to the client (who is standing facing the screen) and curtly beckons with a wave of his arm and an outstretched index finger while sneering, "Come here." At this point the script directs the client to show displeasure with such disregard by turning his/her back resolutely to the insulting person. Next there is a crashing sound accompanied by a curse, as the man has dropped one of the glass containers onto the floor and it has broken into several pieces. The client turns deliberately to face him, and for the most part the remainder of the simulation is devoted to the client being blamed by the harasser for what occurred but answering with such responses as "I don't mind helping, but no one likes to be ordered around," and "Next time you want help try asking in a decent way." The antagonist finally becomes conciliatory and departs, leaving the client dominating the scene.

In the foregoing simulation the turning away from the insulter is quite important. Following several rehearsals of this nonverbal response, it seems that clients develop a certain *bearing* that conveys self-regard; they appear sensitized to derisive messages and are intolerant of them. The client does not actually seem to make the back-turning response with any frequency thereafter though; it is more a matter of a discernible readiness to take such action with an abusive person that seems to make a positive difference in interpersonal relations. In the case of a twelve-year-old male with a complaint of constantly being baited and teased, this simulation seemed particularly beneficial.

The verbal responses as well are obviously quite important in this simulation. Fluent delivery with appropriate voice control of such lines as those illustrated above would definitely enhance social skills.

Incidentally, the emphasis on nonverbal as well as verbal responses seems particularly achievable in videotape simulations. It is a matter of the richness that the production of such simulations permits. Initially, considerable thought is given to a script that may be written as bountifully as the ingenuity of those involved allows. Then this same potential for richness is available in the staging, casting, and acting of the simulation. That the videotape simulation is indefinitely usable thereafter makes such carefulness worthwhile.

In addition to hand and facial gestures, interactive videotape simulations have included such nonverbal responses as drinking (while talking), dancing, seating oneself in a preferred position relative to a group, untentatively walking away from a person feeling ill will towards one, and maintaining eye contact as well as generally attending to a correspondent.

An alternative to looking at social skills in terms of verbal and nonverbal responses is to divide a social interaction into initiation, maintenance, and termination phases (cf. Dawley and Wenrich, 1976). In the majority of social skill video simulations produced by the present author, the client rehearses the initiation of interpersonal relations. Three examples are a preadolescent gaining entrance to a peer group conversation in the school lunchroom, a manager contacting a subordinate to inform him of dissatisfaction with his work, and a male approaching a female in a night club. Of course with the videotape figures and background, the corresponding milieux are quite realistic; the preadolescent is talking to peers in a lunchroom filled with bustle and noise, the manager has the view of a person sitting at a desk in an office as he/she telephones the subordinate to ask him to come to the manager's office, and the man finds colored lights, loud music, a bar, bartender, and patrons in addition to the woman with whom he is initiating contact.

Maintenance of a social contact is also well represented in the social skill scenarios. Some examples include telling a personal anecdote at a cocktail party, discussing current events with new acquaintances, and in a more formal context, chairing a meeting. As in the case of simulations illustrating initiation of social interaction, these are also quite lifelike.

While the previous two phases are often sources of concern, termination of social contact seems most problematical. One seems often to observe previously composed individuals become either curt or effusive in their praise of a host or hostess on departing; such reactions are presumed to indicate anxiety towards performance involving termination of the interpersonal contact. Probably the type of simulation that has engendered the most adverse emotionality on termination, however, has been the instances when the screen figure exhibits irritation or annoyance with the client. For example, one client invariably needed to clear his throat when saying, in essence, that he would be glad to discuss a particular matter in the morning rather than at that time. Only following a considerable number of rehearsals was the person finally able to avoid esophageal dysfunction. Some further examples of termination included in simulations are ending a committee meeting by alertly scheduling the next one with all the members at hand, leaving one group at a cocktail party to join another, and, again in a context of strife, a manager who has reprimanded a subordinate permits him to leave without seeking conciliation.

CONCLUSION: POTENTIAL OF
HARDWARE SUPPORTED THERAPY

Thus far applications of behavior rehearsal to videotape simulations have ranged widely. The greatest effort, including months of writing scripts and casting more than 100 roles, has been devoted to the confrontation management and emotional self-control program of the Houston Police Department. Other uses, either underway or imminent, are further police as well as business management, student teacher, and employment interviewer training.

The support of hardware in videotape-mediated behavior

rehearsal has important advantages. The preeminent one would probably be that several successive behavior rehearsals may be accomplished through a largely automatic process. Rather than a therapist enacting a certain therapeutically desirable role, an appropriate videotape simulation performs this function. Meanwhile the therapist is free to formulate further treatment directions while in the midst of observing the client engage in responses to situations meaningful to him/her. This would seem to provide an active practice format while concurrently permitting the therapist to be sufficiently free to consider the significance of client responses in some depth. It could be argued that prior to hardware-supported therapy, wherein the burden of effective active practice could be relieved from the therapist through automation, the combination of significant quantities of rehearsal and considerable reflection on the client's behavior were simply beyond any real achievement. Hence, perhaps artificially, clients received therapy that was constrained to emphasize either active practice as in usual behavior rehearsal and feedback or a more passive client role involving deeper understanding as found in insight therapies. This might be the point in time for termination of such trade-offs to be seriously contemplated.

Interestingly, notwithstanding the potential of hardware-supported therapy, there has been little active rehearsal but heavy emphasis on self-confrontation in the interest of self-insight; even when videotape or film simulations have been used, this has been the case as illustrated in the Interpersonal Process Recall (IPR) System of Kagan (1978). While having been applied astutely to a number of areas including counselor, medical, and police training, IPR predicates that "if a person is videorecorded while he/she is relating to another and is then shown the recording immediately after the interaction, the person is able to recall thoughts and feelings in amazing detail and depth." Thus videotape or film simulations were a convenient means of presenting a lifelike correspondent to whom trainees could respond so as to "understand better their interpersonal behaviors." In sum, it seems readily within the reach of current technology to provide active practice to correspondents in circumstances quite conducive to treatment gains. At the same time, though, this potential generally has not been realized. It is perhaps ironic that insofar as the client is concerned, preparation for the rehearsal to videotape simulations usually requires little more than pointing out the opportunity for active practice therein.

If the current technology of video projector systems possesses potential for active rehearsal in therapy, then future developments seem likely to increase the possibilities even more. Of particular interest in this regard is the likely development of completely solid-state television receivers, which would eliminate the picture tube and permit the entire unit to be contained in a panel that, being perhaps 10cm in depth, would resemble a picture hung on a wall. There would then be no need for a projection system, and one commerical firm has indicated it will have a color unit in a wall-screen panel measuring 1-1 1/2m diagonally within three to five years (Lochenbruch, 1979). Needless to say, such a unit would lend itself very nicely to interactive simulations.

The most exciting prospect, though, would be the development of three-dimensional displays. The effect would be to provide simulations that are breathtaking in their verisimilitude. Through holography such television has already been developed with "excellent results" (Caulfield and Lu, 1970). The impact of such displays in interactive videotape simulations would be truly astonishing.

In conclusion, this chapter has indicated a number of applications of behavior rehearsal to videotape simulations. In addition, the techniques of accomplishing them have been presented in some detail. In terms of outcomes, the data collected in two studies strongly suggest that approach is effective. Suffice it to say more research is needed, but interactive videotape simulations have progressed to a point where the approach cannot be overlooked. The capacity for active practice in circumstances especially designed to be conducive to treatment gains could well make this approach a watershed in videotherapy.

REFERENCES

Berne, E.: *What do you say after you say hello?* New York, Grove, 1972.

Caulfield, H. J. and Lu, S.: *The applications of holography.* New York, John Wiley & Sons, 1970.

Coleman, J. C.: *Abnormal psychology and modern life.* Glenview, Il., Scott, Foresman and Co., 1978, p.426.

Danish, S. J. and Brodsky, S. L.: Training of policemen in emotional control and awareness. *American Psychologist, 25:*368-369, 1970.

Dawley, H. H., Jr. and Wenrich, W. W.: *Achieving assertive behavior: A guide to assertive training.* Monterey, CA., Brooks/Cole, 1976.

Doyle, P. and Hall, R: Behavior rehearsal to videotape simulations: an interpersonal skills training technique with police. Unpublished paper presented at the annual meetings of the Association for the Advancement of Behavior Therapy, Chicago, November, 1978.

Doyle, P. and Klinge, V.: Field test of the stimulus specific conception of the generalization of assertive training. Unpublished paper presented at the annual meetings of the Southwestern Psychological Association, Dallas, April, 1977.

Doyle, P. and Shafritz, J.: *Personality dominance inventory.* Houston, 1977.

Doyle, P. Smith, W., Bishop, P., and Miller, M.: Simulated Interaction Training: Application to returning college students. In *Social competence: Interventions for children and adults,* Rathjen, D. J. and Foreyt, J. P. (Eds.), New York, Pergamon, 1980.

Galassi, M. D. and Galassi, J. P.: Assertion: a critical review. *Psychotherapy: Theory Research and Practice, 15:*16-29, 1978.

Hoffman, L. W.: Fear of success in males and females: 1965 and 1971. *Journal of Consulting and Clinical Psychology, 42:*353-358, 1974.

Horner, M. S.: Feminity and successful achievement: A basic inconsistency. In *Feminine personality and conflict,* Bardwick, J. M., Douvan, E., Horner, M., and Gutmann, D. (Eds.), 1970.

———: Toward an understanding of achievement-related conflicts in women. *Journal of Social Issues, 28:*157-175, 1972.

Kagan, N.: Interpersonal process recall: media in clinical and human interaction supervision. In *Videotape techniques in psychiatric training and treatment* (rev. ed.), Berger, M. M. (Ed.), New York, Brunner/Mazel, 1978.

Kroes, W. H.: *Society's victim — the policeman: An analysis of job stress in policing.* Springfield, Thomas, 1976.

Lochenbruch, D.: What's new and what's coming. *Television Guide,* Feb. 17, 1979, 29-30.

McFall, R. M. and Lillesand, D. B.: Behavior rehearsal with modeling and coaching in assertion training. *Journal of Abnormal Psychology, 77:*313-323, 1971.

Menninger, K.: Are policemen supermen? *The Police Chief, 32(9):*26-27, 1965.

Osgood, C. E. Suci, G., and Tannenbaum, P.: *The measurement of meaning.* Urbana, U. of Illinois Press, 1957.

Phillips, E. L.: *The social skills basis of psychopathology.* New York, Grune & Stratton, 1978, p. 3.

Rathus, S. A.: A 30-item schedule for assessing assertive behavior. *Behavior*

Therapy, 4:398-406, 1973.

Willems, E. P.: An Ecological orientation in psychology. In *Contemporary issues in developmental psychology*. Endler, N. S., Boulter, L. R., and Osser, H. (Eds.), New York, Holt, Rinehart and Winston, 1968.

CHAPTER 9

THE USE OF VIDEO IN ASSERTIVENESS TRAINING FOR WOMEN

L. Elaine Tomlinson and Patricia G. Ball

INTRODUCTION

THE purpose of this chapter is to explore the use of video in helping women develop assertive skills. Because women have traditionally been socialized to be passive, nurturing, and supportive, many women have difficulty responding assertively to a variety of situations. They lack the words as well as the appropriate gestures and body language necessary for assertion. Consequently, women need practice and feedback if they are to develop new behaviors that are honest, direct, and appropriately assertive. Video can be a very effective tool for developing these new skills.

Through role play and modeling techniques using video, trainers and therapists can give women immediate reinforcement when they approximate assertive behavior. Video can be used to develop these skills by providing immediate visual and auditory feedback about the quality of their responses. Video can therefore assume a major role as a teaching aid in both individual and group therapy for women who are seeking new, assertive behaviors.

This chapter will explain why women have traditionally been nonassertive, review the cognitive and behavioral components of assertiveness training, and specifically discuss the use of video. Ethical issues relating to assertiveness training and the use of video will also be reviewed.

SEX-ROLE SOCIALIZATION VS. ASSERTIVENESS

In the majority of world cultures women have been discouraged from being assertive. Although the socialization process reinforces women for being sensitive to others' feelings and needs, women have not been reinforced for expressing their own feelings and needs. In some cases women may actually be suppressing parts of their own identity. For example, women in our culture have not been reinforced for being ambitious. Sex-role stereotypes, which narrowly defined what is female, are growing more flexible as we see our society reexamine what is female and what is male.

However, recent studies show that traditional femininity still excludes assertiveness. The "ladylike" woman should be always cheerful, compassionate, understanding, warm, yielding, polite, passive, and compliant even at the expense of her own feelings. Her role is to nurture others. She is not a leader. She has difficulty in making decisions, in defending her beliefs, or in taking a risk.

Butler (1976) found that American women are significantly less assertive than men. It is important to point out that in becoming more assertive many women fear losing the positive aspects of the feminine role such as nurturance, warmth, and sensitivity. Laws (1975) points out that the traditional view in psychology or sociology assumes that a person is either masculine or feminine. In reality, women can be forceful while still displaying sensitivity and warmth. Assertiveness training affords women a chance to learn to express themselves as androgynous people. Phelps and Austin (1975) report that many women fear the loss of femininity in developing assertive behaviors. Assertive behaviors often include exhibiting positive traits such as ambition, autonomy, independence, and self-expression, which are usually thought of as appropriate traits for men only.

Women need the tool of assertive behavior to deal with the challenges that are present in our society. In previous years, individuals and families were not faced with the many life-style options that are possible today. Today's woman faces decisions and situations that her grandmother and perhaps even her mother did not encounter. A typical assertiveness training group may find the issues of career, marriage, children, sexual performance, dating behaviors, basic communication problems, and job-seeking behaviors all topics of concern to the participants. Each woman who enrolls in workshops or classes has her own specific needs and concerns. The practical skill training offers help to women in coping with their personal and professional lives. For many women, the lack of assertive skill diminishes chances for getting the position of their choice in an already tight job market (Ball and Nelson, 1979). The working woman may feel inadequate to handle certain situations such as sexual harassment and job promotions. The recently divorced woman or single woman may have difficulty in adjusting to a new set of social mores and dating behaviors. The reentry student may fear the bureaucracy of the university or lack the courage to interact with younger classmates and professors.

THE RATIONALE FOR ASSERTIVENESS TRAINING

The rationale for assertiveness training is based on several theories that postulate the notion of behavior change fostering changes in feeling and/or attitudes (see Paul, 1965; Thorenson, 1969). Wheeler (1977) pointed out that the goal of assertiveness training is to help people learn how to exercise their legitimate rights, to assist them in developing an expanded repertoire of behaviors, and to act in their own best interests. Assertiveness training assumes that changing a behavior pattern such as nonassertiveness or aggressiveness will result in greater feelings of self-worth in addition to greater freedom in choosing a style of interaction (Ball, 1976). Assertive persons will experience a feeling of greater control over their lives than will passive or aggressive individuals.

The methodologies used in assertiveness training groups are indeed varied. Debate in the literature continues on the issue of single sex groups or coeducational groups, positive feedback only as opposed to positive and negative feedback, and responsible assertive responses versus indiscriminate assertive responses. Most trainers, regardless of format, do address three basic issues.

The first and perhaps most important topic for discussion is what constitutes assertive, nonassertive, and aggressive behaviors. The trainer has the responsibility for distinguishing the components of each of these behaviors so that clients can readily identify their responses as assertive, aggressive, or nonassertive. The following definitions can be used as a guideline in this presentation.

The *nonassertive,* or passive, life-style is characterized by such terms as inhibited, helpless, and powerless. Alberti and Emmons (1978) define nonassertive behavior as behavior exhibited when you do not openly express your thoughts or feelings but instead keep quiet for the sake of peace and try to avoid conflict. A person exhibiting nonassertive behavior typically feels disgusted with her/himself for not speaking up and angry for letting the other person take advantage of her/him. A person with this behavior may have learned not to respond in the moment and thinks of a response after the situation has occurred. Lange and Jakubowski (1976) point out that nervousness and anxiety are often consequences of nonassertiveness.

The *aggressive* person is characterized by such terms as obnoxious, vicious, or egocentric. Such people habitually speak up in such a way that attacks, depreciates, humiliates, or belittles other people. The indirectly aggressive woman uses trickery, seduction, or manipulation to get what she wants. Aggressive statements often include dishonest, inappropriate comments, which violate the rights of others. The aggressive person typically feels deeply misunderstood, unloved, unlovable.

The *assertive* person is characterized as spontaneous, honest, and direct. The assertive individual conveys respect rather than deference for the other person's rights and feelings. Alberti and Emmons (1978) define assertive behavior as that which allows a person to express honest feelings comfortably, to be direct and straightforward, and to exercise personal rights without denying the rights of others and without experiencing undue anxiety or guilt. Bloom, Coburn, and Pearlman (1975) find that assertive people usually achieve their goals, and even when they do not, they feel good about themselves, knowing that they have been straightforward.

Next, trainers and therapists must explain personal rights and help women begin to develop their own assertive belief system. Because women have traditionally not expressed their rights, they have often forgotten what rights they do have. For this reason, several authors have compiled lists of basic rights.

Baer (1976) notes seven basic inalienable rights of women:

1. The right to have rights and to stand up for them.
2. The right to dignity and self-respect.
3. The right to consider your own needs (your needs are not always considered last).
4. The right to self-fulfillment (to be competent).
5. The right to accept challenges (includes the rights to make mistakes and take risks).
6. The right to determine you own life-style.
7. The right to change yourself, your behavior, values, and life situation.

Smith (1975) has also compiled a bill of rights that seems especially applicable to women:

1. You have the right to judge your own behavior, thoughts, and emotions and to take responsibility for their initiation and consequences upon yourself.
2. You have the right to offer no reasons or excuses for justifying your behavior.
3. You have the right to judge if you are responsible for finding solutions to other people's problems.
4. You have the right to change your mind.
5. You have the right to make mistakes—and be responsible for them.
6. You have the right to say "I don't know."
7. You have the right to be independent of the good-will of others before coping with them.
8. You have the right to be illogical in making decisions.
9. You have the right to say "I don't understand."
10. You have the right to say "I don't care."

A more complete list of universal human rights is to be found in Alberti and Emmons (1978).

The *get permission syndrome* occurs in many women who seldom stand up for their rights (Baer, 1976). To act on their rights, these women must first get permission from their man. Often these women express the feeling that they have no rights or, if they do, such rights exist only in abstract form (such as the right to be happy) and never seem to apply to any specific information.

Another attitude that prevents women from acting on their rights is called by Phelps and Austin (1975) the *compassion trap*. This attitude describes women who feel that they exist to serve others and who believe that they must provide tenderness and compassion at all times.

Assessment is the third major component necessary for an assertiveness group with women. To address the individual needs of group members, trainers and therapists must know which skills and behaviors clients already have and which skills need to be developed in the training process.

Many groups use paper and pencil methods of assessment to provide pretest and posttest information on the assertive skill level of each participant. Assertiveness Inventories have been developed by Alberti and Emmons (1978), Rathus (1973), Baer (1976), and Phelps and Austin (1975). Osborn and Harris (1975) present a sixty-item Assertive Behavior Assessment of Women inventory, which includes a Likert-scale choice of answers. Less readily available scales include the Wolpe-Lazarus Assertion Questionnaire (Wolpe & Lazarus, 1966), the Lawrence Assertive Inventory (Lawrence, 1970), and the Constriction Scale (Bates & Zimmerman, 1971).

After the group members have a basic understanding of the meaning of assertiveness, a belief system that permits them to be assertive, and specific information about which skills need to be developed, the trainer can move on to develop her format for teaching the group. The format usually includes a combination of lecture, discussion, role modeling, behavioral rehearsal, feedback, coaching, and homework.

METHODOLOGY USING VIDEO

The opportunities to use videotape in the initial sessions of assertiveness training groups are limitless. After an initial discussion and/or lecture on the philosophy of assertiveness training, the trainer can use taped vignettes to demonstrate more explicitly the content and body language of assertive, non-assertive, and aggressive behavior. By using examples that are taped, the trainer frees herself to respond to the group. She also eliminates the need for a cofacilitator or a group member to serve as the model in the role-play situation. Another advantage to taped presentation is that the tapes can be replayed if group members have questions about a particular scene. The trainer can stop the tape and explain, point by point, the reasons that she has labeled a particular type of behavior as assertive, aggressive, or nonassertive. The tapes can be shown several times until all group members undertand the particular components (verbal content and body language) that characterize the three types of behavior.

As the group moves into role-play exercises and behavioral rehearsal (usually by the second group session), video feedback becomes even more important. As women in the group begin to practice specific situations, whether they are designed in advance by the trainer or whether the women use their own situations, feedback on individual content and body language becomes crucial. Although this information can be presented by the trainer/coach and/or by group members, the learning process can be enhanced when the woman can actually see how she performs. Since her role play is captured on tape, she can review and clarify behaviors that she would like to change.

Although in some group members the taping may cause anxiety, the trainer can point out the positive nature of this stress. If a group member can respond assertively under the pressure of being videotaped, she increases her chances of being successful in the real situation.

Because feedback about verbal content and body language is vital to the development of an assertive style, most women are not able to develop assertive skills from merely reading about the techniques. In fact, surprisingly few of the self-help books on assertiveness elaborate on the importance of body language. However, good presentations can be found in Butler (1976) and Phelps and Austin (1975).

The following descriptions of nonverbal components of assertion, aggression, and nonassertion are adopted from Lange and Jakubowski (1976) and can be used as a reference for trainers coaching group members:

Nonverbal Assertive Behavior

The nonverbal behaviors that are congruent with the verbal messages:
    Eye contact is firm but not a stare-down;
    Gestures that denote strength are used, e.g. hand and facial gestures for emphasis, expressiveness;
    Body posture is erect but relaxed.

Nonverbal Nonassertive Behavior

The nonverbal behaviors that convey weakness, anxiety, pleading, or self-effacement:
    Evasion of eye contact;
    Gestures such as hand wringing, twisting the fingers, playing with a pen, hair;
    Clutching the other person;
    Stepping back from the other person as the assertive remark is made;
    Hunching the shoulders;
    Covering the mouth with a hand;
    Wooden body posture;
    Facial gestures may include raising of the eyebrows and inappropriate smiles, especially when expressing anger.

Nonverbal Aggressive Behavior

The nonverbal behaviors that dominate or demean the other person:
    Eye contact that tries to stare down and dominate;
    Parental body gestures such as excessive finger pointing, hand on hip, folding arms;
    Other idiosyncratic nonverbal behaviors, e.g. coyness, winking, holding by the arm, leaning forward.

Video enables the trainer to point out and coach more assertive nonverbal responses. For instance, some women cannot maintain direct eye contact because they have been taught that more feminine behavior is looking down or looking away. On tape, the trainer can demonstrate the impact of eye contact by delivering an identical message with and without the eye contact. The trainee can easily see the increased power that eye contact produces when she watches the replays.

Other women may require extensive practice before they will be able to express anger or disapproval without smiling. Facial expressions can be captured on tape by using close-up shots to demonstrate appropriately assertive responses.

Assertive posture can also be facilitated as group members study their postures on tape. The posture should be firmly, not rigidly, directed toward the listener. Leaning slightly forward with both feet on the ground adds to an assertive posture. Each trainee should experiment to find the distance at which *she* is most comfortable when delivering an assertive message. This distance is different for each person.

For some women, too many or not enough gestures also detract from an assertive message. When looking at videotapes, many people discover nervous gestures that they can reduce through practice and feedback.

Other specific behaviors that can be identified by clients after watching their tapes include voice volume, rate of speech, pitch, and fillers. In some situations the trainer may ask a woman who speaks too softly to exaggerate her voice volume while she is being taped. At first, she may think her behavior is aggressive, but feedback from the videotape as well as group members can help her see the behavior as assertive rather than aggressive.

For other women, the tape will provide the needed stimulus for slowing down the rates of speech to give a more relaxed impression or to lower the pitch of the voice, since purring or squeaking are perceived as nonassertive. Fillers are words without meaning, such as "you know," "and uh," and "really," which usually indicate tentativeness. Often the speaker who overuses fillers is unaware of their frequency. Videotape allows the trainer to demonstrate how fillers detract from an assertive style.

The manner in which the video equipment is introduced is an important part of the assertiveness training program. In our experience, one of the major blocks in using video equipment is the lack of trainer knowledge in the mechanics of operating and setting up the system. Many universities and colleges offer beginning courses in audiovisual aids. Some institutions even provide personnel to operate the equipment for staff. This is certainly convenient, but there is no substitute for first-hand knowledge! Each trainer should be *very* familiar with the video equipment and how to correct the "typical" problems. Assertiveness training groups using video are most efficiently run when one facilitator leads discussion while the other operates the equipment. To reduce the trainer's anxiety, the equipment should be set up and tested early (more than five minutes before the group begins). Lack of knowledge can make you appear anxious to the group because you are.

Share information on how the cards, buttons, and lenses work with interested group members. Almost every group participant will be feeling some anxiety about seeing herself on tape even if she is not assertive enough to verbalize her reluctance or fear to act out situations on camera. For many participants, this is the first time they have seen themselves on camera. The group can be somewhat desensitized through the presentation of some of the introductory didactic material on tape.

Another possibility would be to ask the group to view short clips to identify the correct nonverbal components of assertive behavior. By instructing participants in identifying appropriate assertive content and body language of taped models, the trainer is preparing the groups to give feedback to individuals during later videotaped behavior rehearsal scenes. Lange and Jakubowski (1976) used role-play vignettes to check group members' understanding of various behavioral responses. The situations averaged twenty to thirty seconds each. After each vignette, participants were asked to indicate whether the behavior was nonassertive, aggressive, or assertive.

These short vignettes can be easily adapted to videotape as a discrimination exercise.

Lange and Jakubowski (1976) also recommend the use of taped models. In some situations, watching taped models has the effect of giving group members "permission" to act assertively. They also discuss the use of presenting "self-talk" in modeling sequences on tapes to show how models use cognitive coping strategies. In these "self-talk" modeling sequences, in addition to the actual behavior and speech of the model, her personal thoughts about the approaching situations are also verbalized. In these scenes, participants see the model cope with her own fears about asserting herself and then talk herself into acting out her assertion.

In producing videotaped models, the trainer should be careful to select actors who are similar (sex, race, age, etc.) to the participants in the group. Serber (1977) points out the desirability of using people who previously have taken assertiveness workshops. Galassi and Galassi (1977) offer possible situations that could be used. If the trainer chooses to develop her/his own sequence it is important to remember that the scenes should be replicable and easy to recall. The trainer should try to develop scenes that have positive, reinforcing results if participants are expected to want to emulate the modeled behaviors. To point out the significant behaviors, the trainer should include a narrative before the role-play scene. The narrative serves to highlight the crucial, assertive elements of the scene (Lange and Jakubowski, 1976).

An advantage of group training as opposed to one-to-one is that group members profit from observing others practicing on the videotape. The group situation also provides an opportunity for members to practice "coaching." Flowers and Guerra (1974) found that practice as a coach is important in learning new skills.

Another technique suggested by Serber (1977) is the use of what he calls the "silent movie." In the "silent movie," trainees are instructed to use only facial expressions and gestures to express their feelings. The trainer first models the technique for the group, and then each woman is taped for a two to three minute segment in which she responds to a situation without speaking.

After several trials with video feedback, the participant begins to have more appropriate assertive expressions and gestures. She can then move on to more complicated role play, using words as well as gestures.

Because of the increase in popularized forms of assertiveness training, it is important that both the group facilitators and group members adhere to the ethical standards when using videotape. Participants should be made aware in an individual screening session that video equipment will be used. Participants may be asked to give written permission. Plans for the use of the tapes should be discussed in terms of who will be viewing the tapes and when the tapes will be erased following the completion of the training session.

Videotape provides a creative method for giving women feedback about their own styles of response. If offers immediate, accurate data about specific behaviors. In addition, video also facilitates the replicating of specific scenes for discussion and allows women to watch their progress from earlier tapes as they develop new, more assertive skills. Each trainer or therapist can find unique ways to use video as a teaching tool in her/his own work.

REFERENCES

Alberti, R. E. & Emmons, M. L. *Your perfect right.* San Luis Obispo. California: Impact Publishers, 1978.

Baer, J. *How to be an assertive (not aggressive) woman in life, in love, and on the job.* New York: The New American Library, 1976.

Ball, P. G. *The effect of group assertiveness training on selected measures of self-concept in college women.* Unpublished doctoral dissertation, the University of Tennessee, Knoxville, 1976.

Ball, P. G. & Nelson, E. A. Assertiveness training for job-seeking skills: A model training program for law students. *Journal of College Placement Council,* 1979, Winter Issue.

Bates, H. D. & Zimmerman, S. F. Toward the development of screening scale for assertive behavior. *Psychological Reports,* 1971, *28,* 99-107.

Bloom, L. Z., Coburn, K. & Pearlman, J. *The new assertive woman.* New York: Delacorte Press, 1975.

Butler, P. E. *Self-assertion for women: A guide to becoming androgynous.* New York: Harper & Row, 1976.

Flowers, J. V. & Guerra, J. The use of client-coaching in assertion training with large groups. *Journal of Community Mental Health,* 1974, *10,* 414-417.

Galassi, M. D. & Galassi, J. P. *Assert yourself! How to be your own person.* New York: Human Science Press, 1977.

Lange, A. J. & Jakubowski, P. *Responsible assertive behavior: Cognitive/behavioral procedures for trainers.* Champaign, Illinois: Research Press, 1976.

Lawrence, P. S. *The assessment and modification of assertive behavior.*

Unpublished doctoral dissertation, Arizona State University, 1970.

Laws, J. L. A feminist view of marital adjustment. In A. Gurman & D. Rice (Eds.), *Couples in conflict.* New York: Jason Aronson, 1975.

Osborn, S. N. & Harris, G. G. *Assertive training for women.* San Luis Obispo, California: Impact Publishers, 1975.

Paul, G. K. Strategy of outcome research in psychotherapy. *Journal of Consulting Psychology.* 1965, *31*, 109-116.

Phelps, S. & Austin, N. *The assertive woman.* Fredricksburg, Virginia: Impact, 1975.

Rathus, S. A. A 3-item schedule for assessing assertive behavior. *Behavior Therapy,* 1973, *4*, 398-406.

Serber, M. Teaching the nonverbal components of assertive training. In R. E. Alberti (Eds.), *Assertiveness innovations, applications, issues.* San Luis Obispo. California: Impact Publishers, 1977.

Thorenson, D. C. Relevance and research in counseling. *Review of Educational Research.* 1969, *39*, 263-281.

Wheeler, K. Assertiveness and the job hunt. In R. E. Alberti (Eds.), *Assertiveness: innovations, applications, issues.* San Luis Obispo, California: Impact Publishers, 1977.

Wolpe, J. & Lazarus, A. A. *Behavior therapy techniques: Guide to the treatment of neuroses.* New York: Pergamon Press, 1966.

BIBLIOGRAPHY

Alberti, R. E. (Eds.) *Assertiveness: Innovations, applications, issues.* San Luis Obispo, California: Impact Publishers, 1977.

Alberti, R. E. & Emmons, M. L. *Stand up, speak out, talk back.* New York: Pocket Books, 1975.

Bem, S. L. & Bem, D. H. Training the woman to know her place: The power of a nonconscious ideology. In M. Garskof (Eds.), *Roles women play: Readings toward women's liberation.* Belmont, California: Brooks/Cole, 1971.

Bach, R. C. R., Lowry, D., & Moylan, J. J. *Training state hospital patients to be appropriately assertive.* Proceedings of the 80th Annual Convention of the American Psychological Association, 1972, 383-384.

Ball, P. G. & McLoughlin, M. E. Assertiveness training for job-seeking skills, *Tennessee Education,* 1977, *7* (1), 5-15.

Bardwick, J. M. & Douvan, E. Ambivalence: The socialization of women. In V. Gornick & B. K. Moran (Eds.), *Woman in sexist society.* New York: Basic Books, 1971.

Bart, P. B. Depression in middle-aged women. In V. Gornick & B. Moran (Eds.), *Women in sexist society,* New York: Signet, 1971.

Bloomfield, H. H. Assertive training in an outpatient group of chronic schizophrenics: A preliminary report. *Behavior Therapy,* 1973, *4*, 277-281.

Bolles, R. N. *What color is your parachute?* Berkeley, California: The Speed Press, 1978.

Bower, S. A. & Bower, G. H. *Asserting yourself. A practical guide for positive change.* Reading, Massachusetts: Addison-Wesley Publishing Co., 1976.

Bureau of Labor Statistics. *Occupational outlook handbook.* (1978-79 edition) Washington, D. C.: U. S. Department of Labor, 1978.

Cheek, D. K. *Assertive black . . . Puzzled white.* San Luis Obispo, California: Impact Publishers, 1976.

Cotler, S. B. Assertion training: A road leading where? *The Counseling Psychologist,* 1975, *5* (4), 20-29.

Cotler, S. B. & Guerra, J. J. *Assertion training.* Champaign, Illinois: Research Press, 1976.

Cotler, S. B. & Cotler, S. M. Four myths of nonassertiveness in the work environment. In R. E. Alberti (Eds.), *Assertiveness: Innovations, applications, issues.* San Luis Obispo. California: Impact Publishers, 1977.

Division of Counseling Psychology of the American Psychological Association. Assertion training. *The Counseling Psychologist,* 1975, *4,* 2-96.

Ellis, A. *Humanistic psychotherapy: The rational-emotive approach.* New York: Julian Press, 1973.

Fensterheim, H. & Baer, J. *Don't say yes when you want to say no.* New York: Dell, 1975.

Figler, H. *PATH—A career workbook for liberal arts students.* Cranston, Rhode Island: Carroll Press, 1975.

Freeman, J. The social construction of the second sex. In M. Garskof (Ed.), *Roles women play: Readings toward women's liberation.* Belmont, California: Brooks/Cole, 1971.

Gibbs, D. N. Reciprocal inhibition therapy of a case of symptomatic erthema. *Behavior Research and Therapy,* 1965, *2,* 261-266.

Harragan, B. L. *Games mother never taught you.* New York: Warner Books, 1977.

Hennin, M. & Jardim, A. *The managerial woman.* Garden City, New York: Anchor Press, 1977.

Irish, R. K. *Go hire yourself an employer.* Garden City, New York: Anchor Press/Doubleday, 1973.

Jongeward, D. & Scott, D. *Women as winners.* Reading, Massachusetts: Addison-Wesley, 1976.

Lazarus, A. & Fay A. *I can if I want to.* New York: William Morrow and Co., 1975.

Lomont, J. F., Gilner, F. H., Spector, N. J. & Skinner, K. K. Group assertion training and group insight therapies. *Psychological Reports,* 1969, *25,* 463-470.

Manderino, M. A. *The effects of group assertive training procedures on undergraduate women.* Unpublished doctoral dissertation, Arizona

State University, 1974.

McFall, R. M. & Twentyman, C. T. Four experiments on the relative contribution of rehearsal, modeling, and coaching to assertion training. *Journal of Abnormal Psychology*, 1973, *81*, (3), 199-218.

McGovern, T. V., Tinsley, D. J., Liss-Levinson, N., Laventure, R. O. & Britton, G. Assertion training for job interviews. *The Counseling Psychologist*, 1975, *5*, (4), 65-68.

Molloy, J. *Dress for success*. New York: Warner Books, 1976.

Salter, A. *Conditioned reflex therapy*. New York: Creative Age Press, 1949.

Seitz, P. J. Dynamically-oriented brief psychotherapy: Psychocutaneous excoriation syndromes. *Psychosomatic Medicine*, 1953, *15*, 200-213.

Seligman, M. E. P. *Helplessness: On depression, development, and death*. San Francisco: W. H. Freeman and Co., 1975.

Smith, M. H. *When I say no, I feel guilty*. New York: Bantam Books, 1975.

Taubman, B. *How to become an assertive woman*. New York: Pocket Books, 1976.

Walton, D. & Matcher, M. D. The application of learning priniciples to the treatment of obsessive-compulsive states in the acute and chronic phases of illness. *Behavior Research and Therapy*. 1963, *1*, 163-174.

Walton, D. & Matcher, M. D. The relevance of generalization techniques to the treatment of stammering and phobic symptoms. *Behavior Research and Therapy*, 1963, *1*, 121-125.

Weinman, D., Gelbart, P., Wallace, M. & Post, M. Inducing assertive behavior in chronic schizophrenics: A comparison of socioenvironmental, desensitization and relaxation therapies. *Journal of Consulting and Clinical Psychology*, 1972, *39*, 246-252.

Wolpe, J. The instigation of assertive behavior: Transcripts from two cases. *Journal of Behavior Therapy and Experimental Psychiatry*, 1970, *1*, 145-151.

———. *The practice of behavior therapy*. New York: Pergamon Press, 1969.

———. *Psychotherapy by reciprocal inhibition*. Stanford, California: Stanford University Press, 1958.

———. Supervision transcript: Mainly about assertive training. *Journal of Behavior Therapy and Experimental Psychiatry*, 1973, *4*, 141-148.

CHAPTER 10

USE OF VIDEO AND SUPER-8 FILM WITH DRUG DEPENDENT ADOLESCENTS

Christine C. Reese

THERE is little written concerning the use of videotape or super-8 film in the treatment of adolescents with drug dependency or those with the diagnosis of character disorder. This chapter describes experience with audiovisual media in an innovative program for drug dependent adolescents.

This chapter portrays how these adolescents used audiovisual media, and their quick facility in using them as creative tools, as recorders in activity group therapy sessions, and as tools with career potentials. These adolescents were resistant to the then available mental health services. They were self-destructive and had been presented by the Juvenile Court with the forced choice of inpatient treatment in the program or serving a sentence in a reformatory. The audiovisual media were effective therapeutic modalities in helping to involve them quickly and intensely in the treatment program. This report is about one of the five years of the Adolescent Drug Dependency Program (Reese, 1974), a thirty-day, six-bed inpatient, federally funded pilot program designed to study and develop a treatment program for such individuals.

SHORT-TERM PROGRAM

The Adolescent Drug Dependency Program was started in 1970 by a pediatrician of the University of Connecticut Health Center, Hartford. At that time, the age sixteen and under drug dependent youths were excluded from existing drug programs because of their age (Kramer, 1972) or from mental health services, as they did not choose treatment voluntarily. The purpose of the statewide program was to withdraw the adolescents from drugs as well as from the noxious environment of home and community, and for induction to therapy at voluntary facilities. The program was designed to divert them from the criminal justice system to the mental health services.

Most cases were referred through the court. Deviant behavior included breaking and entering, stealing, dealing in drugs, prostitution, or running away from home. Most were living on the streets and with trouble-prone peers. They left homes because of severe conflicts with or ineffectual parents. They were out of school through suspensions. In addition to serious drug abuse with opiates, stimulants, sedatives, hallucinogens, and inhalants, there were suicidal gestures, depression, deliberate overdose, wrist and arm slashing, and reckless behavior.

Up to six adolescents were admitted to the program every thirty days. There were six beds in two ward rooms and a small recreational room allocated to the program at one end of a pediatric ward in the health center. The program had the professional services of the pediatric staff of physicians and nurses. Funding provided a full-time youth coordinator, a half-time social worker, and the part-time occupational therapist. Youth volunteers were recruited by the volunteer director. The treatment services included a complete behavioral and physical history, physical examination, psychological testing, individual and family counseling, group discussions, occupational therapy, educational and recreational activities. With the completion of four weeks of treatment, the patients were discharged. With a good home situation, an adolescent returned home and was involved with the parent(s) in family outpatient treatment. When the home situation was not considered suitable, some patients entered a long-term voluntary residential facility for rehabilitation. This was opened by the state and based on the pediatrician's efforts and the effectiveness of the program. Some patients were accepted into private psychiatric facilities, which allotted a small number of beds for welfare patients. Later, with more alternatives for continued therapy and experience, continued improvement after discharge from the program reached a high of 80 percent (Reese, 1974).

Cases: Diagnoses and Problems

Upon admission, the clinical psychologist routinely administered the Wechsler Intelligence Scale for Children, the Draw-A-Person, Incomplete Sentences, Thematic Appperception, and Rorschach tests. Almost all the adolescents had the diagnosis of character disorder based on their responses.

The diagnosis *character disorder* has also been termed *antisocial* or *sociopathic* or *psychopathic personality*. Persons with this diagnosis were described in one psychiatric textbook (Kolb, 1977) as having an essential defect in the character structure that resulted in the failure to develop a socialized superego and ego ideals. A study of the problems these persons present was described by Marks, Seeman, and Haller (1974) in their book of the use of the Minnesota Multiphasic Personality Inventory. The problems were similar to the problems that adolescents presented in the inpatient program.

The adolescents had very poor self-concepts. Due to parental abuse or neglect, they often exhibited a "battered ego." They liked getting high on drugs. They were hyperactive and sought immediate gratification of needs by acting out. They swung from mature to childlike behavior, and charm was their forte. Denial, projection, and rationalization were their defenses. There were incongruous actions for feelings, such as laughter for anger, braggadocio for anxiety, hostility for affection.

In task performance, there was near-illiteracy, low ability in verbal and written self-expression, no achievement goals, and no routine habits. For tasks, there was no planning. They were slow to get started. During work efforts, they regressed to childish behavior and were then hard to stop. Fear of being sent to prison was a deterrent to problem behavior and gave authority to personnel.

Creative Therapy

The therapist's responsibility was to use art to give the adolescents feelings of achievement derived from creative acts and artistic products. They were to be stimulated by creative experiences. The pediatrician himself was an artist.

The therapist's goals were to establish a trusting relationship as a warm yet authoritative figure. Within the creative therapy group sessions, provision for ego-building tasks and relationships were undertaken. Boundaries for behavior and social relationships, feedback for good and poor behavior, assistance with honest verbal expression of needs, and learning skills were also developed. Problem-solving and decision-making situations occurred, and these adolescents were given support as they experienced self-disclosure with initial underlying anger and depression. They sensed improvements in their lives, which occurred with continued therapy.

Biomedical Communications Department

The Director of the health center's Biomedical Communications department introduced the therapist to audiovisual media. He provided a Portapack® video camera and recorder, a monitor for playback, a super-8 Kodak® instamatic camera with zoom lens, a movie projector, and a film splicer. Tapes and cartridges were charged to the budget at minimal cost.

The director was creative and humanistic. He taught an adolescent to use a camera or other equipment by handing it to him or her with a brief demonstration and with apparent respect and belief in his or her ability. At times the equipment was left on the ward over a weekend for a project. None of the equipment was stolen, and there was much concern by the adolescents if even a simple repair was needed.

Patterns in Treatment

The therapist worked three afternoons a week for a total of ten hours. The adolescents were scheduled for creative therapy group sessions on each afternoon for about one and one-half hours, or three hours for planned community trips. Attendance was required as part of their admission agreement to participation in treatment. A pattern emerged for the therapeutic activities for each group's month-long stay. Such a pattern had value for evaluative purposes. The principal treatment method was the small group process. The audiovisual tasks were as follows:

Super-8 Filmmaking

Each adolescent was given one film cartridge to use individually or with the group. Planning was done the first week, shooting the second, developing the third, with time to view the film the fourth week before discharge.

Portapack Videotaping

Each group had a thirty-minute tape to film as a shared group experience or project. This was usually performed in the second and third weeks. With about twelve treatment sessions during thirty days, there was time to allow for spontaneous sessions when one individual needed support, to have fun and relieve tensions, just to get off the ward, and yet complete the audiovisual tasks.

There was also a pattern with the process of each treatment session. The first fifteen to twenty minutes were usually spent helping them shift from whatever they had just been doing, or easing the pain of what had happened that morning or over the weekend. The group session started from where the adolescents were emotionally. At times this was the focus of the work done during that session.

As hard as it was to get started, it was equally difficult for them to stop without upsets or regressing. Release of tension took about fifteen to twenty minutes. The therapist's aim was to help them to have good times and to be receptive to the positive experiences that could happen.

Creative Tools

One aspect of creativity is to bring into existence an observable tangible object or work that has evolved from the person's own thoughts or imagination. Carl Rogers (1961) defined the creative process as the emergence in action of a novel relational product, growing out of the uniqueness of the individual on one hand, and the materials, events, people, or circumstances of his life on the other. In creative activities, the adolescents were presented with the medium, given basic instructions, the time to experiment, and to produce.

Videotape "Mod Squad"

With one group, the Portapack camera and recorder were left with them on Friday. The group task was to produce their own thirty-minute tape over the weekend. On Monday afternoon, the recorder was connected to the television set and both the program and ward staff gathered eagerly with the adolescents to watch their show.

The show was named the "Mod Squad" after the long-running television series. The star trio was two girls and one boy. The show was filmed on the pediatric ward. One of the patient's rooms became the emergency room of a hospital where a drug addict (the youth coordinator) arrived o.d. (overdosed) on a stretcher. The "Mod Squad" members transferred him to a bed, and a doctor (an adolescent) sought to revive him, which included straddling him on the bed and vigorously pounding his chest. Interns and nurses (the actual staff) were at bedside helping by not laughing and yet saving the patient from the "doctor's" ministrations.

The adolescents were all too familiar with overdosing and had first-hand knowledge needed to produce the story. They wrote the scenario and directed the actors. At the end of the film, the "Mod Squad" walked with their arms around each other into the lens, obviously pleased with their success. Their identification with positive characters was very important.

This production did much to increase the pediatric staff's respect for the intelligence and skills of the adolescents. For the adolescents, it was a satisfying creative experience. They were proud of their work and became more responsible members of the ward community. It was also an interesting rather than a boring weekend spent in a hospital.

Super-8 Filmmaking

With one group of adolescents, the therapist gave each an open-ended task of using a film cartridge as he/she wished. The adolescents chose to work together, and they photographed scenes on the ward over several days. One film was a series of scenes, faces and bodies of pediatric staff, adolescents, and children. Another was of adolescents doing "weird things" (their title), such as painting their faces with paints, standing in odd positions, filming multicolored water as it swirled down the toilet bowls.

One film was of a pink plastic Pepto-Bismol® bottle, tied on long purple yarn, and filmed from the fifth floor open window as it was lowered several floors, swung wide, swung in circles, raised. The pink bottle on purple yarn against green treetops produced a nice color effect in the movie. The adolescents then devised their own zoom effects by throwing pink fluffy slippers out the window and filming their descent, and then other objects. Next the film showed a security officer leaving a building below, walking past the pile of thrown objects on the ground, and then his back was seen as he left the ward — after warning them to stop throwing objects out the windows.

In another film of ward life, there was a close-up of a large poster on one of their doors. As one watched, the poster caught fire, and the next scene was of fire engines pulling away from the hospital five floors below. The poster had caught fire from the heat of the sun gun on the camera, and this was what had brought the fire engines to the hospital and firemen to the ward.

The two latter films were taken on a Friday morning. When the therapist arrived at 1:00 PM, she was greeted at the elevator by adolescents who were quite excited about filmmaking. They had tales to tell of security officers and firemen coming to the ward. Filmmaking certainly met their need for excitement. The pediatric staff, on the other hand, had mixed feelings upon greeting the therapist. They needed relief from caring for the adolescents, but they did not share the excitement about filmmaking on their ward.

Activity Psychotherapy Tools

Super-8 Filmmaking

The therapist presented a film cartridge to each one in a

group of four adolescents, to be used as he/she wished. Rather than a nondirected creative activity, however, the action was planned and carried out in the group activity therapy sessions when the therapist was present.

One scenario was to enact the parts of a "narc squad," a pusher and a buyer, and to film a buy taking place on a street in the inner city. The therapist determined that each knew a number of persons in the area who could fit the parts. She also reviewed the risks attendant with such filming. Each of the adolescents was surprised at the knowledge the other had of such people in the downtown area, and each began to discuss his or her own drug abuse. Three were fifteen years old and one was sixteen.

Carol lived in the downtown inner city with her mother and two brothers. Her mother had come from Puerto Rico and was on welfare. One brother, a thirteen year old, had banked more than $5,000 profit from heroin sales the previous year. She said that anyone who lived where she did was on drugs. Sharon was of Polish descent and lived in a predominantly blue-collar, working-class city with her mother and six younger children in an apartment in a housing project. She described her use of drugs. So did Paul, from a poor family with three brothers who lived in an affluent community near the New York border, and Arthur, who lived with his parents, two older sisters, and a younger brother in an upper middle-class suburban integrated city.

Capturing their respective lives in the different communities became the subject of filming. On four successive Wednesday and Friday afternoons, the therapist was to drive them to their communities for location footage.

As part of their planning, each was asked to write a scenario. Carol listed the places where she would go, "my house, my school, pig station, downtown." Sharon wrote "(state boys' reformatory), (state) Park Tower, (adult drug rehabilitation house), (city) high school, (city) police station." Paul listed his places on separate index cards: "my house, the school, the (town) Green, town folks, downtown, all the freaks." Arthur wrote his topic first and then a description of himself:

"THE TOWN I DEALT IN"

I supply most of (the city) with illal drugs like LSD, Grass and hash. My involment with drugs is a wide span. I did coke, hash, grass, acid, Mesline, Pilybin, speed, downs, opium, up's, cigerettes, coffee and baladona." (sic)

Arthur also listed the places we were to film: "my house, my dogs, the school, town green, pig shop, new mall, pond."

Paul's. The first trip was to Paul's community — a lovely historical New England town. Paul's house was built into the side of a steep hill and overlooked the valley and his school. There was no yard except for the front driveway. No one was at home, but Paul insisted his parents knew of and approved of our visit. The interior of the house was remarkable for its clutter of clothing, papers, and objects so that one room was not distinguishable from another except that one had a stove, refrigerator, and sink. His mother was an alcoholic and his father, the school custodian, was ineffectual. After discharge from the drug program, Paul did not return home but was accepted for further treatment in a private school for troubled youth.

We toured Paul's school, where he was greeted affectionately by many students and teachers. He introduced us to some of his friends and teachers, as well as to the principal and the school nurse. The nurse had befriended Paul, and she told him she would visit him at the health center. "He looks good," she said to the therapist. (Doesn't he usually look good?) "No, sometimes he looked quite bad."

We drove to the town's green, a large block surrounded by colonial houses. It was then we remembered the camera! Home and school had been very emotional and no one had remembered to start filming. Following his outline, Paul then filmed from car windows as we drove, for there was little time left. He filmed the green, townsfolk, some youth in cars, smoking and clearly upset at having the small camera aimed at them. As we had hastily predicted, their faces were not clear on the developed film.

A stop was made at a hamburger stand on the way back and the adolescents' behavior regressed as they started to mess with the condiments. Quick and firm instructions restored appropriate behavior. In the car, they were quiet and introspective. Carol said she felt funny being in an all-white school.

Arthur's. For the second trip, the group was eager to leave as soon as the therapist arrived. Carol was not with us, as she was visiting her mother, who had suffered a mild heart attack. At Arthur's house, as at Paul's, there was no one home, although our visit had been discussed with the parents. It was a large, well-appointed house with a large yard in a neighborhood of similar houses. Arthur informed us "there were two good-looking chicks next door." His two dogs greeted us. In his room, Arthur was shocked, for it had been stripped bare of his possessions, wall posters, etc. Only a few clothes and phonograph records were left, and his mouse was dead. Arthur's usual braggadocio was gone, and he was sad and subdued. He had had a long history of rebellious behavior and drug dealing, and his parents were no longer able to cope with him. He too, when discharged, went to a private boarding school for further treatment.

His school was a barracks-like building with long hallways and classrooms, starkly utilitarian and lacking any beauty. Camera in hand, Arthur led the way to the principal's office, where he introduced us as being from the University of Connecticut Health Center's adolescent drug program and stated that we were doing a film project on where the adolescents lived. The principal smiled for the camera, shook our hands and approved our trip into the school. Arthur walked through the school as "cock of the roost," greeting "kids I was busted with," and the attractive girls. He knew few teachers, as he had spent little constructive time in school. To the gym teacher, he shot, "Have you any team left?" The teacher bristled and went on. As Arthur photographed one teacher in a woodworking shop, the teacher said he did not know why he was being filmed. Arthur replied, "You got me busted and reported me last month." He toured the male locker room with Paul and then took us outside to a wall near the parking lot ". . . where we dealt. . . . We'd sit here and be high, and the teachers would ask us if we were high." The adolescents shared laughter at this.

We drove through the city. Arthur had us stop in the police

station parking lot. He pointed out the "narcs changing shifts," policemen getting in and out of squad cars. He wanted to film inside the police station, so he walked over and asked this of one of the policemen, who told him to ask the chief in the station. Arthur and Paul went inside the station, and Sharon and the therapist waited in the car. After five minutes they returned and we left.

Arthur was angry. One of his posters that had been in his bedroom at home was hanging behind the police chief's desk. Arthur asked why the therapist had not gone in with them. She said that her experience to date with police had been to avoid getting tickets for speeding and avoidance in general. Arthur talked quite a bit about Lt. ————, "a pig." The therapist listened and ventured to tell him what she heard him saying — that he really liked the lieutenant. The adolescents howled at this. Yet it did seem that this person had served over a period of time as a concerned but strict father figure to Arthur, and Arthur kept searching him out by visiting the police station when he was at home, albeit with a belligerent attitude.

Sharon's. On the third trip, this time to Sharon's house, we stopped at a local restaurant, where the therapist's education began about the stream of alienated youth that flowed from community to community, and from this fast-food restaurant to another. As we ate, the adolescents identified the kids in booths who were high, and on what. These kids would be joined by other kids, and some of them would leave. Arthur said they were never kicked out, as they brought business. We did not film them.

At Sharon's school, we were ushered right into the principal's office. After introductions, he leaned back in his chair and asked, "You want to take my picture?" Paul just sat there with the camera and required a nudge from the therapist to take this principal's picture.

Sharon, like Paul, had a number of friends who were glad to see her. They said they missed her and that they had heard she was in the hospital. Later, the therapist asked what they thought she was in the hospital for, and she replied, "drugs." With one male teacher, there was obvious mutual fondness and respect. Mostly, the students were white and dressed "straight."

Arthur commented that they had never seen a hippie before him, and Carol again talked of her discomfort in an all-white school.

From there, we went to the city hall, where the police station was. The therapist had overcome her middle-class bias by then and went inside with the four adolescents. She was pushed to give the by now routine introduction of where we were from and what we were filming. The adolescents appreciated the respect we received in this role. The humorous aspect came after giving this speech, when we produced the small insta-matic camera and a clamp-on light!

Sharon asked for Lt. ———, who was not there. The sergeant ushered us into his office. He told us he was in street clothes because he had just returned from the Rotary club, where he had given a speech on drugs. The adolescents led him on, feigning innocence about drugs. As he talked, Paul set up the clamp-on light to film him. However, the light was a little 40-watt bulb! The adolescents had exchanged the large floodlight with the 40-watt bulb taken from over the sink in the residents' washroom in the hospital. (We were to hear about that on our return!) After this, the therapist learned to check out the equipment more carefully before we left on future trips.

The adolescents asked the sergeant to see the display case of drugs. It seemed every police station in Connecticut had one. After we left, Paul displayed a plastic marijuana leaf that he had stolen from the display case before our eyes. This had been the objective in seeing the display case. They said they now had three for their own collection. More were to come.

As we left the sergeant's office, we met Lt. ——— in the hall. As with the male teacher, there was good rapport between Sharon and the lieutenant. He commented that Sharon "had a lot on the ball, and that she could be a leader." Later, Sharon said, "They tell me I'm smart and good looking. It makes me angry." Her self-concept was so poor she could not accept compliments.

As we toured the communities, the therapist observed and discussed with the adolescents that although they reviled "the pigs," there was usually one who served as a warm but firm father model. The adolescents listened, began to examine that observation, and then later began to establish good relationships with these persons.

Sharon's mother lived in a low-income housing project. She was separated from the father, who was a compulsive gambler and who spent all his money. The mother, one brother, and two sisters were waiting for us with a late lunch. Sharon and her mother looked very much alike, which was pointed out by Carol. The mother smiled and said, "Do you hear that, Sharon?" Sharon groaned. Sharon's mother picked on her constantly. "Did you go to your school dressed like that? . . . Why were you so late? . . . Don't eat like that." The other children were quiet. Sharon was hostile to her mother and snapped back. When we left, she huddled in the back seat of the car in tears. The whole group was quiet. Halfway back, she began to query us about where she lived, seeking our approval, "Don't you like (the city)? You don't? I love it."

Back at the hospital, when we were discussing the trip, Sharon said she really loved her mother. She did not like her father and his gambling. "We all get along at home until he's there and then they fight. I hate him. I love my mother." Carol said she was surprised to hear that, as Sharon did not act as if she loved her mother. "I didn't?" Sharon asked, looking at the therapist. (No.) "I think I'll call her and apologize." All the adolescents said no one ever apologized in their families but they would start to do this themselves.

Again, we had found the events so emotional that most of the film shots were taken as we drove off of persons walking in the streets, some of whom waved back and smiled.

Carol's. When we visited Carol's home in the inner city, Arthur stayed behind. While he acted with much braggadocio in the suburbs, he was afraid in the inner city where this kind of behavior provoked physical violence.

Carol's mother lived in a second floor apartment on a street adjacent to a state highway that went through the city. Although in a slum section, the apartment was bright and cheerful, with yellow and orange colors used in covers on furniture, tablecloths, curtains, plastic flowers, and live birds. Paul had become the group's cameraman, and he took pictures of everything. With the mother was a male friend, a neighbor boy of twelve, and the mother's probation officer.

We sat in the kitchen, and Carol acted as an interpreter for her mother with the probation officer. The probation officer turned to the therapist at one point and said that Carol's mother "had been a *bad girl*," as she had not been reporting in. He informed us that Carol's brother was in jail again, "booted." We had a cold drink and cookies.

We did not go to Carol's school or the police station. She said she had had too many fights in school to go there, and if she went to the police station, they would keep her there. As we drove through the run-down area where Carol lived, it was hard for Sharon and Paul to believe how bad it was. Paul would get out of the car and photograph the deteriorated buildings, garbage in the streets, derelicts. The others stayed in the car.

Carol then took us to the downtown office of a Community Renewal Team to see a woman for whom she had worked. The woman was not there, but the staff was friendly and liked Carol.

Videotaping

For this group's thirty-minute videotape, they decided they would tape a group therapy discussion of what had happened to them on the community trips. The Biomedical Communications office was contacted and an appointment made for the use of the Portapack. On the afternoon of the taping, a technician arrived with the equipment. He offered to film the session.

It was a poignant session as each person told the others of his/her reactions. They described their emotions, made comparisons, and named each other's problems while at the same time being very supportive of each other. They told how much each had come to mean to him or her. Much warmth and sensitivity had been generated within the group.

There was some levity. Midpoint in the session, the camera had been passed around and each did some filming. Later, on playback, we saw the girls' breasts and legs as they talked as that was where the fellows had focused the camera.

When the group was summarizing the session, the technician asked if he could add his comments. He said he was very disappointed. Weren't they supposed to be more honest with each other and not so friendly? Why hadn't they gotten angry and told the truth? The adolescents were startled and did not respond. The therapist pointed out that it had been important for them to talk about good feelings and that it had been a fine sharing session.

The filming trips and the taping had caught the interest of the center's public information staff. It was arranged that they and the program director would view the films in the BMC office. The super-8 films were not documentaries, and did not show what had happened on our trips. They were like home movies, meaning something only to those of us who had been there. When the videotape was shown of the group as they sat on their beds in the ward and talked, the sound we heard was "Days of Our Lives." The adolescents had dubbed the soap opera over their voices and erased the caring statements about each other.

SUPER-8 FILMMAKING IN INDIVIDUAL THERAPY

Shana was a fifteen-year-old, well-developed, attractive girl. She lived away from home, was on drugs, and prostituted herself for money to buy drugs. On the ward, when a man was near, she would become highly seductive, and the man would respond with obvious sexual interest. On psychological tests, there was major confusion about males, rejection of females, and doubts that she herself was a girl. As a young child, she had been sexually assaulted and had had a forced abortion. Being female to her meant being damaged and open to further attacks. There was pervasive hostility. She was a "bad girl." Shana lacked mothering; her own mother's behavior was immature.

The therapist saw her in individual sessions. Shana had an immediate and totally positive response to super-8 filmmaking. She used her film cartridge to film flowers in a city rose garden on a trip with the therapist. She filmed flowers of all types and colors, from near and far, and zoomed in on open blossoms. After the film was developed, she learned to splice and edit it, hanging strips of film as she worked. Her film was successful.

There was a fine sense of form and color. The filming was symbolic of her own maturing as an attractive, flowering female. It was also instructional and indicated her cognitive abilities in planning, editing, and producing her own film. She came to accept that she needed to continue in therapy and upon discharge was placed in a residential treatment program.

VIDEO AS A VOCATIONAL TOOL

Several adolescents discovered that they had talent in using the videotape equipment and explored their skills for career possibilities and vocational training. One adolescent served as the therapist's camera technician to tape a group discussion she led with elderly residents in a home for the aged on the topic of death and dying. Other adolescents liked operating the monitoring panel of video cameras in dental clinics in the School of Dentistry as a job station for rehabilitation counseling. One boy was especially eager to start work early every weekday. We discovered that a young nurse used one of the dental clinics to undress and change into her uniform when she arrived for work.

Later, when the drug program expanded, a vocational rehabilitation counselor found videotaping an excellent medium for motivating adolescents toward vocational opportunities.

MEDIA FOR YOUTH

The excitement adolescents have for filmmaking was described by Kahn in an article in the *Super-8 Filmmaker* magazine (1974). The article described a fifth grade class in a private school filming the American Revolution. Included were Paul Revere's ride and the battles of Lexington and Concord. A newly hired filmmaker-educator at the school set the sole admonition to the fifth grade teacher, which was to let the children do the thing themselves. There were many problems but the pupils were ingenious in their solutions. There was also a lot of learning. The task was made easy. The cameras were simple Kodak super-8 instamatic with a zoom lens. The project was reported as helpful for nonverbal children who had trouble in school and yet were eloquent in making visual statements. Children needed to express themselves through film, and they became more interested in the written word as a result of filmmaking.

Case (1974) presented the idea of making a portrait of someone with super-8 film, not an oil painting to be hung on a wall or a still photograph of someone frozen forever in a more or less characteristics expression, but a record of the variety of expressions and movements and gestures that make up one's impression of another person. Life, he wrote, is motion, and (only) the movie camera comes close to capturing its vitality. He advised planning the portrait — movements, expressions, and activities. Ask others what to film, get clues from possessions, furniture and hobbies, and ask one's self how the person lives and why. Look at him through the camera's eye, separating all the bits and pieces, and thinking of him as camera problems, and you would be well on your way to a better understanding of the person and to more knowledge of what movies can be. Special technical devices on the super-8 camera, such as slow or fast motion, zoom lenses, macro close-up lenses, and planning ahead of time can eliminate much editing.

An article in the *Hartford Courant* newspaper, May 1974, described a program in a public school, in which each student developed a project idea to videotape. Each student initially wrote it down in outline form, acted it out in pantomime, made a series of drawings, and then performed it before the camera. The purpose of these steps was to improve thought processes, develop writing skills, gain self-expression, and improve self-image and confidence.

In 1969 in *Art in America*, Margolies wrote that the first generation of television babies were reaching maturity. Ninety-five percent of American homes had television sets. The generation that grew up with television had evolved a new perception of processing information in which the individual relied more on visual and aural sources than on printed information. The new attitude was called process level perception that affirmed direct sensory perception, as contrasted with content level perception, which was determined by individual relevance. The television camera, and cameras in general, were fantastic tools for teaching people to see, he wrote. The lens could be considered an extension of the eye and could guide the eye in ways that it did not normally take.

DISCUSSION

During this year, the work of the therapist as a part-time employee was, for the most part, isolated from that of the treatment team. Reliance for relevance of her work came from the adolescents' responses that carried over into other therapeutic interactions, from the therapist's intermittent contacts with individual staff members, and from documentation in the case records. She found that the involvement in the audiovisual media by the adolescents was an effective therapeutic modality, as it caught the interest of the other staff, thereby bridging her work and theirs.

The adolescents, who were life dropouts, responded to these media with obvious emotion and to the treatment sessions with intense interest and anticipation. The excitement came from the creative acts of producing personal film, their self-portraits, and from having their work accepted by the therapist and one another. The therapist and the eye of the camera were witnesses to who they were and how they lived.

For the therapist, filmmaking and videotaping proved to be an excellent projective technique for evaluation and treatment. The adolescents photographed meaningful objects in their lives and experienced how they related to these objects.

> There was a child went forth every day
> And the first object he look'd upon, that object
>   he became,
> And that object became part of him for the day or
>   a certain part of the day,
> Or for many years or stretching cycles of years.
>   Walt Whitman
>   "There Was a Child Went Forth"

Therapeutically, the adolescents gained insight into how they viewed themselves and others, experienced emotions appropriate to events, and attempted productive behavior. Media therapy facilitated their induction into long-term therapy. It was fun as well as a deeply moving experience for the therapist and adolescents.

One problem that was not satisfactorily resolved was that of the cameraman. With a trained cameraman, filming our visits into the communities could have produced a documentary film. There would have been a need to orient the technician to the psychodynamics of what was occurring. Another technique could have been the assignment of the adolescent to film his/her own portrait of his/her home and community to show others, rather than making it a group experience. The newness of the media to the therapist meant that she was learning with the adolescents. With more knowledge of and experience with the media, there would have been better products.

SUMMARY

There appears to be little use of video by activity psychotherapists and rehabilitation counselors. Cline (1972) wrote that the use of this media to document behavioral change over the course of time was still relatively undeveloped.

Wachtel, Stein, and Baldinger (1979) considered it crucial that the therapist be adequately prepared for the use of video playback and comfortable with the video equipment, and that training for this had to include full exploration of his feelings about self-image. They also said that these feelings had to be monitored throughout the work with video replay.

Audiovisual media are therapeutic and creative tools for adolescents in short-term therapy, are relatively inexpensive, easy to use, and pertinent, with tangible products for feedback in therapy and for patient data.

The disadvantages seem to lie with the need for training and experience by the therapist, whether for use in creative projects with patients or in psychotherapy — two different yet interrelated approaches. The cameraman's training and experience are also critical for good results. There are possible negative effects upon patients' self-concepts if this is not handled skillfully.

There may be more use of these media by creative therapists than appears in the literature. One reason for the lack of known popularity with creative therapists may be the mechanical nature of the equipment and also the therapists' discomfort in viewing themselves. If the latter is true, the writer suggests that activity psychotherapists risk experimentation with videotaping in creative activities knowing that the initial experience may be harrowing. It is most helpful in short-term therapy, and when the resistance phase is supervised and worked through, a period of considerable growth is possible for both patients and therapist.

Videotaping and filmmaking are highly personal media for self-expression. Both are excellent for use as projective techniques. Both present permanent testimony of events, and there is an intense level of audience participation. It would seem these media would be beneficial as a treatment modality with other patient populations and different diagnoses.

REFERENCES

Case, William: Making family portraits. *Super-8 Filmaker,* 2:50-51, March/April, 1974.

Cline, D. W.: Videotape documentation of behavioral change in children. *American Journal of Orthopsychiatry,* 42:40-47, January 1972.

"School Uses Film, TV to Develop Writing," *Hartford Courant,* 26 May, 1974.

Kahn, Carole: The American super-8 revolution. *Super-8 Filmaker,* 2:35-38, March/April, 1974.

Kolb, L. C.: *Modern clinical psychiatry.* Philadelphia, W. B. Saunders Co., 1977.

Kramer, Robert A.: A design for a state-sponsored therapeutic program for the treatment of adolescent drug dependency. *Connecticut Medicine,* 36:623-627, November 1972.

Margolies, John: TV — The next medium. *Art in America,* 57:48-55, September-October, 1969.

Marks, P. A., Seeman, W., & Haller, B.: *The actuarial use of the MMPI with adolescents and adults.* Baltimore, Williams and Wilkins, Co., 1974.

Reese, Christine C.: Forced treatment of the adolescent drug abuser. *American Journal of Occupational Therapy,* 28:540-544, October 1974.

Rogers, Carl R.: *On becoming a person.* Boston, Houghton-Miflin Company, 1961.

Wachtel, A. B., Stein, A., & Baldinger, M.: Dynamic implications of videotape recording and playback in analytic group psychotherapy. *International Journal of Group Psychotherapy,* 29:67-85, January, 1979.

CHAPTER 11

SOCIODRAMA:
VIDEO IN SOCIAL ACTION

LINDA GREGORIC AND MICHAEL GREGORIC

As practiced today, sociodrama joins together social work and the dramatic arts. The profession of social work provides the content; the art of theatre and video produces the form.

The coupling is natural. Each discipline is concerned with the emotional needs of society on a large scale; each discipline is involved with human conflict; each discipline is aware of a marketing need. Necessitated by the proliferation of social problems and prompted by a flourishing communication technology, the sociodrama merger addresses a larger audience than that possessed by any classroom or theatre. Pragmatically as well as aesthetically, sociodrama does two jobs, better.

In part one of this essay, by Michael Gregoric, we intend to define the principles of sociodrama and to bring its methodology into historic focus. In part two, by Linda Gregoric, we will outline sociodramatic procedure.

THEORY AND PRINCIPLES

First, the word.

The "father" of psychodrama, J. L. Moreno, used the term *sociodrama* as early as 1923. Sociodrama

> ... is differentiated from a "social drama," the brain products of an individual playwright only vaguely related to the audience and the playwright himself.... The difference between psychodrama and sociodrama is one of structure and objective. Psychodrama deals with a problem in which a single individual or a group of individuals are *privately* involved. Whereas sociodrama deals with problems in which the collective aspect of the problem is put in the foreground,

244

the individual's private relation is put in the background. The two cannot, of course, be neatly separated. (Moreno, 1973, p. 127)

We agree, but we do suggest a stronger and more contemporary distinction. While acknowledging the pioneer contribution of this creative scientist and his spirit of intellectual merger, we use the term *sociodrama* in a different context. Moreno's work itself, in theory and practice, evolved from a theatre of spontaneity — an impromptu, or improvised, or immediate theatre — to a therapeutic theatre. We merge the aesthetic commonality of theatre and film with social need. We have evolved a contemporary union of the mobile-image and a mobile-society.

Moreno attempted to combat the traditional theatre — what he called the *drama conserve* — with a theatre of spontaneity (1973). He offered in place of psychoanalysis (what he called "an artificial psychotherapy of two") psychodrama, whose "spontaneity" and "action" would produce a "liberation and cure" (Renouvier, 1958).

We are eager to liberalize the *drama conserve,* but we are not willing to abandon it for psychodrama. Like the "alternative-theatre" trends of the Environmentalists, or the *auteur*-actor examples in film, such as Marlon Brando, sociodramatists share an involvement with the process that begins before the product, or the script.* Like them, we work from improvisation to a "piece."†

However, unlike theatrical Events, Happenings, or the political pieces from the eponymous Open Theatre, sociodrama eschews sensationalism, embraces commercial technology, and provides training in social work.

We do see, both philosophically and in practice, sociodrama

---

*By definition, a "piece" is a produced play that is realized from improvised group "workshops." A play, traditionally of course, is written by a playwright and interpreted in "rehearsals."

†In terms of film criticism, it is highly debatable that even the universally recognized *auteurs* aesthetically did it all. Certainly, Orson Welles was indebted to writer Herman Mankiewicz and cinematographer Gregg Tolland and musician-composer Bernard Herrmann. John Ford was indebted to Dudley Nichols and Winton C. Hoch and Bert Glennon, among others.

as operating in the political arena. Indeed, after more than a decade of working in such sensitive social service areas as corrections, human resources, and social welfare, we cite politics as the first principle or law of sociodrama. Before one can practice, an artist must be allowed an instrument on which to play. Before a sociodramatist can work, he or she must be allowed in the field.

Hence, for the sociodramatist, the first need exists to know the employer as well as the employee, the trainer as well as the trainee, the audience as well as the performer. The sociodramatist must gain field experience in both social work and the dramatic arts.

For too long there have been snobbish and shameful academic schisms. A debilitating vacuum of aloofness exists between the social scientist and humanist, between the performer and the business person, between the aesthete and the entertainer, between the artist and the crafts person, between professional and amateur, between evaluation and analysis. The standard should be a matter of relative criteria, not exclusivity. The concern should be with the objective articulation of significant crisis, be it in social work or in artistic form. Survival, basically and aesthetically, bureaucratically and philosophically, is the goal of social welfare recipients as well as audiences everywhere. It is usually for selfish, provincial reasons that the means to survival — a better working relationship of the delivery systems — have been kept apart. Sociodrama joins means, as television threatens established boundaries.

The basic purposes of sociodrama are to clarify and to ventilate critical incidences, as they are found in social service work. Through the means of video technology, sociodramatists and their actor-clients *see* into the conflicting emotions that lie behind the need for social treatment. Through the use of drama — a thing done — we *do* in the social services. Do, not do-in: language overload is our very reason for being. Words can be wrong; language can be less revealing than tone or body language. Or, more precisely, words are too exact or too restrictive in dealing with ambiguous actions or deeds rich in contradiction, to use Kenneth Burke's insight. Words are also too limited in transmitting emotional shadings or ethnic differences. Problems of cultural conditioning and language translation are frequently found in social work. Video, with its voice-over, split screen, *mise-en-scène* capacity, offers powerful social as well as artistic tools.

Perhaps the word *social-video* or *socio-video* could serve as descriptive appellations for our work, but all of these hyphenations are not as complete or as resourceful as the fundamental word *sociodrama*. In content, the amalgams *social-video* or *socio-video* (besides sounding like a disease) imply the broader entertainment area of public television. While some of our training films have been on PBS, such screenings are only an adjunct benefit of the sociodramatic final product. The earlier training process must not be ignored.

While we, as dramatic artists, are respectful of the huge demands inherent in pointing a camera, and while we are interested in communication theory associated with film and television, we, as sociodramatists, are not the Baxters, much less the Bunkers (Edith and Archie).

Nor, as earlier implied, are sociodramatists psychotherapists. Neither by training nor by inclination are we prepared to tear into the psyches or dark personal labyrinths of those in need of psychiatric help. This lack of clinical orientation is what separates us from some of those practitioners working in the area of drama therapy.

This is not to imply that the training provided by the Moreno Institute is not important to us. In fact, we are indebted to Moreno for much of our terminology: role playing, role reversal, group therapy, interpersonal relations (his interpretation thereof), as well as the basic term *sociodrama*. The concept of *tele* ("insight into," "appreciation of," "feeling for," the "actual makeup" of another person), which Professor Zerka Moreno, J. L. Moreno's widow and professional associate for many years, masterfully teaches, is part of our training program at the University of Connecticut.

Also, sociodramatists are not involved with clients on a one-to-one basis, as psychotherapists and drama therapists often are. The distinction between theory and practice becomes finer here but, essentially, sociodrama is a team effort, a group process that produces a product.

Group dynamics in sociodrama necessitates a further distinction between Moreno's methods and ours. Moreno, differentiating between group therapy and group psychotherapy, theorizes that

> . . . the term group is used to designate the therapy which takes place as a by-product from other primary activities without the specific intention of the participants and without a scientific plan; in this sense group therapy may take place, among others, in a physical hospital, in a school, in a church, in a workshop, or in any social setting *without group participation*. The term group psychotherapy is used *exclusively* whenever the process is a medicine for the group treated, when the therapeutic welfare of the group is the *immediate and sole objective*, and when these ends are attained by scientific means, including analysis, diagnosis, prognosis, and prediction. (Moreno, 1950, p. 119; italics mine)

Sociodramatic methodology uses both approaches, employing its own pet terms, *process* and *product*. In early sociodrama workshops group psychotherapy goes on, if Moreno's qualifiers "exclusively" and "immediate and sole objective" are excepted. The individuals participating in the workshop do receive therapy through the means of the workshop, but they are also "improvising" and even rehearsing with an artistic, if not a scientific, plan.

In the later sociodrama workshops, and in the final recording, group therapy goes on not only for those participating, but group therapy is extended for all those who, in subsequent screenings, will vicariously experience the film.

In short, we would have our cake (group therapy) and eat it too (group psychotherapy).

Another distinction that characterizes sociodrama is that the process derives from both Moreno and Stanislavski in regard to the Category of the Moment and the concept of recalled emotion. Moreno's Category of the Moment

> . . . must be differentiated from the "present." The present is a universal, static and passive category, it is a correlate of every experience, so to speak, automatically. As a transition of the past to the future it is always there. The present is a *formal* category in contradistinction from the moment which

is dynamic and a *creative* category; it is through a spontaneous-creative process that the formal category of the present attains dynamic meaning, when it turns into a moment. A completely automatic and purely mechanical process as for instance the repetition of a film, has just as well a "present" as the most intensive creative experience. (Moreno, 1973, pp. 126-127)

Stanislavski's famed principle of recalled emotion for the actor was first translated into English in 1936.

Just as your visual memory can reconstruct an inner image of some forgotten thing, place or person, your emotion memory can bring back feelings you have already experienced. (Stanislavski, 1948, p. 158)

Moreno states that Stanislavski "limited the factor of spontaneity to the re-activation of memories loaded with affect. This approach tied improvisation to a past experience instead of the moment." (Moreno, 1973, p. 101)

Again, present-day sociodrama is somewhere between improvisation tied to a past experience (Stanislavski) and the spontaneous creative moment (Moreno). The significant difference is in terms of a prewritten script. Stanislavski's pupils (and their present-day legatees in the Actor's Studio and beyond) recall their own related emotions so as to deliver more effectively actions previously dictated by a playwright. Sociodramatic performers, real-life persons such as an inmate or a parole officer, spontaneously role play themselves — intellectually recalling and emotionally recreating their own past experiences. However, sociodramatic performers do, in their capacity of scenewrights, provide for the future. Sociodrama extends the moment, through the present, from the past, to the future.

In actual practice, this temporal parlay is quite simple. Be the situation a theatre rehearsal of the *drama conserve* or a sociodramatic workshop using actual characters gendering their own "script," the improvisational atmosphere is not dissimilar. Acting is acting.

The heaviest distinction between drama, psychodrama, and sociodrama occurs in the domain of directing. The basic goal of the sociodramatist is similar to that of a nondidactic director of *drama conserve*, who strongly uses the Category of the Moment. Conversely, the dictatorial stage director has no place in sociodrama. The egotistic "I want . . . " theatre martinet who is concerned with "his" or "her" production has not the makings of a sociodramatist.

A flexible but firm sociodramatist, like any good director in the theatre, film, or television, will work with individuals from a point of view. His first responsibility is to work in collaboration with a qualified social work trainer. In addition, the sociodramatist must interface with designers, musicians, graphic artists, electronic engineers, etc., in concepts of *mise-en-scène*. The most important job of the sociodramatist, like that of the director, is with the whole, with marshalling all the elements of a piece into an energized and truthful unity. As a synergistic director taps the skills of performers and stimulates the imaginations of workers behind the curtain, the sociodramatist releases the concerns, reveals the social dialectic in such highly complex areas as planned parenthood, minority-action groups, and prison reform.

The self-effacement of persona instead of professional aggrandizement, the willingness to accept being a team player instead of an "artist individually free to express himself — or herself," is not easy for many neophyte (or mature) artists. We respect independence, but it has no place in sociodrama.

The analogy of the commercial film director is closer to the interdependence that is characteristic of the sociodramatist. If we agree that film is a collection of crafts, or artists working together, then the status of the sociodramatist is clear. However, the sociodramatist's persona-parameter is like that of a film director who is sensitized to social work as well as the artistic crafts of sight and sound.

Nonetheless, the sociodramatist is not an audiovisual specialist, or a technologist trained in instructional media and assigned to a social service agency. The sociodramatist must be *trained in social work* and schooled in the aesthetics of film and video. The ability to diagnose social problems, the sensitivity to organic form, and the concomitant techniques to direct a production constitute the foundation of sociodrama.

Also, although fact and mimesis are both parts of the sociodramatic process, sociodrama is not docu-drama. Docu-drama, as we know it from television, combines biography and history with large dosages of fiction. "Roots," "Holocaust," and the recent bicentennial offerings use professional actors, a script-writer, and a director to suggest a dramatic but fictive recall of our past. Sociodrama uses professional or amateur "actors" only in roles that cannot be filled by the actual persons.

Sociodrama cannot be sensational exposé, as is frequently the case in journalistic, paparazzi-like electronic newsgathering. While sociodrama is alert to recording reality, with revealing truth in current crises, the films or tapes are not intended to be inflammatory or revolutionary. In fact, to tell the story of both the administrator and the person on the knife-edge of direct contact, sociodramatists cannot be crusaders from without.

This inside status separates the sociodramatist from sociologists, anthropologists and *cinema-verité* film document-arians. While most of these professionals must work within an academic-governmental-foundational system and are hardly without strings, they do — more or less — objectively look at the tensions within a society from the outside. They may, for a time, immerse themselves in a community or a social boil, but they must write or film as observers or viewers.

Sociodramatists work from within. We subjectively involve the actual participants in their own roles and situations. We are here or there to tell the story through the first person, by the first person, for the first person. They learn by doing. We learn by doing and viewing. We all learn by viewing. By working with social workers through video, the community at large, in experiencing broadcast-quality training tapes, ultimately benefits.

THE PROCESS

The process of sociodrama is as important as the video product. In both of its educational phases, the procedural development and the final videotape or film, the primary tool is the video camera. Through the process, the camera evaluates and trains the participants. The tangible tape that ultimately results permits the recycling of insights and information to new groups. During the workshops, the individual is trained, while, over the course of time, the product as well as the fruits of the process promote and constructively develop social change and understanding.

Video, of course, represents a major force in our daily lives. The medium of television shapes our minds, stirs our emotions, and patronizes our intellect. We are told by any number of network-appointed authorities what to think, what to feel, and what to do on almost any social issue. How ironic that this television medium has been so underused by the real experts, those in the field of social work and human resources.

For too many therapists and social trainers, the video camera, if used at all, is limited to recording individual and/or group behavior. Video documentation is kept on file for personal or legal reference and for periodic examination to measure client growth. However, the camera is allowed only to receive and collect information. At no time does the camera actively participate in the scene.

In sociodrama workshops, however, the camera becomes a participant — a facilitator, a monitor, a seemingly neutral, nonthreatening observer of events. After the first flush of embarrassing self-consciousness, the performer begins to accept the lens as another person and motivation is facilitated. At the same time, the third eye of the video system objectively as well as subjectively monitors the action. By videotaping critical incidents, as they are role played through improvisation by staff professionals and/or trainees, the playback capacity then allows participants to re-view more objectively their subjective review of the scene. Thus, the camera becomes and serves as the communication link between director and participants (role players), role players and other trainees, and trainees and trainer.

It is the role of the sociodrama director to structure and set in motion the scene. It is the responsibility of the social work trainer to direct the discussion that follows. In this media manner, the workshop procedure, aided by camera process, promotes group discussion and individual evaluation. By experiencing and seeing one's self in a situation with others, individual social work skills and techniques can be improved.

Specifically, the process requires an expertise behind the camera, for in the early stages of the sociodrama workshop the cameraperson cannot be cued by the director while the scene is in play. There must be no technical intrusion. More importantly, the person on camera must be sufficiently knowledgeable about social work methods as well as cinematography to understand the importance of focussing on body language as well as the spoken scene. In addition, the person must know when to follow the reaction as well as the action. (Such decisions in the final taping with multiple cameras are made in conjunction with the director through the use of headsets. In the beginning workshops, the single camera is fairly autonomous.) Learning to look, select, and interpret — all basic to any social work training — is intensified by the selectivity of the video camera.

Throughout the workshop process, as in any kind of practice, there are false stops and starts. The issues are tough. The situations selected for role play are those which represent the nerve endings of relationships and complex social situations. These are the points at which social workers often disagree, philosophically, as to approach, diagnosis, and treatment. As a result, these critical moments are often shunned or not dealt with in general training programs. Politically, these incidents often represent the "hot spots." Strategically, it is far easier for human nature to ignore these moments altogether or to put them aside in the false hope that they will not fester and erupt at a later, and possibly more detrimental, stage. Sociodrama does not permit procrastination or avoidance. The process demands confrontation and involvement.

Herein lies a therapeutic value for the individual participant, be he or she trainer or trainee. Sociodrama subscribes to the belief that even "normal neurotics," as are we all, need ventilation of feelings and frustrations. By allowing staff or trainees to act out job-related tensions and problems on camera, an individual is moved to act, to feel, and to respond. Through instant replay, the participant immediately becomes an observer. This visual distancing permits an objectivity after the subjective catharsis occurs, to the degree that there is one. The dual objectivity of situation and self promotes clarity and understanding of the role, the reverse role, and the problem.

By repeating the scene on camera, role players can test options and techniques. Often role reversal is used to stimulate new ideas and insights. This might mean, for example, a parole officer changing roles with his supervisor, or even role playing his parolee. By acting out these roles, staff members become more sensitive to themselves and to the problems and, therefore, more aware of client needs and possible solutions.

These insights are then shaped into a coherent scenario, and the participants, once again, replay their roles — still extemporaneously — in the final taping. For nonactors (and most actors) the learning of lines is a large credibility hurdle that can be avoided in sociodrama. Some polish is lost, but greater truth is achieved. The resultant "moving picture" developed by the videocamera and the group can still be shared with the public. The following summary in outline form shows the overall flow of the sociodramatic process and suggests its many rich potentials.

Definition of Sociodrama

A group process relying on the skills of dramatic artists and the knowledge and experience of social service agents.

Goals of Sociodrama

1. Provide in-service training through workshops.
2. Develop permanent, professional, open-ended training tapes based on the critical incidences dramatized in the workshops.

Planning

1. Meet with agency representatives.
2. Review current training programs.
3. Discuss, identify, and assess agency needs and problems.
4. Schedule a flexible workshop series that will permit maximum staff and/or trainee involvement.

Workshops

1. A six to eight week training program.
2. One two-hour session per week. (A maximum of two sessions per week.)
3. Move staff and/or trainees through planned, structured improvisations.
4. Role play critical problems and situations.
5. Record with one camera role-played scenes on 1/2 inch videotape for immediate group analysis and discussion.
6. Repeat scene. Reverse roles or add new role players. In video playback, identify new points of view and options.
7. Construct new scenes that grow out of group discussion.
8. Recycle and continue the process to the conclusion of the workshop session.

Final Taping and Evaluation

1. Evaluate workshop videotapes with trainers.
2. Design a final training scenario.
3. Cast primary roles from the training group. Supply professional supporting actors only when absolutely necessary.
4. Rehearse the scenario improvisationally using a multiple camera, 1/2 inch video system.
5. Tape the final scenes on 3/4 inch color tape in a broadcast-quality studio and/or film on location, generally with 16mm equipment.
6. With trainer or social work professional design and develop an accompanying training guide.

Distribution

1. Develop an announcement brochure.
2. Generate mailing lists for social agencies and schools.
3. Preview, demonstrate, and distribute the training product.

The star-studded professional television dramas dealing with social problems, written by professional writers, may sharply whet our appetites, but rarely do they offer much in terms of instructive reality.

Sociodrama relies on real, as opposed to reel, people to tell the stories that cry to be told. The former "actors" know their "roles" and their rhythms. They know the social dynamics of their "scripts." All they lack is a means of getting from Act I to Act II. Sociodrama provides the continuity.

All kinds of "video" involve the union of substance and form. Theoretically and commercially, television is the technologic presentation of active raw material called "talent," or persona. Sociodrama similarly involves people in an effective and contemporary delivery system. The goal of sociodrama is to render a dramatic representation of social reality.

REFERENCES

Moreno, J. L. *Group psychotherapy*, vol. III, 1950.
— — —. *The theatre of spontaneity*. Beacon, NY: Beacon House, Inc., 1973. This enlarged second edition of the 1947 first edition is an adaptation and translation from the German original, *Das stegreiftheater*. Potsdam, Germany: Gustav Kiepenheuer Verlag, 1923.
Renouvier, P. *The group psychotherapy movement, J. L. Moreno, its pioneer and founder*. Beacon, NY: Beacon House, Inc., 1958.
Stanislavski, C. *An actor prepares*. Translated by Elizabeth Reynolds Hapgood. New York: Theatre Arts Books, 1948.

CHAPTER 12

INSTITUTIONAL CLOSED CIRCUIT TELEVISION

Tom Emmitt

IN institutional uses of closed circuit television, two broad general divisions can be recognized. One has come about in most cases when a member of the professional staff who has gained access to television equipment has begun to experiment with applications to his or her immediate professional tasks. This has led to many small, individual examinations of narrow areas of use (Evans, 1968abc; Evans, Goertzel, and Emmitt, 1968). There is very little evidence of efforts to use television to affect large segments of an institution or cluster of institutions.

For better or worse, the second area was the arena of endeavor I chose for myself (Emmitt, 1973). The choice was not wholly mine. The Camarillo State Hospital was wired for a master antenna system, which fed commercial television signals to every patient area in the hospital. The design also provided for the input of a signal from a source within the hospital on the frequency of Channel 6. As soon as this became known, salesmen descended on the hospital to sell transmission equipment. One finally succeeded. The hospital purchased a control center, two cameras, two camera cables, two cheap lavolier microphones, and nothing else. There were no lights, no sound proofing, no provision for visual aids, and no staff.

Eventually I was appointed to run the facility, and with a patient staff of forty, in 1961 it was begun (Emmitt, n.d.). I had been in the audience of a television studio once and knew absolutely nothing about engineering. I was sent to visit a few facilities, but I learned the most from my patient staff, who were assigned to me through what was then called Industrial Therapy. So, we began, forty patients and I. We began to try anything and everything that promised benefit for the patients of the hospital. This approach has continued to the present time, although the Telecommunication Center today operates very differently from the way it did in 1961.

The philosophy under which the patient staff of the studio operated was not complex. The reasoning upon which it was based was that anyone could feel better if he had stimulating and rewarding work to do. Particularly the mental patient, with the feelings of incompetence that were typical, needed a chance to establish or reestablish himself in his own eyes. It was not uncommon for a patient to enter a hospital and show signs of great improvement in an atmosphere that was highly protective and relatively free from pressure. The return rates that were the common problem of all psychiatric institutions would seem to indicate that the patients were not generally able to hold their gains with any predictability in the world outside the hospital, where stress was unavoidable. The studio gave patients meaningful work to do, which was worth doing for its interest and to which they had to adjust and with which they had to deal. They worked in a small studio that was crowded with equipment and people. They became a part of a team whenever they did a show, no matter what their particular job was in relation to that show. Others depended on them, and they had to cooperate with the others on the team and communicate with them. How they did the job that was given to them depended on their ability to work on a team and assume full self-responsibility. In other words, the structure of the work of the studio was the opposite of an overprotective environment.

One fortunate aspect of this work situation was that there were many levels of involvement. Assignments varied in several ways: in the complexity and skill level, in the amount of responsibility they demanded, in the expertise involved in their performance, and in the amount of interpersonal relating they demanded. In any case, as the patient approached a work experience in the studio he had, well in the background, a therapist who was present when the work was done and was immediately available for support when needed. In very rare cases, if the therapist felt that the pressure of the moment was too severe, he relieved the patient of the assignment and then spent the necessary time to help him understand what had happened to him.

Patients were not sheltered from failure. Failure is a part of life, and it is completely unrealistic to expect to avoid its impact. The studio therapist made a very special point, however, of helping the patient to use failure as an opportunity for learning. Since job assignments were rotated with great frequency, the patient who tried to learn from failure today could look hopefully to a chance to succeed in tomorrow's new assignment. A list of the jobs to be done in the studio will give some idea of the scope the therapist had in grading tensions to the patient's tolerance level.

1. Producer
2. Director
3. Video Operator
4. Audio Operator
5. Audio Tape Operator
6. Video Tape Operator
7. Camera Man
8. Cable Puller
9. Microphone Boom Operator
10. Announcer
11. Newscaster
12. Property
13. Floor Manager
14. Teacher
15. News Editor
16. Reporter
17. Secretary
18. Script Writer
19. Typist
20. Tool Room Keeper
21. Lighting Technician

In this list of jobs to be done in the studio, no effort was made to rank them in order of difficulty. Experience taught us that the most difficult assignment was not the same for each patient. One patient might do very well at writing scripts, or even at such a complicated job as directing, and be acutely anxious as an announcer. The personality problems of the individual patient were all-important in making these determinations. The crucial problem was that the therapist had to find ways to use the various work assignments to enable the patient to build or rebuild a picture of himself as a competent person who could deal with interpersonal problems and meet the requirements of a job at the same time.

From the beginning of Camarillo State Hospital TV, a daily meeting with the entire staff was found to be vital. It became the center for interchange of information, and it afforded a means of keeping group identity strong and morale high. In this thirty minutes between 9:00 and 9:30 AM each day, many things occurred. The work of the day was planned, problems were discussed, future plans were explored, and the staff gave consideration to any and all problems affecting the work of the studio. These might involve discussing a conflict between two staff members, or it might be a discussion of how to increase the effectiveness of some program that was being done on the circuit that day. The meetings varied in value. Some were very productive and others were thoroughly routine. All were vitally important to assure that the patient group became fully aware of the entire range of problems in the studio and that there was complete freedom of communication. The group meetings contributed to the patient's increasingly clear self-image and were essential to group morale.

Out of the meetings came the work assignments, which were posted on a call sheet. It was demanded that the individual examine the call sheet and ready himself to meet the duties to which he was assigned. If, in an emergency, a staff member from the employee group worked a position on a show, he had to meet the same demands as any other staff member and in the same way.

A very real effort was made to keep a patient working at a job that was challenging to his best efforts. The ideal was not realized, but a constant effort was made in this direction. It was in this area of job assignment that the responsibility of the therapist in the studio became apparent. It was his therapeutic judgment that determined the work assignments. He had also to decide when it was necessary to relieve a patient of responsibility and how this should be done. Every effort was made to make the patient aware of the therapist as a supportive figure who was always available on need. Our experience made us very aware that the patients working in the studio had to be very certain that the therapist staff members were concerned about them as individuals, over and beyond their concern for the patient's contribution to the actual television programs. A constant stream of letters and visits from patients who had left the studio was evidence that this attitude was felt.

As the program of the studio evolved and we refined our techniques of working with patients, we saw considerable numbers of staff members leave the hospital. In fact, the turn-over made the ceaseless training of replacements a major problem. It would be inaccurate to leave the impression that there were no other problems. We were not able to reach every patient who came to the studio. We were conscious of patients who came to us in whom we sensed a great potential, but whom we did not reach therapeutically. They went to other work assignments within the hospital, leaving us with an uneasy feeling of having failed. We felt a growing need to evaluate the factual situation in regard to the effectiveness of this work on the patient staff within the studio. However, we felt it was necessary to wait long enough to gain perspective. So, months slipped by as staff and patients worked together, making mistakes and learning from them, trying new programs, keeping some and discarding others and, hopefully, learning.

As this learning process continued, changes were occurring within the hospital and outside that made major changes in the function of the studio. Tranquilizing drugs came on the scene in great abundance with parallel reduction in hospital population. Also at this time (the mid 1960s) there began to be serious stirrings of the idea of community treatment of the mentally ill and a massive growth of treatment programs for the developmentally disabled, who were then referred to as mentally retarded.

Possibly the impact of these changes can be most vividly seen as they affected the studio by examining a typical week's program from the early 1960s and another from 1979.

WEEKLY SCHEDULE — CAMARILLO STATE HOSPITAL TV
(Early 1960s)

MONDAY:
1000 Psychodrama — Dr. Vogeler (T*)
1045 See Hear News — Staff
1100 Way of Life — Mr. Joe Jelikovsky
1330 Etiquette Program — Nursing Service (T)
1400 Christian Science Readings — Mrs. Mahoney
1415 See Hear News — Staff
1430 Talk Back — Panelists

NOTE: (T) indicates videotape recording
      (R) indicates videotape rerun

1500 Psychodrama — Dr. Vogeler (R*)

TUESDAY:
1000 Good Grooming — Jean Paul (T)
1040 See Hear News — Staff
1055 Drop In Clinic — Dr. Hart (R)
1330 Are You Speaking My Language? — Mrs. Phillips (T)
1400 See Hear News — Staff
1415 Group Psychotherapy — Nursing Service
1500 Etiquette — Nursing Service (R)
1900 Songsters — Nursing Service
1930 See Hear News — Staff
1945 Orientation — Nursing Service

WEDNESDAY:
1000 Recovery Inc. — Social Service
1045 See Hear News — Staff
1100 Let's Go Home — Social Service
Wednesday Afternoon ——— Closed for Maintenance
1400 T.V. Consulting Committee
1900 See Hear News — Staff
1915 Division Special — Division I, II, III, IV (T)

THURSDAY:
1000 Wonderful Home — Nursing Service (T)
1030 See Hear News — Staff
1045 Orientation — Nursing Service (R)
1330 Drop-In Clinic — Dr. Hart (T)
1400 See Hear News — Staff
1415 Sewing Made Easy — Mrs. Miles
1500 Good Grooming — Jean Paul (R)

FRIDAY:
1000 Music for Everyone — Mr. Beasley
1045 See Hear News — Staff
1100 Who's Who — Staff
1330 Group Remotivation — Nursing Service (T)
1400 See Hear News — Staff
1415 Division Special — Division I, II, III, IV, VI

TYPICAL WEEKLY ACTIVITIES — TELECOMMUNICATION CENTER
(1979)
(Three full-time employees, no patient staff)

MONDAY:
0800 Staff Meeting
0900 - 1700 Tri-Counties Director arrives to edit videotaped material with one staff
　　　member
0800 - 1700 One staff member copies videotapes for loan and sale
0900 Half-time secretary arrives, processes mail, mails videotapes to various re-

questing agencies

1000 28 staff in studio to view Cardio-pulmonary Resuscitation tape

1000 15 visitors from Ventura College arrive to view Management of Assaultive Behavior tapes

1030 2100 Play Fire Safety tape for hospital-wide

1400 0200 system. Continue schedule for 5 days

1500 0400 at these times

2000

TUESDAY:

0800 Engineer repairs and adjusts equipment

1000 Record Psychodrama. 16 students from Los Angeles observe.

1300 Psychodrama played back over hospital system

1330 27 psychiatric technicians view Psychopharmacy Update

1400 4 training officers review Infection Control: Microbiology

---

WEDNESDAY:

0800 Pick up van, organize equipment for travel to remote location for recording (2 staff)

0830 If You Loved Me and One Day shown for psychiatric technicians

1100 Tape and class on Management of Assaultive Behavior

1400 Tape on Bedmaking for hospital workers

THURSDAY:

0800 Two staff on remote location

0930 Record Psychotherapy group of alcoholic patients in Center

1030 Playback for alcoholic group

1300 Tape on Blood Withdrawal for nursing staff

1500 Mock Orals for social workers preparing for examinations

---

FRIDAY:

0800 Transfer of film to tape for Training Office Dubs

1000 Record interview of patient and therapist

1300 Play Psychological Characteristics of Alcoholism over hospital system especially for alcoholic program

1400 Psychiatric technicians view Cerebral Palsy

1500 Staff return from remote location. Unload and return van.

These schedules clearly show that the function and mission of the television project underwent radical revision. Direct therapy for patients was originally one of the chief functions of the studio. It has almost totally ceased. In the first years, we served the local hospital only. Now we serve the entire state as the Telecommunication Center. We now prepare videotapes of general information and for training for the entire California system. We also still do therapy groups for therapists who bring groups to the studio as part of our continuing service to the local hospital. Beyond this, however, our responsibility has come to be that of preparing training and treatment materials for other therapists. All of these experiences and these broad shifts of mission have left us with a series of experiential convictions.

In broad, general terms we have found that television can have wide-ranging effects based on videotape recording in three areas:

1. *Therapy*

Most forms of nonmechanical, nonchemical treatment may be enhanced by the self-viewing component of television using videotape playback for self-viewing.

2. *Education*

Many patients leaving hospitals do not have vital information they need to survive: where to go for emergency help, where to go for guidance, and where to go for help in various personal emergencies all constitute information they usually do not have. Retarded patients need to be able to recognize traffic signals, identify bus stops, count change, and do many other things that the individuals living in the community take for granted.

Striefel, in his paper "Television as a Language Training Medium with Retarded Children," addresses the issue of teaching the retarded using closed circuit television (CCTV). The study done by the writer gives support to attitude changing and teaching through the use of CCTV.

3. *Training*

Recorded material on CCTV provides an ideal training medium for staff. There is almost no limit to the treatment techniques that can be learned from this audiovisual source. Recently, recordings of cardiopulmonary resuscitation techniques were used to train hundreds of persons in a nearby community. Students viewed the videotapes, which were played over the community cable system. Then they came to various centers for testing. Similar things have been done in the Camarillo State Hospital (Evans, 1969).

Anyone who has had any amount of experience as a psychotherapist knows that the single greatest task of the therapist is to get the patient to see himself clearly as he reacts both to others and to internal problems. It needs to be recognized that clarity of self-perception is as great a problem for the therapist as for the patient. To the writer's knowledge there exists no better instrument for solving the problem of self-perception than videotape recording. Within minutes of the completion of a therapy session the therapist and the patient or patients can be reexperiencing the treatment hour just completed, the difference being that patients and therapist alike see the happening as spectators. In addition, experience has shown that if the self-viewing reveals insights the patient is not ready to deal with, they are ignored.

In recent years researchers have been calling on psychotherapists to modify their claims of therapeutic results from verbally oriented therapies. Research data do not support the curative claims commonly made. I do not find this in any way disturbing, since every mode of treatment fails to some extent. It is important to note that when excessive claims are eliminated, there still remains a solid residue of benefit. Additionally, this effectiveness can be enhanced by videotape recording and self-viewing.

Another area of effectiveness lies in modeling. Here too, as in the area of verbal therapy, caution must be exercised. Modeling must be based to some extent on understanding. The following quotation has bearing on this issue.

> Do patients understand the message in TV broadcasts? Patients may turn on a receiver, but if they do not tune in mentally, production and equipment costs are wasted. In recent months, we have evaluated the ability of over 1200 adult mentally ill patients to understand brief, simple, and apparently interesting programs under better than average viewing conditions. Of these patients, only about one-fourth gave us reliable indication that they could comprehend what was shown on the screen. The implications of this finding for the number of patients who can be reached and the complexity of material broadcast are obvious.
>
> What about the effect of [therapeutic] TV programs for those who can understand? We assessed opinion change following a series of three programs among patients we knew could understand what was being presented. We found statistically significant changes in a therapeutic direction. However, on closer inspection we discovered that this difference occurred only among women. Also opinion change varied with the diagnosis of the patient. (Evans, 1968b, p. 5)

It may at this point be fair to say that the patient who cannot understand the program cannot model on it or learn from it. Such seems to be Dr. Evan's contention. If the patient actually does not understand, he is probably quite right. If, however, the problem is with an inhibition in the response mechanism rather than a failure of comprehension, he would not be right.

Some years ago I was working with a chronic schizophrenic woman who was assigned to the television studio with me. We planned a field trip to reward the patient staff for a period of effective work. This patient dressed for the trip and then lapsed into a catatonic episode. I went to the ward to evaluate her condition. She was standing in the day room, quite rigidly immobile and verbally unresponsive. I went to her, told her that the bus would be leaving in fifteen minutes and that we wanted her on the trip. She gave no response, verbally or other-wise, but she was on the bus when it left and enjoyed the trip. It would seem that a comprehension test given to her during her catatonic episode would have elicited no response, but she obviously did comprehend.

I would contend that everyone models and that we model on things we do not understand as well as things that are compre-hended. Patients exposed to material showing problems being solved do tend to model on the solutions just as large numbers of teenagers model on popular television series. Whether they understand the material or not is debatable.

Some writers (Evans, 1969) hold that patients and normal people respond to information differently. This would also apply to material stimulating modeling. I would argue that this particular distinction between patients and nonpatients is erroneous. I see people in the broadest sense as a continuum in which learning and modeling take place as the result of various factors including culture or the capacity of the organism, not the status of patient or nonpatient. If this concept of a contin-uum of comprehension is used, it is possible to hypothesize that what is being dealt with in the patient is a difference in degree and not in kind. Of course this would clearly not apply to patients with massive brain damage and would probably apply to retarded patients only under special circumstances. I would, therefore, argue most strongly that material televised to a patient, with the above possible exceptions, will have a learning and modeling effect at some level. Of course, patients who are asleep, stunned by medication, or deliberately avoiding will be exceptions.

Two areas in the Camarillo State Hospital make ongoing use of the Telecommunication Center for therapeutic purposes. One is the distinguished Alcoholic Treatment Program. Here patients are brought to the Center and recorded so they can see themselves reacting in various social situations without alcohol. Another area is devoted to psychodrama. No research has been done here in either of the two areas mentioned. However, we have seen some remarkable things happen. Here we have seen patients reacting at one level and have seen that level deepen and intensify as they see playback. The psychodrama recording is played so as to be available to the entire hospital. We have no data on effectiveness.

The examples mentioned above are only some of the areas in which I see CCTV having value in a hospital setting (Emmitt, 1973). In listing three broad general areas of value, I have mentioned patient education. My experience of almost thirty years in the field of mental hygiene has convinced me that patients have only two kinds of experiences, therapeutic and antitherapeutic. Any learning a patient acquires that increases the ability to deal with any problem strengthens self-respect and is, therefore, therapeutic. For the mentally retarded patient to be able to read traffic signs, make change, use public transportation, and so on makes for therapeutic progress. By the same logic, information on health care, handling money, paying taxes, and seeking assistance makes positive contributions to the welfare of both mentally ill and mentally retarded patients.

Lest there be a misunderstanding, let me say that I do not regard CCTV as universally useful. It is a tool to be used as part of the armamentarium of treatment just as chemotherapy, verbal forms of psychotherapy, behavior modification, and other techniques are tools. Patient education or training is a form of treatment for anyone with a treatment philosophy similar to mine. Patients leave hospitals by the scores without adequate information to use to survive in the community. They do not know where to go in the event of an emergency. They do not know where to go for assistance in job hunting. Many have had unfortunate experiences with the police. Prerecorded material on CCTV can do much to inform and allay fears.

It has been part of the philosophy of the Telecommunication Center from the beginning that any training provided to staff has an ultimately beneficial effect for patients. Consequently, we have in our library training material on videotape in a host of areas too numerous to be fully listed here. However, a small selection of titles may be instructive.

1. Issues in Service Delivery to the Developmentally Disabled — William Wilsnack, President's Council on Mental Retardation
2. Fiesta Educativa (in Spanish) — Various Presenters
3. The World of Jody and His Friends (A documentary on a residential care facility for the developmentally disabled) — Introduction: Allan D. Toedter, Department of Developmental Services
4. Operant Conditioning, Parts 1 and 2 — Ivar Lovaas, Professor of Psychology, UCLA

Over the years as the applications of CCTV in which I have been involved have developed, training has come to be one of our major areas of work. Now a new area is developing. We are being asked to go throughout the state and develop documentaries on various outstanding programs to use these recordings as teaching tools.

It would be dishonest to leave this discussion without discussing problems connected with the use of CCTV in mental hospitals. The main source of difficulty is similar to that met in education. Teachers and therapists, for a variety of reasons, are reluctant to use the medium. Some administrators feel that teachers see television as a tool to replace them and, therefore, they resist its use. Therapists tend to avoid the medium. Some frankly feel insecure in having their therapeutic activity shown. Some honestly feel the medium is antitherapeutic. Still another group avoid the medium because nothing in their training prepares them for the experience of self-viewing. All of these reasons ignore research evidence and the ongoing practice of many progressive educational institutions.

Trainers tend to resist the use of audiovisual materials, preferring a classroom and a live teacher. In a study we did on the issue, we found that the resistance of the trainers was not based on fact. We trained one group by the use of videotaped material and another in the classroom. The tests covering the material showed no significant difference in the level of learning. The television teaching was vastly cheaper and more economical of staff time. It has, however, proven impossible to persuade the training staff to continue this use.

Finally, rather than use Dr. Evan's title, *Therapeutic Television, an Effective Tool or a New Toy?*, I would seek another more relevant to the use of the medium. One that occurs to me again and again is *Closed Circuit Television, A Neglected Treatment Tool.*

REFERENCES AND BIBLIOGRAPHY

Alger, I. et al.: The use of videotape recording in conjoint marital therapy. *American Journal of Psychiatry, 123*:1425-1430, 1967.

Bandura, A., Ross, D., and Ross, S.: Imitation of film-medicated aggressive models. *Journal of Abnormal Social Psychology, 66*:3-11, 1963.

Barrington, H.: A survey of instructional television researches. *Educational Research, 8*:8-25, 1965.

Benschoter, R. A.: Modern communications to assist a state hospital. Progress Report, Grant MH 01573-04, National Institute of Mental Health, December 1, 1964-November 30, 1967.

———: Multi-purpose television. *Annals of the New York Academy of Sciences, 142*:471-478, 1967.

Benschoter, R. A., Wittson, C. L., and Ingham, C. G.: Teaching and consultation by television: I. Closed circuit collaboration. *Mental Hospitals, 16*:99-100.

Brandon, J. R.: An experimental television study: the relative effectiveness of presenting factual information by the lecture, interview, and discussion methods. *Speech Monograph, 23*:272-283, 1956.

Carpenter, C. R. and Greenhill, L. P.: An investigation of closed circuit television for teaching university courses. In *Instructional Television Research.* University Park, Pa., Pennsylvania State University, 1958.

Cornelison, F. J. et al.: A study of self-image experience using videotapes at Delaware State Hospital. *Delaware Medical Journal, 36*:229-231, 1964.

Davis, T. S.: Closed circuit television in a mental hospital. *British Medical Journal, 5318*:1531-1532, 1962.

Emmitt, T.: CSH-TV — a pioneering project in the psychiatric use of closed circuit television. Mimeograph, no date.

———: Final report summary. Applied Research Grants Program, National Institute of Mental Health. Mimeograph, no date.

———: Television and the health services information gap. *exChange, 1*:5-12, 1973.

Evans, J. R., Goertzel, V., and Emmitt, T.: An evaluation of television as a therapeutic tool. Mimeograph, 1968.

Evans, R.: Psychopathology and persuasibility. Mimeograph, 1968a.

———: Television research progress report. Research Progress Report, Grant MH 14983, Camarillo State Hospital. Mimeograph, 1968b.

———: *Therapeutic television (TTV): An effective tool or a new toy?* Paper presented at a symposium of the 76th Annual Convention of the American Psychological Association, San Francisco, 1968c.

———: *Attacking urban social problems through the mass media.* Paper presented at the Twenty-Second Annual Convention of the California State Psychological Association, Newport Beach, California, 1969.

Evans, Richard I., Roney, H. B., and McAdams, W. J.: An evaluation of the effectiveness of instruction and audience reaction to programming on an educational television station. *Journal of Applied Psychology, 39*:277-279, 1955.

Evans, R. I.: An examination of student's attitudes toward television as a medium of instruction in a psychology course. *Journal of Applied Psychology, 50*:32-34, 1956.

———: *Resistance to innovation in higher education.* San Francisco, Jossey Bass, 1968.

Frity, J. O.: Film persuasion in education and social controversies: a theoretical analysis of the components manifest in viewer-film involvement as they affect the viewer's urge to further inquiry into social controversies. *Dissertation Abstracts, 17*:2221, 1957.

Geertsma, R. H. and Reivich, R. S.: Repetitive self-observation by videotape playback. *Journal of Nervous and Mental Diseases, 141*:29-41, 1965.

Goldstein, M. J., Acker, C. W., Crockett, J. T., and Riddle, J. J.: Psychophysiological reactions to films by chronic schizophrenics: I. Effects of drug status. *Journal of Abnormal Psychology, 71*:333-334, 1966.

Gunn, R. L., Navran, L., Sullivan, D., and Jerden, L.: The live presentation of dramatic scenes as a stimulus to patient interaction in group psychotherapy. *Group Psychotherapy, 16*:164-172, 1963.

McGuire, F. L. and Stizall, T. T.: Psychotherapy by television: a research paradigm. *Psychotherapy: Theory, Research and Practice, 3*:159-162, 1966.

Mikulich, W. H.: Some aspects of a film program adjunctive to total psychiatric treatment. *Journal of Psychiatric Social Work, 24*:17-104, 1955.

Minear, V.: An initial venture in the use of television as a medium for psychodrama. *Group Psychotherapy, 6*:115-117, 1953.

Moore, F. J. et al.: Television as a therapeutic tool. *Archives of General*

Psychiatry, 12:117-120, 1965.

Myerhoff, H. L.: *Review of settings in which video tape feedback has been explored.* Paper presented at Western Psychological Association Meeting, San Francisco, 1967.

Robinson, M.: *Effects of differential feedback on self-concept among group therapy participants.* Unpublished manuscript, 1966.

———: Effects of videotape feedback versus discussion feedback on group interaction, self-awareness, and behavioral change among group psychotherapy participants. *Dissertation Abstracts,* University of Southern California, 1967.

———: Feedback as a therapeutic tool. *The Quarterly of Camarillo, 2:*14-24, 1966.

———: *Performance mirror — a gut level experience.* Paper presented at a symposium of the American Psychological Association Convention, New York, 1966.

Robinson, M. and Jacobs, A. A.: *Research study investigating the effects of videotape feedback on group interaction, self-awareness, and behavioral change: Methods, results, implications.* Paper presented at Western Psychological Association Meeting, 1967.

Schiff, S. B. and Reivich, R.: Use of television as aid to psychotherapy supervision. *Archives of General Psychiatry, 10:*84-88, 1964.

Schweitzer, H. C., Jr.: Comparison of color and black and white films in the modification of attitudes. *Dissertation Abstracts, 24:*874-875, 1963.

Spietz, R. A.: Films and mental health: principles for the use of motion pictures for teaching mental health. *Bulletin, World Federation for Mental Health, 4:*35-40.

Stoller, F.H.: Focused feedback with videotape: extending the group's functions. In G. M. Gazda (Ed.), *Basic innovations in group therapy and counseling,* Springfield, Ill., Thomas.

———: Group psychotherapy on television: an innovation with hospitalized patients. *American Psychologist, 22:*158-162, 1967.

———: *Reconsiderations of therapeutic concepts in the light of video tape experience.* Paper presented at Western Psychological Association Meeting, San Francisco, 1967.

———: Use of focused feedback via video tape in small groups. *Explorations in Human Relations Training and Research, No. 1.* San Diego, National Training Laboratories, National Education Association, 1966.

Striefel, S.: Television as a language training medium with retarded children. *Mental Retardation, 10:*27-29, 1972.

Wilmer, H. A.: Innovative uses of videotape on a psychiatric ward. *Hospital Community Psychiatry, 19:*129-133, 1968.

Yonge, K. A.: Use of closed circuit television for teaching of psychotherapeutic interviewing to medical students. *Canadian Medical Association Journal, 92:*747, 1965.

Zucker, H. D. et al.: The impact of mental health films on in-patient psychotherapy. *Psychiatric Quarterly, 34:*269-283, 1960.

Part Three
Professional Considerations

CHAPTER 13

APPLICATION OF VIDEOTAPE IN PSYCHOTHERAPY TRAINING*

David M. Schnarch

THE application of videotape recording (VTR) in training psychotherapists and counselors has proliferated in recent years. This development is rooted in the early 1940s when audiotape recording was first used (Rogers, 1942; Bloom, 1954; Gaier, 1952). At the time, training considerations were as unsophisticated as the equipment being used. Questions regarding surreptitious recording with hidden microphones in those early days evolved into more complex questions of optimal strategies for student development.

As the medium of television developed, a few educators experimented with new ways to train students in the mental health fields. In the late 1950s closed circuit television was used in teaching psychotherapy (Fleishmann, 1955; Moore, Hanes, and Harrison, 1961) and clinical psychiatry (Holmes, 1961; Kornfield and Kolb, 1964).

As the technology of videotape recording (VTR) became readily available, it was used in teaching basic courses in clinical psychology and psychiatry (Suess, 1966; Ryan, 1966). Widespread application of VTR in psychotherapy training, however, was somewhat slower to develop. Historically, psychotherapy supervision has focused on discussing what was done or what to do, with little direct observation (Schmidt and Messner, 1977). Personal psychotherapy was sometimes used to augment the student's understanding of the therapeutic process. Teaching psychotherapeutic techniques, however, is a relatively new field. As recently as 1966, there was essentially no

*The author wishes to thank Judith Barnes, Thomas Wolf, and Valerie Wolf for their advice in the preliminary stages of writing this chapter. Thanks also go to Virginia I. Howard of the L.S.U. Medical Center Editorial Office, and Sharon Barre' for their aid in preparation of this manuscript.

research regarding effective and efficient teaching of psychotherapy (Matarazzo, Wiens, and Saslow, 1966). No doubt many supervisors were disinclined to use the new medium of VTR because it was totally alien to their own educational experiences.

The explosion in VTR application for psychotherapy training is attributed to three factors. The first is increased knowledge about how students learn best. VTR allows students to progress at their own paces, increases the personal relevance of the material, and stimulates students' aspirations to learn. With VTR, students can receive highly specific and relevant feedback on their behavior and progress. Behavior and feedback can be presented in close temporal proximity to maximize knowledge of the results (Stoller, 1968). Videotape also permits students to engage in self-instruction, whether by reviewing preprogrammed material, or by recording their own activities. Self-confrontation and self-examination from reviewing their own videotapes often enhance students' self-esteem as well as their knowledge, which perhaps accounts for students' increased receptivity and involvement in their own training when VTR is used (Benschoter et al., 1965; Greunberg et al., 1967). Some educators report that videotaping also helps sharpen student perceptions and sense of involvement in the treatment process (Kornfield and Kolb, 1964). Walz and Johnston (1963) found that counselors who viewed themselves on videotape reported this to be the most significant experience in their practicum supervision.

The second factor in the increased use of VTR is the relatively recent trend to regard psychotherapeutic effectiveness less as a form of art or magic and more as a behavioral science. Teachable therapeutic skills have been identified and empirically validated (Carkhuff, 1969; Kagan and Krathwohl, 1967), as have the importance of therapist characteristics and variables in therapist-patient interaction (Strupp, 1960; Strupp, 1962; Strupp, Wallack, and Wogan, 1964). VTR is adaptable for use in those areas.

The third factor in increased VTR use is increased recognition of the need for counseling skills among a wider range of health-care providers. The field of medicine has become more aware of the role of personality and emotions in the cause and treatment of physical disorders. Moreover, medical education has focused more attention to helping physicians become aware of their personal style and impact on their patients.

Today, VTR is widely used in psychotherapy training at academic universities, medical schools, mental health clinics, and professional conventions and workshops. It has been used to teach psychiatric fundamentals and family therapy to family practitioners (Lurie, 1978; Schmidt and Messner, 1977), interviewing and diagnostic techniques to medical students (Hunt, MacKennon, and Michels, 1975), and fundamental skills to nurses, pastoral counselors, and paraprofessionals. VTR is also increasingly used in advanced training for clinical psychologists, psychiatrists, and social workers. In 1979, the American Association of Sex Educators, Counselors, and Therapists introduced VTR in training programs for sex therapy supervisors. VTR has been a prominent aspect of the annual convention of the American Group Psychotherapy Association for many years. Reviews of videotape materials in mental health journals also reflect the growing application of VTR in psychotherapy training.

VTR APPLICATIONS IN PSYCHOTHERAPY TRAINING

Methods of videotaping student activities in psychotherapy vary greatly. Some institutions are fortunate to have complete studios with multiple cameras and mixing consoles. More common is the interview room with a camera operated from an adjacent room through a one-way mirror. A basic operation would use a portable camera and recording equipment in the interview room itself. With a wide-angle lens, the camera can be preset so that only the client and therapist are present. Zabarenko, Magero and Zabarenko (1977) suggested that recordings made with the camera operated by a third person (usually a supervisor) in the interview room are less intrusive and more "authentic" than tapes made in the studio. Supposedly the paitent and the student experience the supervisor-cameraman as a positive and supportive presence. That theory remains to be documented.

Information storage and dissemination are two of the advantages of VTR in psychotherapy training. VTR libraries preserve unusual case material for future use and preclude the last minute search to "find a patient" in interviewing courses. Objective demonstrations to a larger group of students than could be physically accommodated in a clinical interview are also possible. Prerecorded interviews can illustrate patient (or therapist) defense mechanisms, unconscious processes and security operations, verbal and nonverbal communications, psychopathology, or specific interviewing techniques. VTR permits specific segments of behavior to be reviewed repeatedly. Some equipment allows "stop-action" playback so that a single moment can be examined in minute detail.

The medium of VTR is flexible to meet the needs of students at various stages of their training. The degree of a student's participation in the clinical interaction can be modulated to maintain an effective but not overwhelming degree of anxiety in the training process, and can be increased as the student's clinical skills develop. VTR allows students to observe particular types of patients or problems before they are ready to conduct their own interviews. Neophyte therapists are often better able to develop basic observational and diagnostic skills for dealing with patients' verbal content, affective tone, and nonverbal behavior, when they do not have to carry on a dialogue at the same time.

Videotape is highly useful in helping students develop skills of empathy, genuineness, respect, warmth, and appropriate self-disclosure. Lewis (1978) conceptualizes these as "intimacy" skills, which are distinctly different from the "detachment" skills of observation and diagnosis. Intimacy skills seem to be relatively more difficult for neophyte therapists to develop. Directed information-gathering interviewing, such as that used in history taking and mental status examinations, appears easier for neophyte therapists to learn than collaborative, exploratory interviewing, perhaps because information-gathering interviews can (although less than desirable) be conducted with relatively fewer empathic responses and more structured, close-ended questions. The tendency for medical students to conduct mental status examinations that offer little support and no feedback to the patient may reflect their relative lack of empathy. Relative difficulty in accurately recalling and assessing patients' emotional functioning may further reflect this lack.

Neophyte therapists can enhance their abilities to recognize patients' manifest feelings and communicate this understanding by watching brief segments of videotaped interviews or prepared vignettes. After three or four minutes of observations, the VTR is stopped and students are asked to state their impression of what the patient is feeling and thinking and the degree of intensity of those feelings and thoughts. In variations of this process, the students' perceptions can be written, recorded on audio cassettes, or selected from pre-evaluated multiple-choice items. The VTR segment can be replayed with only the audio or video content present as a means of helping students identify the determinants of their perceptions. Students can also be asked to formulate empathetic responses to the patient, and the response can be registered in the various ways outlined above. The students' responses can be reviewed immediately or at a later time, and the review can be conducted individually with a supervisor or in group discussion. The simple rating system developed by Carkhuff (1969) is additionally useful in helping students assess the accuracy of their perceptions and the relevance of their reflective responses.

In conducting their first psychotherapy interviews, students are confronted with the complexity of the therapist's functions. For some, accurately perceiving the patient, remembering the events transpired, making facilitative responses, and conceptualizing and hypothesizing become competitive rather than complementary processes. For many, their ability in any one area of functioning is somewhat diminished or inhibited. For most, it is a time of exhilaration and anxiety.

Review of videotaped sessions allows the student to master the complexities that originally escaped him/her and to practice new skills. In reviewing content and sequence, the student can make previously unrecognized observations, formulate appropriate questions and responses, and identify multiple opportunities for interventions. Occasionally, the student realizes that the patient actually gave him/her few opportunities to intervene, or discouraged any intervention at all. The opportunity for students to self-correct and teach themselves is one of the major advantages of VTR. Recognition of appropriate responses and timing, like observational accuracy, often first develop from retrospective examination.

Videotaped sessions facilitate self-awareness of the student's interview behavior. Few persons are aware of how their behavior appears to others. VTR allows the student to distinguish his or her actual behavior from (perhaps cherished) fantasies of a therapeutic "appearance." Heretofore unrecognized mannerisms, body posture, and aspects of general appearance are often reported. Teaching a student how to convey genuineness, warmth, and respect is extremely difficult. The absence of these behaviors, however, is often apparent on videotape. Judgmental behaviors and extreme abstractness or emotional detachment are also commonly recognized by students reviewing their own sessions. Fortunately, VTR permits the student to evaluate his/her own behavior rather than necessarily being confronted with an evaluation by the supervisor. Live observation without VTR does not permit the therapist to review for himself or herself the events on which he or she is receiving feedback.

As the student masters the skill of client observation and the anxiety of self-observation, training can advance to the more complex examination of student behavior from the standpoint of its effectiveness and impact on patients. The "meaning" of the therapist's behavior to the patient often differs from the intention of the therapist. Reviewing the patient's reaction both identifies the patient's perspective as an important aspect of the interview to monitor and helps develop the student's skill to accomplish such monitoring. "Rapport," like "assurance," is not a single statement given to the patient, but rather must be developed, and that development can be observed on videotape replay. VTR allows the student to examine not only what was done to establish a working relationship, but how successful it was in stimulating further collaboration. The effectiveness of the therapist's empathetic behavior can be assessed by the outcome in further collaborative exploration. Moreover, the timing and accuracy of interventions can be monitored in the impact on the rhythm and flow of patient-therapist interactions. Kagan (1978) uses a direct approach to increase the student's awareness of his/her impact. In the review of the videotaped session, the patient is present (as is the student) and is encouraged to recall his/her reactions to the student's behavior at specific points in the session.

VTR also facilitates recognition of the latent or process meaning of behavior, which is evident only over the course of time. The nuances of facial expression, hand gesture, body movement, or frozen posture of both patient and therapist are easily identified and recognized as an intricate ballet of purposeful and meaningful communication. VTR can powerfully demonstrate nonverbal communication to students rigidly wedded to verbal content. Silences, discontinuity, and periods in which "nothing seems to be happening" in the dialogue often take on new meaning and illustrate new ways of looking at the interaction. VTR allows opportunity to examine and integrate multilevel messages of verbal and nonverbal content. VTR also records the context and precursors of behavioral signaling, which are critical to understanding the specific meaning of nonverbal communication. The meaning of verbal content is often clear only when the process or context in which it emerges is also considered, and often this recognition begins during retrospective examination of videotaped sessions. A common illustration is in the first therapeutic interview. Although the patient's initial verbalizations contain requests for treatment, it is often only in review of contradictory messages in verbal content, affect, and nonverbal behavior that students begin to recognize and respect the ambivalence that patients manifest but rarely articulate directly.

Neophyte therapists often attempt to maintain a "neutral posture" or project a "blank screen." Students with some inclination towards psychoanalytic theory may make extreme attempts to remain "detached" from their patients, often at the expense of productive use of the students' creativity and ability for therapeutic intervention. The VTR can demonstrate that despite his or her intentions, the student is *not* "blank." It remains for the supervisor to teach the student that, excluding psychoanalysis (for which the neophyte student is not likely to be in training), the two-way communication of perceptions and needs is a realistic part of the therapeutic alliance.

VTR has been used to teach students how their personal needs and reactions to their patients are an inherent part of functioning as a therapist and can, if unrecognized, impede his/her clinical effectiveness. One educator plays prerecorded sessions to groups and polls their interpretations to show that their personal values, even basic concepts of mental health, affect how they react to the patients (Lewis, 1978). "Affect stimulation" vignettes, which confront students with the "therapeutic nightmares" of seduction and anger occurring in simulated interactions, have been developed. By reviewing their verbal and internal responses to these situations, students confront the fears, needs, and reactions they bring to such encounters (Kagan, 1978).

Kagan (1978) reported that students' needs for acceptance by patients, and students' attempts to reduce their own anxiety often reduce their recognition or confrontation of conflictual topics. In recalling their feelings, perceptions, and associations during playback of their own videotaped interviews, students recognized how their feelings and needs led them to "tune out" particular communications from the patient.

Finally, VTR is helpful in developing the most difficult of abilities — that of using one's feelings, fantasies, and subjective reactions to the patient as a useful clinical tool. Students develop subjective evaluations and feelings towards their patients, and it is often by tape replay that they are able to identify the behaviors that validate or contradict their budding clinical sensitivity. The anger, for example, that students feel when they think they have been "manipulated" is often difficult for them to use productively. Nevertheless, such feelings can facilitate the treatment if the behaviors that comprise the "manipulation" can be identified and reinterpreted as behaviors which the patient has found effective in coping with significant figures in the past and which the patient is now using to evoke similar reactions in the student. Moreover, it is helpful if the therapist can review both the current context and the antecedents of these behaviors to understand what is creating the need for the client to use these "eliciting behaviors" (Kell and

Mueller, 1966). Such understanding is often a major step in the development of a therapist. Although VTR by no means guarantees that the therapist will gain such understanding, it can certainly facilitate the process by providing the data for the collaborative efforts of the student and supervisor.

The applications of VTR to psychotherapy training outlined here are illustrative rather than exhaustive. Moreover, the focus in training is usually multifaceted rather than sequential as implied here. The purpose of this discussion is stimulation rather than prescription, and supervisors must use their own creativity and judgment in appropriately applying VTR to programmatic training in psychotherapy.

VTR IN PSYCHOTHERAPY SUPERVISION

VTR and the Student

Experienced supervisors can readily identify the issues and dynamics inherent in training and supervision of psychotherapists. These issues and dynamics include student fears of inadequacy, defensive strategies to cope with the anxiety of self-exposure and intimacy of supervision, and fears of being controlled or dominated by the supervisor. They arise as a result of the personal and professional developmental tasks involved in becoming a therapist and are colored by the unique personality, strengths, and weaknesses of each student.

The characteristics of VTR tend to highlight these issues. That phenomenon is often advantageous to the training process, because issues are then more clearly defined. Moreover, VTR can aid in resolving these issues, to the enhanced development of the student.

In the following discussion, common issues and situations arising in VTR supervision will be considered. Such issues are not an inherent aspect of VTR, but rather processes inherent in psychotherapy training that are highlighted by the application of VTR. Supervisors should not erroneously reject VTR as the complicating factor in supervision but rather make further efforts in the supervisory relationship.

Anxieties About Being Taped

The initial suggestion to tape and review their therapy sessions generates varying degrees of anxiety in students. Protests regarding equipment availability and set-up time are often the initial expressions of personal concerns. Where portable equipment is required, equipment handling can add a half hour to the student's schedule. Once experienced in its operation and once the benefits are enjoyed, however, most students become willing if not eager to tolerate this minor irritation. Supervisors should be aware that complaints about recording facilities often mask the student's fears regarding his/her therapeutic abilities.

A common fear among students is that VTR will complicate their jobs as therapists. This fear is sometimes consensually validated by supervisors who overidentify with the students' anxieties. One author, who advocated the use of TV media in teaching general psychiatry, believed it was "inconceivable that it will ever be possible to demonstrate office psychotherapy in anything resembling its actual form" (Holmes, 1961). Nevertheless, experience with VTR has revealed that it does not have a detrimental impact on the therapy process.

Review of the literature reveals no reports of VTR producing a "strain" on patients, precipitating acting-out or psychosis with less stable patients. Moreover, there were no reports of VTR creating problems with particular populations, such as paranoid patients. Schiff and Reivich (1964) and others reported that the advantages of VTR far outweighed the minimal disruption of treatment, and that the use of VTR might enhance therapy. Gruenberg, Liston, and Wayne (1967) reported an instance in which both the patient and the therapist believed that progress in treatment "slowed down" when VTR was discontinued for several sessions. Stoller (1968) reported that introduction and usage of video in group therapy caused minimal intrusion and disturbance, the bulk of which passed in ten minutes when focus turned to more substantive group issues. Anxiety, if present, has been observed to be evident in the first or second session, after which it rapidly declines (Benschoter et al., 1965; Gruenberg, et al., 1967). Usually, both the student and the patient focus less on the VTR and more on the business of therapy. In fact, continued attention to the recording process may reflect resistance to engage in a therapeutic alliance.

Students' anxieties can be both reduced and used to advance their development as therapists in several ways. First, the supervisor can nondefensively introduce VTR to the student. Second, the student's fears can be identified, legitimized as common, and discussed as a useful expression of his or her expectations for therapy and supervision. Third, the supervisor can share his/her experience with VTR or cite the information that VTR is generally helpful and nondestructive to the therapeutic process. Finally, role playing the introduction of VTR, wherein the student takes the role of the patient, often elicits the student's fears and provides an opportunity for considering possible solutions. The supervisor can also model the role of the therapist and demonstrate techniques for coping with possible patient resistance. Zabarenko et al. (1977) believe the key to rapid patient acceptance of VTR is to present it as a natural and comfortable part of the clinician's work.

Having faculty and supervisors share tapes of their sessions effectively minimizes student resistance to videotaping. It also enhances modeling and helps clarify the covert attitudes supervisors may have about training and the use of videotape. Initial resistance to the TV camera by faculty and students has been overcome by having the department chairman give case demonstrations (Kornfield and Kolb, 1964). Several authors recommend that supervisors model the process of being videotaped, e.g. Lurie, 1978; Gladfelter, 1970. Certainly, the climate of trust at an agency will affect the acceptance of VTR.

My own observations concur with those of other authors, e.g. Greunberg et al., 1967, that the student is often more anxious about VTR than the client is. Ryan (1966) reported that student acceptance of VTR was good, but that anxiety about it tended to be increasingly greater for students at higher levels of training. She reported that this anxiety diminished with exposure to the benefits of the medium. Zabarenko et al. (1977) reported that physicians may be more troubled than their patients when their work is recorded. Generally, the anxiety that students sometimes feel when VTR is introduced is actually a crystallization of their fears regarding doing psychotherapy, receiving supervision, acknowledging his/her training status, fears of rejection by the patient, and the setting of ground rules for therapy. Such anxiety is usually not attributable to VTR, per se.

Numerous reports confirm my own experience that patients rarely refuse to permit recording (Ryan, 1966; Schmidt and Messner, 1977). Ryan (1966) reported that patients are generally unconcerned about who will review the tape as long as they are not known to the patient.

The supervisor should be prepared to help the student in the rare instances in which the patient does refuse to permit recording. Patients sometimes attempt to immobilize student therapists by expressing concerns of being "guinea pigs" who are only valued as a required training experience. When patients seize on VTR as "proof" of these complaints, students can mistakenly focus on the "recording issue" rather than the patient's fears of rejection, motivation for treatment, and concerns about self-disclosure that underlie the protests. In the process of addressing the therapeutic issues involved for the patient, the student often recognizes his/her own desire to be accepted by the patient and the personal needs and goals he/she brings to the therapy. As students confront their own anxieties, which are aggravated because the introduction of VTR underscores their need for supervisory input, they are often better able to empathize with the patients' fears that by entering therapy they are declaring incompetency. Ultimately, the best way to allay students' fears about VTR is to provide instances in which it is helpful in establishing new adequacies.

Student Differences in Response to VTR

All students do not react similarly to playback. Whereas VTR review is more productive for some trainees, it can be more stressful for others. For some, previewing a tape of a therapy session before supervision reflects investment and motivation. For others, it reflects a defensive maneuver to "plug up" inadequacies and take the sting out of anticipated supervisory criticism. Yet for others, it is an attempt to ward off all supervisory input and a struggle for recognition from the supervisor.

VTR supervision does not diminish the need for awareness of students' uniqueness but rather may increase it. Roesche (1978) pointed out that presentation of psychiatric material evokes an idiosyncratic emotional response in each student, whose awareness and acknowledgement of this impact is limited by the personal implications of the response to the student.

One recently published study actually examined the differences and relationships between a person's defense style and the degree and direction of distortion in observing VTR playback. Persons whose defenses characteristically involved projection less accurately evaluated their own behavior on VTR than did those characterized by self-deprecation, intellectualization, or acting-out. Self-deprecatory persons underestimated the quality of their own performances. Interestingly, no relationship was found between personal defensive style and accuracy in evaluating another person's behavior on VTR, presumably because anxiety was not sufficient to trigger the defensive response (Kipper and Ginot, 1979).

Students differ in how they respond to seeing themselves on VTR and how they cope with their feelings. Students may assess the observed behavior of patients more accurately than their own, but this difference is likely to vanish when their anxiety is at its highest level. This commonly occurs when patient behavior is similar to the student's coping style, particular content is threatening to the student, or focus is on the interactive process between the patient and therapist. The supervisor must remain sensitive to the multiple impacts that VTR material has for a particular student and be ready to handle these problems as appropriate to allow the continued professional growth of the trainee.

Decisions in VTR Review

Kornfield and Kolb (1964) suggested that supervision with VTR relieves the therapist of the dual role of treatment agent and observer. Those abilities, however, are exactly the ones that the student needs to develop, and if VTR were used to undermine the student's participant-observer role, its use would be misguided. This point lies beneath the decision of the supervisor to review the student's tapes in the student's absence. Generally, such review is not helpful. First, the tape is for the student's benefit and use, not merely the supervisor's. Second, review of VTR is not simply for the purpose of the supervisor getting the "data," but for the student to learn *how* the supervisor integrates cues and events. The student learns the *process* of observation by collaborative review with the supervisor.

Who decides if a particular tape should be seen at all? The student should be able to exercise some control over reviewing an *occasional* tape that he/she is embarrassed to show. On the other hand, student difficulties in therapy or supervision are sometimes expressed as perpetual embarrassment, repeated problems with VTR equipment, or "forgetting" tapes for supervision. At these points, the supervisory focus ought to address the origin and meaning of the therapist's embarrassment; his/her feelings toward himself/herself, toward the patient, toward the supervisor; and the effect of those factors on treatment. A similar approach is indicated at times when only "good" tapes are presented for review.

Students sometimes hand their tapes to the supervisor at the outset of the meeting, as if they were handing over control of their adequacy, and their alliance with the patient. Therapy and supervision are interrelated and often reflect parallel processes. If a student approaches supervision with the attitude of "accounting" to the supervisor, he or she will probably conduct therapy with more attention to the supervisor than to the patient. In such cases, the student attempts to "treat" the supervisory relationship through his/her interactions with the client. Some students are overeager to play their tapes, hoping to avoid committing themselves to definite statements about their perceptions, reactions, and conceptual understanding. Other students turn on the tape and sit back awaiting the supervisor's judgments. For these students, the supervisor should convey that what the student thinks and feels is at least as important as what the supervisor sees on tape. It is often beneficial to start the supervisory meeting with discussion of the student's recall, reactions, questions, and concerns. Such discussion emphasizes that the student is the primary authority and also gives the supervisor valuable information about the student. The discussion will also allow the supervisor to develop a perspective from which to view the VTR, or perhaps to decide it is better *not* to view the tape at all.

Student dependency and passivity can be diminished in several ways. Students who become documentors of verbal content can benefit from video-only replay of VTR. The student can also be encouraged to focus on his/her own affective reactions to tonal quality and nuances, so as to emphasize his/her reactions rather than the "events" recorded on tape. A simple "heuristic supervision" form (Thorton, 1975), which requires the student to focus on conceptualization and goals before the supervision session, is effective in stimulating active participation. In Interpersonal Process Recall (I.P.R.), students perform the role of an active inquiring colleague ("inquirer"). The inquirer, rather than a faculty supervisor, helps the therapist recall his/her thoughts and feelings during the therapy session as the VTR is reviewed. Students can be trained as "inquirers" in less than a ten-week period (Kagan, 1978).

Students often complain that their supervisor never sees a whole tape, or that they "never get beyond the first ten minutes." Certainly the first few minutes of therapeutic interaction is extremely important and rich in "compacted communication" (Kell and Mueller, 1966), but it is counterproductive to focus on the supervisor's reaction to the first ten minutes, to the exclusion of the ten minutes about which the student is concerned. The student must be an active presenter and collaborator, and not a passive spectator. The use of VTR must encourage the trainee to collect data, remain sensitive to his/her own personal reactions, and generate hypotheses and formulations. The student should be discouraged from relying on VTR to provide a record of events or as the primary means to discover the meaning and implications of behavior.

Sometimes students feel inadequate when they gain much clarity in supervision. They may marvel at the wisdom of the supervisor in teasing out the nuances apparent on VTR. It is vital to point out that few therapists can be as insightful, articulate, and poised during the therapy hour as they can be when reviewing sessions retrospectively (and particularly when it is someone else's tape). New insights must enhance self-esteem rather than highlight past oversights. "The task of the supervisor is to be alert to these conflicts and to engage the . . . therapists in the struggle to assume the full role of the therapist with its inherent limitations" (Gladfelter, 1970).

VTR and the Supervisor

Few approaches can match the benefits of VTR in psychotherapy supervision. A major advantage of VTR is that the data received by the supervisor are not subject to the conscious or unconscious editing or retrospective distortions of events by the student. Distortions aside, VTR permits the supervisor to receive information about the session that the student never recognized, and thus to gain additional information about the student. Often a student's difficulties lie in events that have gone unnoticed or unexamined. Without VTR, the supervisor often can do little more than augment the basic data the student presents with the manner in which the data are presented.

VTR can also improve the quality of the supervisory relationship. The supervisor who has a clear picture of the therapeutic exchange is often more relaxed, honest, and genuine in his/her interactions with the student. Students perpetually scan the countenance of the supervisor and can sense this feeling of security and often internalize it to cope with their own fears. Certainly an anxious supervisor often makes for an anxious therapist. Students who are certain their supervisors accurately understand what has transpired place more faith in the supervisors' feedback and value their support all the more.

The Supervisory Role

"Audiovisual material can be a potent educational experience. However, the development and utilization of any video material must be considered within the context of the author's theories about learning" (Roesche, 1978). The supervisor's theoretical concept of his/her role has critical impact on the way in which VTR is used in supervision and the degree to which it facilitates or debilitates the student's growth.

Certainly, some supervisors resist the use of VTR. Never

having used it in their own training, some consider VTR as alien. Other clinicians have no more knowledge about supervision than their memories and emotional reactions to their own training experience. Others may resist VTR out of lack of clarity about their role and goals as a supervisor, whereas others may be rigidly locked into theoretical biases. Persons using VTR to supervise others would be wise to be experienced at being recorded on VTR and seeing themselves on TV.

The diverse ways in which VTR can be used may make greater demands on, and more readily highlight, supervisory competency. As the student becomes more involved in addressing specific aspects of his/her psychotherapy sessions, the supervisor may be expected to become more involved in the analysis and resolution of specific situations. VTR will not make up for deficits in the supervisor's investment or skill in supervising. In fact, the use of videotape may require greater supervisor sensitivity to the situational and personal concerns of the student.

The optimal role of the supervisor is that of a professional "sponsor" for the trainee, rather than critic or overseer. The supervisor should make the necessary evaluations from the perspective of an auxiliary ego rather than superego. The student and the supervisor must enter into a collaborative relationship, wherein they are "peers by profession" although they differ in experience (Berger, 1978). Both have skills and adequacies as well as limitations that need to be acknowledged and accepted as part of the supervisory relationship. The student's recall, the student's reaction to videotape playback, the supervisor's perceptions of the videotape, and the emotional climate of the supervision are all sources of data to be used in the collaborative process. One source of data is not superior to another.

The foundation of the supervisory relationship must be a mutual commitment to enhance and develop the skills and adequacies the student has at the outset. To facilitate this, there must be a basic trust in the therapist to be helpful with the particular client in question. The goal of supervision thus becomes enhancing these abilities and addressing blockages that limit the therapist's abilities to use his or her own creative and therapeutic abilities.

Pitfalls

ROLE MISCONCEPTIONS. Certain authors advocate the preceptor model used in training surgeons as the ideal for psychotherapy supervision (Kornfield and Kolb, 1964; Gruenberg et al., 1967). In the "surgery model" of supervision, VTR is seen as a means of allowing the supervisor to become a quasi cotherapist who can protect the patient from the antitherapeutic maneuvers of the student and insure a therapeutic result.

The "surgery" paradigm for psychotherapy training appears to be an unfortunate by-product of attempts to align psychiatry more closely with the rest of the field of medical practice. First, the risk factors of surgery and psychotherapy differ. Second, unlike surgery, most psychotherapy is doomed to failure if the patient is passive (or unconscious) and a nonparticipant in his/her treatment. Third, the therapist cannot assume the total responsibility for the outcome of the "procedure" as does the surgeon, and the dominance-submission roles characteristic of the surgeon and the patient would usually insure a failure in psychotherapy. Fourth, psychotherapy training asks the student to be open to, and to use, his/her personal responses and feelings, whereas the training of surgeons focuses on the development of unemotional technical skills. Finally, as a participant-observer, the psychotherapy supervisor has much more of an impact on the student's performance in subsequent therapy than does the surgery preceptor.

The goal of supervision is not to do therapy through the student, but to help the student develop his/her own style of therapy that incorporates his/her affective and cognitive resources. Students sometimes fear they will be replaced by VTR as the authority reporting the events of the therapy. Another fear is that the tape will allow the supervisor to do therapy with the client, with the student as middleman. Many authors, e.g. (Schmidt and Messner, 1977) imply that the purpose of VTR is to help the supervisor develop specific behavioral suggestions for the student to carry out in the next therapy session. Using VTR in this manner, however, often confirms the student's fears.

If the supervisor's major goal is to protect the client from the student's ineptness, the resulting supervisory relationship is more likely to focus on identifying errors than developing strengths. By implication, the supervisor is making his/her major alliance with the patient against the student. Neither surprisingly nor helpfully, that situation often causes students to sit in subsequent therapy sessions with one eye on the patient and the other on the camera. Not uncommonly, students do therapy to please the supervisor rather than to help the patient. It is a result of the supervisory relationship rather than of the videotape per se.

COPING WITH "ERRORS." Certainly in some instances the student can become deadlocked with a client in decidedly unproductive ways, or engage in clearly destructive or unethical behavior, and it is appropriate to suggest that the patient be seen by another therapist. Such difficulties, however, occur in an extremely small percentage of therapy cases, and the focus of the supervisor's anticipation and concern for such problems should be proportional. Students need to understand that "errors" or technical mistakes are common and inevitable. Technical errors are rarely the cause of poor treatment results. Most treatment failures result from inaccurate diagnosis and conceptualization, unresolved pervasive counter-transference, or stalemates that focus only on intellectual quests for insight rather than on affect (Lewis, 1978). By reviewing videotapes of sessions, the student can see how a central theme will resurface many times in a given session, and also in successive sessions. Each repetition is an opportunity for new growth and effective interventions in future sessions. This recognition tends to build the student's faith in his or her ability to use new insights in future sessions and lessens fears of "uncorrectable" (and "unforgivable") errors. The notion of a critical period or a lost opportunity to make a response is quickly dispelled. Students also begin to recognize "healthy resistance" (Kell and Mueller, 1966) or "forgiveness" (Lewis, 1978) that patients manifest to facilitate their own treatment. Relationships are generally tractable and resilient enough for the student to make errors, learn, and still be of help to the patient.

Students must learn that they can afford to make errors and that these errors are understandable in light of their personal needs and needs of the patient. Errors can often be capitalized on, rather than simply minimized. Ineffective behavior can be *understood,* not simply admonished, and can accelerate students' growth as psychotherapists.

Balanced attention to effective and ineffective behavior in psychotherapy helps students gain perspective on their competencies. Supervisors must remain alert to being seduced by students who are overly self-critical during VTR review, or who invite unbalanced "critique sessions." Part of supervision is helping students to recognize their own strengths and unique styles and to accept their expertise appropriate to their levels of training. Supervisors who use VTR to find errors the students may try to hide, or use it to protect the patient from these errors, may be gratified at the student's willingness to self-critique. Nevertheless, it should come as no surprise when the student seems unable to develop any resilience to patient's eliciting behaviors or when the student seems unable to take supervisory interventions without undue deference or superficiality.

SUPERVISING THE VIDEOTAPE RATHER THAN THE STUDENT. Schmidt and Messner (1977) tout the "objectivity" of VTR as providing "considerable insight" to the trainee. Their focus, however, is misleading. The "objective facts" we see on VTR may not be evident to others. Researchers experienced in training raters of videotapes for reliability and validity know the difficulty of getting two people to see the same thing the same way. It is not the objectivity of VTR, but collaborative working through and integrating the data VTR provides, that creates insight in supervision.

In a recent case seminar involving VTR, the clinician whose case was under review reported that the husband and wife being interviewed were on the verge of tears most of the interview. Seminar participants, however, formed a different impression on viewing the VTR of the patients and offered interpretations of therapist counter-transference to explain the discrepancy in perceptions. Shortly thereafter, the case was transferred to another participant of the seminar. Much to everyone's surprise, the second clinician confirmed the patients' tearfulness. This anedote illustrates two main points. First, VTR is not infallible in recording "data," especially small nuances. Second, and most important, the VTR must never replace the observations, feelings, formulations, and intuitive processes of the therapist. VTR can be used to augment, illustrate, and stimulate the clinical skills of the student, but not supplant them.

Consider a common situation in which the supervisory relationship replicates the dynamics of the relationship between client and therapist. The student comes to supervision feeling confused, inadequate, and seeking help, in many respects like his patient. In the course of supervision, the student (like patient) rejects all the supervisor's suggestions and interpretations because accepting aid and acknowledging the supervisor's adequacy are threatening rather than helpful to the student's flagging sense of competency. Reviewing the videotaped interaction between patient and therapist can help the supervisor identify the dynamic meaning of the impasse. Moreover, VTR can help the supervisor and student recognize the anger and frustration the student may hold for the patient.

On the other hand, the increased objectivity and data provided by VTR will not automatically resolve this impasse. If the supervisor uses the tape to "prove" his interpretations to the trainee, that action often exacerbates this impasse rather than helps resolve it. Under such circumstances the student not uncommonly models the experience in the treatment relationship by attempting to "prove" the correctness of interpretations to the patient, pushing for superficial acceptance, and ignoring the patient's feelings, which preclude a cooperative alliance. Supervisory attempts to explain disagreements by interpretations of the student's "pathology" may be similarly modeled in the treatment relationship. Supervisors who have not reviewed tapes regularly may push interpretations of events that are striking to them, without understanding the long-term process meaning of the event (which the student may understand better). Likewise, the supervisor may mistakenly focus more on what he/she would do to cope with the therapeutic situation and focus less on what the student is prepared to do and is comfortable in carrying out.

Emphasis on the objectivity of data presented by VTR sometimes may distract the supervisor's attention from his or her own distortions, needs, and dynamics. Because the supervisor has more direct access to the raw data of the therapy session and is more open to the direct impact of the client via VTR, an awareness of the supervisor's personal response to the patient, to the student, and to their interaction is greatly needed. As patients become more real for the supervisor, sensitivity to the supervisor's possible counter-transference reactions becomes more important. Supervisors who become enamored with "objectivity" sometimes lose sight that what is clear and apparent to them may be unclear to the therapist for any number of reasons. At these times, the supervisor may ignore issues of timing and consideration of the supervisor's own personal needs in presenting input to the student. VTR can be abused by the supervisor to make premature interpretations to the therapist, giving too much too soon for the student's needs.

Confronting Counter-Transference

Introducing discussion of a student's counter-transference is one of the most anxiety-producing topics for supervisors. Usually, the anxiety results from equating this topic with doing therapy with the student. Because VTR presents students' responses to patients in greater clarity and detail than self-report can provide, the use of VTR often increases awareness of counter-transference behavior with attendant supervisory discomfort.

Fortunately, VTR has been used to examine how popular and effective supervisors cope with counter-transference issues. As seen in reviews of videotapes of individual supervision meetings, less effective supervisors tend to avoid counter-transference issues (Goin and Kline, 1978). Although the skills required of the supervisor to discuss a student's counter-transference are similar to those used in therapy (and indeed the discussion should be therapeutic for the student), the purpose and scope of supervision differ from those of therapy. "Probably a clearer understanding that discussion of a therapist's feelings (and their effect on his/her therapeutic interactions) does not necessitate investigation of the origins of these feelings would free more supervisors to talk about counter-transference" (Goin and Kline, 1978). Discussion of the student's transference is never an end in itself (as it might be in the student's therapy), but only a means toward facilitating the student's development as a psychotherapist. The focus of the discussion is continually on the student's work with his/her patients. The discussion is most effective when comments are frank, open, direct, and nonpunitive. Moreover, the discussion should not lead to deeper probing of the student's dynamics. When deeper probing appears unavoidable to achieve resolution, an appropriate recommendation is that the student embark on a separate psychotherapy for himself or herself.

Goin and Kline (1978) found that VTR made other behaviors and styles used by effective supervisors easier to identify. Effective supervisors were active, aggressive, and encouraged students to conceptualize and consider alternative formulations. The more effective supervisors were not satisfied with student's fragmented conceptualizations, and their own clear, concise comments addressed transference, patient dynamics, and interactions between the patient and the student. Supervisors who were shown videotapes demonstrating these behaviors were later rated as more effective supervisors by their students and themselves.

VTR IN CASE CONFERENCE

The foregoing discussion focused on the application of VTR for psychotherapy training via individual supervision. VTR has also been used in case conferences to demonstrate patient symptomatology, therapeutic approaches that vary in degrees of structure and uncovering, and the different techniques of "experts." Such presentations enhance students' identification with their mentors and present auditory and visual data approximating that received by the therapist in the session. Moreover, students can receive input and feedback from more than one "authority," thus benefitting from the varied approaches and expertise of the participating faculty. VTR presentations stimulate discussion, interaction, and staff development.

VTR does not reduce the need for adequate preparation of

the presentation. For case conferences, a videotape is not worth a thousand words. A dozen preselected, two-minute interview segments will fail to convey a composite profile of the patient because the unfamiliar observer does not have a framework in which to comprehend the meaning of what is being seen. This is true for experienced therapists and even more so for neophytes. Segments selected because they illustrate the therapist's conception of the patient do not necessarily inform the conference participants what the therapist's gestalt is. The case-conference presenter must recognize the same principle that was discussed regarding therapy supervision: VTR cannot replace the therapist's understanding and conceptualization.

When VTR is used in case conference, larger segments of ten minutes are needed for conference participants to become oriented. Illustration of thematic or process-related behavior or dynamics requires longer segments. Interpretations by conference participants regarding briefer segments often stem more from the characteristics of the observer than the actual data, which may be desirable in some aspects of training such as development of therapist self-awareness, but not in a case conference. Brief, isolated segments can be used to illustrate phenomena assessable by simple binomial decision making, e.g. whether the event is occurring or not.

EVALUATION OF PSYCHOTHERAPY TRAINING VIA VIDEOTAPE

In recent years, VTR has been used in the evaluation of training. Generally, VTR evaluations fall into two broad categories: clinical observation and judgment tests, and evaluation of student tapes. Clinical observation and judgment tests have been the more common application. Such examinations involve viewing a prerecorded interview, after which students respond to a written or oral examination. The College of Family Physicians of Canada and the American Board of Pediatrics have used simulation interviews in certification examinations, and standardized prerecorded interviews have been part of the certification examination of the American Board of Psychiatry and Neurology since 1975.

Examinations using a videotaped psychiatric interview followed by written examination have been used to evaluate the performance of third-year medical students completing a psychiatry clerkship (Meyerson et al., 1977). The examination assessed observational skills, clinical judgment and decision making, and knowledge of psychiatry. Examination grades were significantly correlated with clerkship grades assigned by faculty providing clinical training. This finding is not surprising given that faculty assigning clinical grades would attend to the same basic skills at this level of training as did the VTR examination. Nevertheless, VTR examinations that assess clinical skill at one level of expertise may not be accurate at more sophisticated levels. Turnblad et al. (1973) used prerecorded VTR interviews with a written questionnaire to assess the clinical ability of medical students. Their test discriminated among the basic skills of preclinical medical students, freshmen, and sophomores but was not effective in assessing skill differences among more sophisticated sophomores, juniors, and seniors. The authors believed their test assessed observational skills and understanding of psychiatric knowledge and theory, but not clinical skills per se.

Clinical observation tests offer the advantages of ease of administration and economy. With VTR, the clinical material presented can be standardized, and the reliability of the test increased. VTR presentations allow examiners of oral examinations to predetermine major areas of assessment and reduce the likelihood of gross examiner error. Finally, VTR permits the use of a standardized examination to record responses.

Weir (1978) argued that tests using preselected videotaped patient interviews were superior to conventional written and oral examinations because VTR provided "actual patient material" and introduced "interpersonal stress and ... countertransference." Other research, however, suggests that prerecorded VTR examinations do not provide sufficient opportunity to assess clinical *style* and personal responses.

Naftulen et al. (1977) found no relationship among performance on oral video-centered examinations, oral patient-centered examinations, and written examinations for twenty-eight psychiatrists preparing for board certification in psychiatry and neurology. With prerecorded video examination, the student lacks the opportunity to demonstrate rapport-building skills, interview style, and elicitation of information expected at higher levels of expertise. Clinical judgment tests cannot accurately predict a student's actual clinical performance with a client.

A criterion for measuring validity of clinical judgment is difficult to establish on VTR tests. Faculty consensus on answers can be used to establish a criterion, e.g. Weir, 1978, but the assumption is erroneous that students who respond similarly have similar clinical skills. Moreover, cutoff points for "passing" and "failing" grades are often the result of relative judgments rather than empirical determination.

In the teaching of psychotherapy, the trainee's increase in clinical ability seems best evaluated by review of VTR of his/her actual performance. Using actors to simulate patients in interviews somewhat standardizes and increases test reliability, while also permitting the student to exhibit interpersonal style, empathy, and elicitation of information. Actors have been used in this manner in certification examination for family physicians in Canada (Lamont and Hennen, 1972), although interviews were evaluated live rather than from VTR. Weir (1978) argued that actors were not effective in evaluations when the student was aware of the simulation. Research suggests, however, that evaluations are not affected by the student's awareness that he/she is interviewing an actor (Naftulen et al., 1977).

The validity and reliability of observer ratings of students' tapes are questionable in this type of evaluation. An observer's rating scale was developed to evaluate communication skills of third-year medical students who conducted taped forty-minute interviews (Waldron, 1978). Such scales are capable of empirical validation and certainly should improve the reliability of tape evaluations. Reliability is further enhanced if judges preview several tapes to reach consensus on the level of ability expected from the students to be evaluated. Using student tapes to assess both clinical skills and knowledge/judgment is generally a poor idea, particularly for unsophisticated clinicians. Poor clinical skills may limit the elicitation of symptomatology or significant history, thus precluding the demonstration of observational and diagnostic skills.

One additional type of evaluation has been developed, which is a hybrid of the standardized observational test and the evaluation of students' tapes. In this third type, students are presented with vignettes wherein an actor-patient is filmed close up and appears to be talking directly to the viewer. A particular situation is presented to which the student then makes some response, which may involve selecting the most appropriate choice from several written possibilities or recording his/her unique response on audio tape. These vignettes often successfully stimulate the student's feelings about dealing with similar situations in real life. The Sex Counseling Education Training Tape (SCETT) (Richards, 1978) is an example of this type of examination, which is accompanied by multiple-choice "responses" that are prerated on the Carkhuff Gross Rating Scale of response effectiveness. The affect stimulation vignettes used in Interpersonal Process Recall (Kagan, 1978) are quite similar, although they were not initially designed for evaluation.

Multiple-choice responses can be validated against criterion measures of clinical ability and/or professional judgment. Verbal responses are more difficult to score, and standardization and validation are serious problems. Verbal responses, however, allow examination of the student's personal style in making responses and allow more opportunity for interpersonal stress and counter-transference to become manifest.

CONCLUSION

Although video technology is an unquestionably significant asset to teaching psychotherapy, it is not the equipment, but the manner and purpose for which it is introduced and used that will determine the degree to which the overall training goals are met. VTR is not a panacea and does not, by itself, necessarily enhance training. VTR, like a computer, advantageously stores large amounts of data; it requires skill to extract this raw information and process it so that it is meaningful for desired purposes.

REFERENCES

Benschoter, R. A., Eaton, M. T., and Smith, P.: Use of videotape to provide individual instruction in technique of psychotherapy. *Journal of Medical Education, 40*:1159, 1965.

Berger, M. M.: *Videotape techniques in psychiatric training and treatment,* 2nd ed. New York: Brunner/Mazel, 1978.

Bloom, B. S.: The thought processes of students in discussion. In S. J. French (Ed.): *Accent on teaching: experiments in general education.* New York: Harper, 1954.

Carkhuff, R. R.: *Helping and human relations,* vols. I and II. New York: Holt, Rinehart, and Winston, 1969.

Fleishmann, O.: A method of teaching psychotherapy: a one-way-vision room technique. *Bulletin of Menninger Clinic, 19*:160, 1955.

Gaier, E. L.: Selected personality variables and the learning process. *Psychological Monographs*: General and Applied, *66*:1, 1952.

Gladfelter, J. H.: Videotape supervision of co-therapists. In M. Berger (Ed.): *Videotape techniques in psychiatric training and treatment.* New York: Brunner/Mazel, 1970.

Goin, M. K. and Kline, F.: The use of videotape in studying and teaching supervision. In M. Berger (Ed.): *Videotape techniques in psychiatric training and treatment,* 1978.

Goldstein, R. H. and Saltzman, L. F.: Correlates of clinical judgement in psychiatry. *Journal of Medical Education, 37*:1101, 1962.

Gruenberg, P. B., Liston, E. H., and Wayne, G. J.: Intensive supervision of psychotherapy with videotape recording. *American Journal of Psychotherapy, 23*:98, 1967.

Holmes, D. J.: Closed circuit television in teaching psychiatry. *University of Michigan Medical Bulletin, 27*:330, 1961.

Hunt, W., MacKennon, R., and Michels, R.: A clinical clerkship in psychiatry. *Journal of Medical Education, 50*:1113, 1975.

Kagan, N.: Interpersonal process recall: media in clinical and human interaction supervision. In M. Berger (Ed.), *Videotape techniques in psychiatric training and treatment,* 1978.

Kagan, N. and Krathwohl, D. R.: *Studies in human interactions: interpersonal process recall stimulated by videotape.* Educational Publications Services, College of Education, East Lansing, Michigan: Michigan State University, 1967.

Kell, B. L. and Mueller, W. J.: *Impact and change: a study of counseling relationships.* Englewood Cliffs, New Jersey: Prentice Hall, 1966.

Kipper, D. A. and Ginot, E.: Accuracy of evaluating videotape feedback and defense mechanisms. *Journal of Consulting and Clinical Psychology, 47*:493, 1979.

Kornfield, D. S. and Kolb, L. C.: The use of closed-circuit television in the teaching of psychiatry. *Journal of Nervous and Mental Disease, 138*:452, 1964.

Lamont, C. T. and Hennen, B. K.: The use of simulated patients in a certification examination in family medicine. *Journal of Medical Education, 47*:789, 1972.

Lewis, J. M.: *To be a therapist: the teaching and learning.* New York: Brunner/Mazel, 1978.

Lurie, H. J.: Videotape demonstrations and exercises in the psychological training of family physicians. In M. Berger (Ed.): *Videotape techniques in psychiatric training and treatment,* 2nd ed. New York: Brunner/Mazel, 1978.

Matarazzo, R. G., Wiens, A. N., and Saslow, G.: Experimentation in the teaching and learning of psychotherapy skills. In A. Gottschalk and A. H. Auerback (Eds.): *Methods of research in psychotherapy.* New York: Appleton-Century-Crofts, 1966.

Meyerson, A. T., Wachtel, A., and Thornton, J.: Evaluation of a psychiatric clerkship by videotape. *American Journal of Psychiatry, 134*:8, 1977.

Moore, F. J., Hanes, L. C., and Harrison, C. A.: Improved television, stereo, and the two-person interview. *Journal of Medical Education, 36*:162, 1961.

Naftulen, D. H.; Wolkon, G. H.; Donnelly, F. A.: Burgoyne, R. W.; Kline, F. M., and Hansen, H. E.: A comparison of videotaped and live patient interview examinations and written examinations in psychiatry. *American Journal of Psychiatry, 134*:1093, 1977.

Richards, D. L.: *Sex counseling evaluation training tape.* Scarborough, Maine: Counseling and Training Associates, 1978.

Roesche, N. A.: Videotape as an educational experience. In M. Berger (Ed.): *Videotape techniques in psychiatric training and treatment,* 2nd ed. New York: Brunner/Mazel, 1978.

Rogers, C. R.: The use of electrically recorded interviews in improving psychotherapeutic skills. *American Journal of Orthopsychiatry, 12*:429, 1942.

Ryan, J.: Teaching by videotape. *Mental Hospitals, 16*:101, 1966.

Schiff, S. B. and Reivich, R.: Use of television as aid to psychotherapy supervision. *Archives of General Psychiatry, 10*:84, 1964.

Schmidt, D. D. and Messner, E.: The use of videotape techniques in the psychiatric training of family physicians. *Journal of Family Practice, 5*:585, 1977.

Simons, R. C. and Rubenstein, M.: The use of film and video in the teaching of human behavior. In R. Simons and H. Pardes (Eds.): *Understanding human behavior in health and illness.* Baltimore: Williams and Wilkins, 1977.

Stoller, F. H.: Use of videotape (focused feedback) in group counseling and group therapy. *Journal of Research and Development in Education, 1*:30, 1968.

Strupp, H. H.: *Psychotherapists in action.* New York: Grune and Stratton, 1960.

———: Patient-Doctor Relationships: Psychotherapists in the Therapeutic

Process. In A. J. Bachrach (Ed.): *Experimental foundations of clinical Psychology*. New York: Basic Books, 1962.

Strupp, H. H., Wallack, M. S., and Wogan, M.: Psychotherapy Experience in Retrospect: A Questionnarie Survey of Former Patients and Their Therapists. *Psychological Monographs*, 78 (whole # 588), 1964.

Suess, J. F.: Teaching clinical psychiatry with closed-circuit television and videotape. *Journal of Medical Education, 41*:483, 1966.

Thorton, D.: Personal Communication, January 10, 1975.

Turnblad, R. J., Muslin, H., and Loesch, J.: A test of clinical learning by medical students. *American Journal of Psychiatry, 130*:568, 1973.

Waldron, J.: A communication skills assessment rating scale. In M. Berger (Ed.): *Videotape in psychiatric training and treatment*, 1978.

Walz, G. R. and Johnston, J. A.: Counselors look at themselves on videotape. *Journal of Counseling Psychology, 10*:232, 1963.

Weir, W. D.: Evaluating psychiatric learning through videotaped patient interviews. In M. Berger (Ed.): *Videotape techniques in psychiatric training and treatment*, 2nd ed. New York: Brunner/Mazel, 1978.

Zabarenko, R. N., Magero, J., and Zabarenko, L.: Use of videotape in teaching psychological medicine. *Journal of Family Practice, 4*:559, 1977.

CHAPTER 14

INVIDIOUS MIRROR?
ETHICAL PROBLEMS IN THE
USE OF VIDEORECORDING

Edward Johnson

> They viewed media as neutral tools & they viewed themselves
> as men who could be trusted to use them humanely. I saw the
> problem otherwise.
>
> Edmund Carpenter
> Oh, What a Blow That Phantom Gave Me!

THIS essay is not a discussion of *legal* questions that may arise regarding the use of videorecording in
scientific or therapeutic contexts. The moral considerations I
shall discuss may well raise legal problems, but I shall not be
concerned with them. Therapists or scientists who are interested *solely* in the legality of their practices would be better
advised to visit a lawyer than to read a philosopher (but see
Oswald and Wilson, 1971).

This essay is also not a compendium of moral *rules*, whether
these be construed as "commandments" or as "recommenda-
tions." Purely abstract judgments about purely schematic cases
have a certain ludicrous futility. Moral decisions actually have
to be *made*; when they are, obnoxious concrete details invariably intrude and derail the rules. A vivid appreciation of this
fact might save us from looking for *rules* in the first place.

However, though there are no rules that will make our moral
decisions for us, there are considerations that we do well to
ponder when we can — considerations that render us more
sensitive, more sensible, more responsible judges, though they
cannot guarantee that our judgments will be correct. Such aids
to moral reflection are less touchstones or paradigms of ethical
correctness than tender spots of the comprehending conscience,

apt for the moral probe. Here, as elsewhere in philosophy, the proof is in the putting of the scruple. It hurts, or it doesn't.

What I *shall* do in this essay is suggest some considerations that scientists and therapists using videorecording technology should ponder — for the sake of their souls, as it were.

These considerations fall into two very general categories. First, there are those considerations which have to do with the application of videorecording technology in particular cases of therapy or experiment. This group includes problems about therapists' obligations to their clients, or experimenters' obligations to their subjects, in such matters as confidentiality and consent. These are, so to speak, questions of professional ethics. The second group of considerations involves questions of social ethics, or public policy. Therapists and scientists must consider what they do not only *qua* professional specialists, but also as citizens who take an interest in the large-scale social effects of the technologies they employ.

PROFESSIONAL ETHICS

The use of videorecording, for therapeutic or other purposes, involves subjects being observed, or observing, or both, all this with or without their informed consent.

Being Observed

People quite often do not like to be observed. Their aversion to being seen, especially to being stared at, finds expression in folk theories concerning the "evil eye." What is supposed to be invidious about an "unblinking" or "all-seeing" eye? One answer might be that such observation involves an attack on privacy (see Schneider, 1977). Privacy, though difficult to define (see Thomson, 1975; Scanlon, 1975; Rachels, 1975), is presumably something that a responsible therapist will want to respect. This is made difficult because therapy by its very nature often requires that the patient let the therapist in on *some* secrets — even the most important ones. (The psychoanalyst, for example, attempts *ex officio* to penetrate into spaces of thought that are off limits to most, sometimes all, of the patient's family, friends, acquaintances.) Videorecording provides an additional, and powerful, technology of exposure. If a nuance of speech or gesture, some subtle but expressive tic, is overlooked on the occasion of its emergence, it can be caught on tape and detected and dissected later. This may be good or bad. It may aid therapy, or it may constitute an intrusion beyond what is sanctioned by therapeutic purpose. No useful general rule can be formulated on this matter. What inquisitions are germane and ingenuous will depend on the details of the case. A caution to the therapist is in order precisely because videorecording may be so effective. Questions of privacy will also arise in connection with the *sorts* of actions that are recorded. There need be no record for there to be invasion of privacy. A forgetful voyeur still invades your privacy. However, the addition of a record may make the invasion of privacy seem greater. In part, perhaps, this is because one's actions are exposed to the scrutiny of an indeterminate audience. There are really no effective *guarantees* concerning what use will later be made of a videotape, or who will see it. (After all, who would be in a better position to insure the privacy of his taped conversations than a President of the United States? But. . . .) How concerned a patient is about such indeterminate surveillance will depend in part, of course, on *what* is exposed to view.

Even though a patient has consented to being watched by at least the therapist, and perhaps by others who are in varying degrees unknown, the patient may still worry. Why? A videotape of some action will, of course, provide a "permanent" record of the action. Someone might well have reason to object to this embalming of what otherwise would be transient and trivial. There are, however, other such "permanent" records. What is specially disturbing about the videorecord?

First, it is much more detailed than other records, because the visual channel carries so much information about the situation. Second, it is more likely than other records to elicit a strong positive or negative response from the viewer, because we are so powerfully moved by what we *see*. Third, there is what I have called "indeterminate surveillance." You cannot tell *who* may see it. Nor can you tell — and this is the fourth point — just *how long* it may continue to be seen. Patients may have the feeling that their actions will never die. Film recordings of the Milgram obedience experiments, for example, would probably leave subjects more uncomfortable (and understandably so!) than other kinds of records of the same facts. Why? Perhaps the illusion of reality is greater. (Imagine what holographic videorecording will mean!)

Observing

Besides being observed — by the camera, by the therapist, perhaps by others — the patient is often also, at some point in the process, an observer. In some cases, patients are supposed to watch the completed videotape and observe their own behavior, their actions and responses. In other cases, patients do not themselves appear in the film at all; rather, as in the "music minus one" phonograph records, it is precisely the patient who is missing, visually and audibly, but is present by virtue of her or his live actions while viewing and by virtue of the "responses" of the film figures.

In both sorts of cases, the chief question concerns the *objectivity* of what is being observed. Is the picture of oneself presented on the videotape true? Objective? Complete? Or is there distortion? People experience various degrees of difficulty in identifying with their video personae. Most people, I suppose, feel some shock of surprise when they first see themselves "on TV." Some never really come to recognize themselves. The problem about objectivity arises because, for most of us at least, videotape *seems* so very objective, though in many respects it is not. I offer no explanation of why it seems so objective, except to suggest that probably it is for the same reasons that make a photograph seem so objective — only more so, since the videotape captures motion and the passage of time as the photograph does not (see Sontag, 1977, on photographs). That videotape is not so objective should be obvious. The camera is selective, to begin with, and editing is still more so. Of course, one might record from a fixed perspective and eschew editing, but even then, the recording gives only one angle, or a few, and not necessarily the best. The introduction of the "instant replay" into sports led some to suggest that this could provide a standard by which to correct the sometimes erroneous calls of umpires and referees. However, aside from the impracticality of the suggestion, it was quickly realized that cameras do not always tell the truth. They tell truly, of course, what they see; but they don't always see the truth. Perhaps the expression on that person's face would look rather different from another angle. The danger lies in taking the videorecord to be more objective than it is.

The camera operator, the editor, the therapist may all mean to present an objective picture. But what they present is unavoidably influenced by subjective perceptions. Even if that were not so, any single visual account would still be, at best, a fragment of the objective facts. Consider also Kafka's remark: "Photography concentrates one's eye on the superficial. For that reason it obscures the hidden life which glimmers through the outlines of things like a play of light and shade. One can't catch that even with the sharpest lens. One has to grope for it by feeling" (Sontag, 1977). Can we asseverate that this does not apply to the videocamera?

I have spoken primarily with reference to the pictures of themselves on videotape with which patients are sometimes presented. Worries about objectivity apply also to "modeling" cases where the viewer may be absent from the film. In the first place, there will of course be an implicit "picture" of the subject (who has not been filmed), defined, as it were, by its shadows, visible in the responses of those figures which do appear in the film. This implicit "picture" may or may not be objective. In the second place, the situation may or may not be objectively presented; it may or may not be artificial, oversimplified, etc.

Of course, objectivity may not always be what is wanted. The therapist who employs videorecording must consider when it is wanted and when it is obtained.

Consenting

The notion of *consent* raises special problems. What *is* consent, exactly, and when has it been given in an *informed* manner? Who must give it? Under what conditions is it required? Such questions inevitably confront any scientist who studies human beings and any therapist who treats them.

Both therapist and experimentalist sometimes use children as subjects or patients. Can children consent in an informed manner? If not, can someone else, a parent or guardian, do it *for* them? I am not asking whether they "can consent" in a *legal* sense. Certainly parents and guardians, can, and often do, consent in that sense, but there is more to informed consent that its legality.

Consider: why is consent important? *Not,* I suppose, just because the laws of our society happen to stipulate it. If the laws were changed, would consent no longer be relevant? Consent matters, and laws that failed to recognize that would be bad laws. Consent matters because it can make morally legitimate what otherwise would not be. Interfering with others, particularly in ways that involve injury or risk of injury to them, is morally noxious. For me, for example, to insinuate chemicals into your body, without your knowledge or approval, or indeed against your will, would be outrageous, however desirable the consequences might be from my point of view. But if you consent, then I am not acting *against* you. Anything less involves fraud or coercion on my part. Of course it is possible that what one wants (and so is willing to consent to) may be opposed to what is in one's "best interests." Nevertheless, one's "best interests" should not be assumed to be identical with the content of someone else's will.

The notion of consent is particularly problematic when one is dealing with children, or with the "mentally ill." Even in the case of competent adults, however, there are general problems about the nature of "informed" consent, problems especially troublesome in the case of experiments by social scientists (see Soble, 1978; Donagan, 1977). Obviously, such problems can only be aggravated, in the use of videorecording, by what I earlier called "indeterminate surveillance." A patient may sign release forms that stipulate some specific employment of the videotape — but those are only as good as the video-factor's *control* over the product, which is necessarily limited.

SOCIAL ETHICS

Now that we have discussed some of the considerations that the therapist must reflect upon *qua* therapist, we must touch certain ethical problems involving the general social consequences (or possible consequences) of videorecording technology. I shall discuss some specific sorts of problems first and then, at the end, mention briefly some larger questions.

Manipulation of Viewpoint

The same week I began to write this essay, there appeared in *TV Guide* an article by Max Gunther on the videorecording of trials for later viewing by juries. (That this appeared in a large-circulation magazine such as *TV Guide* indicates the considerable interest that already exists in videorecording.) One enthusiastic proponent, Judge James McCrystal, sees three advantages in using this taping procedure rather than having "live" trials. First, "there is no need to wait until a lot of busy people can all be scheduled into the court on the same day," since the various portions of the trial need not be recorded at the same time. Second, the trial can be made less time-consuming, since so-called "dead" time can be omitted. Third, the videotape can be edited by the judge before he allows the jury to see it, so as to expunge any improper remarks by counsel or witness, etc. Despite these advantages, the procedure has not found rapid acceptance by judges. There may be various reasons for this — Gunther mentions several — but most important for our purposes is the obvious danger of manipulation of the viewer's (juror's) perceptions of the defendant, witnesses, lawyers, and others involved. I say "manipulation," which implies a manipulator, but there might be just a distortion by the medium. In a study by Gerald Miller and Norman Fontes, of Michigan State University, it was found that jurors were better able to guess whether witnesses were lying when they saw them "live" than when they saw them on videotape. Miller, according to Gunther, felt that "the differences were too slight to have any major significance," but I wonder. Certainly, it would not be very surprising if one were better able to detect lies (or spot truth) in the physical presence of a witness. How much of a person's manner of speaking and sitting and gesturing, how many of the facial expressions and other nonverbal (and, conceivably, nonvisual) cues and clues might be ignored or distorted by the video-camera? Moreover, it is worth asking to what extent watching a witness on videotape encourages the viewer to interpret what is seen and heard in terms of the conventions and stereotypes of commercial television.

The possibility of such intrinsic distortion aside, it is clear that such use of videorecording in court proceedings offers opportunity for intentional or unintentional manipulation of the juror's viewpoint, either by the camera operator, or by the judge (or anyone else) who edits the videotape. Even the elimination of so-called "dead" time might be dangerous, not only because it eliminates the possibility of the juror acquiring useful perceptions of the trial situation during that time, but also because it creates artificial juxtapositions and an artificial pacing and "intensity," just as happens in film drama and television news (see e.g. Sontag, 1977; Epstein, 1973; Mander, 1978.

The responsible therapist must consider to what extent similar problems might arise in the therapeutic context. Among the advantages of film and videotape modeling over live modeling cited in a recent article is this: "And, of course, the therapist has greater control over the composition of the modeling scene because the film or videotape can be reconstructed until the most desirable scene is produced" (Thelen et al., 1979). Obviously, many of the editing advantages provided by the use of videorecording in therapeutic contexts are similar to those in legal contexts, mentioned previously. I discussed earlier the problems about objectivity that arise in the therapeutic use of videorecording. These problems may arise no less in the various paralegal or quasi-legal proceedings that are part of mental health treatment in institutions. The larger the role videorecording plays in therapy, and the more successful it is, the more natural it will seem to use videorecording as a perhaps too-decisive part of these proceedings or as a replacement for "live" contact between administrator and patient. One might want to resist this for the same or analogous reasons that one resists (if one does) the rapid deployment of videorecording to replace "live" trials.

In addition, therapists should consider to what extent their uses of videorecording technology contribute to the general social acceptability of "edited" versions of events, interactions, or personalities. Do we really want to live in an increasingly image-soaked society? We need very much to consider seriously what the interaction of all these media images might be doing to us. Therapists or scientists who employ videorecording technology are not exempt as citizens from considering their contribution (if any) to those general (and perhaps invisible) effects.

Instability of Viewpoint

In the videomedia we find a "characteristically heavy use of changes in camera viewpoint" (Hochberg and Brooks, 1978). What are the effects of this technique? Nobody really knows. These frequent changes of viewpoint may emphasize the passivity of the viewers, perhaps rendering them more "vulnerable" (Sontag, 1977). They may nourish a short attention span or even "hyperactivity" (Winn, 1977). They may instill in viewers an expectation that images (or what the images represent) are essentially fragmented, isolated, and contingent (see Sontag, 1977; Mander, 1978). Perhaps they do none of these things. If they do, however, these would be serious social effects of the media. The present point of interest is that these effects (if they exist) are effects not of the content of the videomedia, but of certain techniques that are a usual, if not indispensable, part of the employment of videorecording technology. Therapists ought to consider whether their own employment of videorecording involves such instability of viewpoint and, if so, to what extent this is desirable.

Unreality of Viewpoint

To what extent do the techniques of videorecording affect the *reality* of the viewer's viewpoint on life in general? Consider that people often say "it seemed like a movie." They say this about an experience to emphasize how real and how unreal it was. As Sontag says, "reality has come to seem more and more like what we are shown by cameras." As Winn says, "once television fantasy becomes incorporated into the viewer's reality, the real world takes on a tinge of fantasy — or dullness because it fails to confirm the expectations created by televised 'life.' The separation between the real and the unreal becomes blurred; all of life becomes more dreamlike as the boundaries between the real and the unreal merge." No doubt such an effect (if it exists) is due mostly to television, perhaps also to the cinema. However, therapists must consider whether their own work in the videomedia contributes to this social effect and, if so, whether they can affirm that. Does the use of videorecording in therapy encourage people to think of themselves and their situations in terms of television (or cinematic) images? *If it does, is that a good thing?* If television is creating an artificial sense of what "real" life is like (in terms of intensity, drama, pacing, etc.), could the increasing use of videorecording technology in the mental health field encourage that?

I do not claim that the videomedia have been shown to have such effects, though there is an interesting case to be made. What I do think is that responsible therapists, concerned with the large-scale social results of their own work and of the techniques they employ, ought to be aware of, and interested in, these possibilities.

Large Questions

It has been argued by Alasdair MacIntyre that the modern corporate organization has altered us fundamentally as moral agents — for the worse. I cannot consider here the merits of that case, but it is clear that modern corporate organization and modern technology go together, enabling each other, like two legs, to carry us where we may not want to go. What moral stance should one take towards the technologies employed by the videomedia? This question is a part of the older and larger question of how one is to feel about technology — or, rather, about a group of technologies that are increasingly complicated, and increasingly out of one's own hands, and possibly out of everybody's hands.

We encounter at this point a fundamental political polarization within the camp of radical social critics. Who or what is the enemy? Is it those who employ a neutral technology to oppress? Or is it the technology itself? Marshall McLuhan realized that technology does things to people, but his suggestive intuitions got lost in cute slogans and apocalyptic optimism. Nevertheless, he said clearly that "'the medium is the message' because it is the medium that shapes and controls the scale and form of human association and action." Jerry Mander, in his radical but unevenly argued critique of television, has dumped the optimism but kept the basic notion of technological influence when he claims that "the basic form of the institution and the technology determines its interaction with the world, the way it will be used, the kind of people who use it, and to what ends." That the technology determines how it is experienced, and so what effects it will have, has been suggestively argued (for television) by Marie Winn and (for photography) by Susan Sontag.

These matters, though large and dauntingly vague, ought to be in at least the periphery of our moral vision when we reflect on the proper role of videotherapy in mental health. To view them directly, and closely, would be beyond the bounds of this essay, but any moral reflection that simply ignores them is parochial — and so, insincere. The ultimate goal of moral philosophy — as opposed to moral and political polemic — must be here as elsewhere, to enable the individual agent to look on the subject with, as we say, new eyes.

REFERENCES

Carpenter, Edmund: *Oh, what a blow that phantom gave me!* New York, Holt, Rinehart and Winston, 1973.

Donagan, Alan: Informed consent in therapy and experimentation. *Journal of Medicine and Philosophy,* 2:307, 1977.

Epstein, Edward Jay: *News from nowhere.* New York, Random House, 1973.

Gunther, Max: Why the courts are resisting TV. *TV Guide,* 21 July 1979, 2.

Hochberg, Julian and Brooks, Virginia: The perception of motion pictures. In Edward C. Carterette and Morton P. Friedman (Eds.), *Handbook of perception,* vol. 10. New York, Academic Press, 1978, p. 259.

MacIntyre, Alasdair: Corporate modernity and moral judgment: are they mutually exclusive? In K. E. Goodpaster and K. M. Sayre (Eds.), *Ethics* and problems of the 21st century. Notre Dame, University of Notre Dame Press, 1979, p. 122.

McLuhan, Marshall: *Understanding media.* New York, McGraw-Hill, 1964.

Mander, Jerry; *Four arguments for the elimination of television.* New York, Morrow Quill, 1978.

Milgram, Stanley: *Obedience to authority.* New York, Harper and Row, 1974.

Oswald, Ida and Wilson, Suzanne: *This bag is not a tot: a handbook for the use of videorecording in education for the professions.* New York, Council on Social Work Education, 1971.

Rachels, James: Why privacy is important. *Philosophy and Public Affairs,* 4:323, 1975.

Scanlon, Thomas: Thomson on privacy. *Philosophy and Public Affairs,* 4:315, 1975.

Schneider, Carl D.: *Shame, exposure, and privacy.* Boston, Beacon Press, 1977.

Soble, Alan: Deception in social science research: is informed consent possible? *Hastings Center Report,* October, 1978, p. 40.

Sontag, Susan: *On photography.* New York, Farrar, Straus and Giroux, 1977.

Thelen, Mark H. *et al.*: Therapeutic videotape and film modeling: a review. *Psychological Bulletin, 86*:701, 1979.

Thomson, Judith Jarvis: The right to privacy. *Philosophy and Public Affairs,* 4:295, 1975.

Winn, Marie: *The plug-in drug.* New York, Viking Press, 1977.

THE EQUIPMENT

MENTAL health workers are not experts in technical matters such as video equipment capabilities and, in fact, are loathe to spend much time finding out about the inner workings of the electronic gadgetry. With this stereotype of the mental health worker in mind, we offer an appendix of sources of information about video equipment. We have deliberately avoided references to highly technical publications. The references cited here are understandable to the novice and should prove to be of value to readers in nontechnical fields.

We include four categories of resources. The first category, Guides and Directories, is the most basic because information in the other categories, plus a wealth of other information, can be found there. Any media center or well-stocked library should have these guides, or they can be purchased directly from the publishers. The second category, Books, is made up of references to primers on the use of video. No prior knowledge of video technology is assumed. The third category, Journals, consists of four journals that may be of special interest to the nonbroadcast user of video in the mental health or medical fields. The fourth category, Manufacturers, includes addresses of the manufacturers of video recorders and cameras. We have not included manufacturers of tapes, editing equipment, or other supplies except inasmuch as the listed manufacturers also provide them.

We have not made any attempt to provide an exhaustive list of resources, nor do we endorse any of the products.

Guides and Directories

Audiovisual Market Place: A Multimedia Guide, R. R. Bowker Company, 1180 Avenue of the Americas, New York, New York 10036.
Audio-Visual Equipment Directory, National Audio-Visual Association, Inc., 3150 Spring Street, Fairfax, Virginia, 22031.
The Video Register, Knowledge Industry Publications, Inc., Two Corporate Park Drive, White Plains, New York 10604.

Books

Caranicas, P. (Ed.). *The Video Handbook, Third Edition.* United Business Publications, Inc., 475 Park Avenue South, New York, New York 10016,

Harwood, D. *Everything You Always Wanted to Know About Portable Videotape Recording.* VTR Publishing Company, 23 Eaton Road, Syosset, New York 11791.

Robinson, J. F. *Videotape Recording: Theory and Practice.* Communication Arts Books, Hastings House Publishers, 10 East 40 Street, New York, New York 10016.

Robinson, R. *The Video Primer.* Links Books Publishers, 33 West 60 Street, New York, New York 10023.

Quick, J. and Wolff, H. *Small-Studio Video Tape Production, Second Edition.* Addison-Wesley Publishing Co., Inc., Jacob Way, Reading, MA 01867.

Journals

Biomedical Communications, United Business Publications, Inc., 475 Park Avenue South, New York, New York 10016.

Video News, Phillips Publishing, Inc., 8401 Connecticut Avenue, Suite 707, Washington, D.C. 20015.

Educational and Industrial Television, C. S. Tepfer Publishing Co., Inc., 51 Sugar Hollow Road, Danbury, Connecticut 06810.

Videography, United Business Publications, Inc., 475 Park Avenue South, New York, New York 10016.

MANUFACTURERS OF VIDEO PRODUCTS

Akai

Akai America, Ltd.
2139 Del Amo Boulevard
P.O. Box 6010
Compton, California 90224
Attention: Video Marketing

Curtis Mathes

Curtis Mathes Sales Co.
One Curtis Mathes Parkway
Athens, Texas 75751

JVC

East
JVC, Professional Video Division
58-75 Queens Midtown Expressway
Maspeth, New York 11378

Midwest
JVC, Professional Video Division
2250 Lively Boulevard
Elk Grove Village, Illinois 60007

West
JVC, Professional Video Division
1011 West Arteria Boulevard
Compton, California

Southwest
JVC Professional Video Division
3400 South Loop East
Houston, Texas 77021

Magnavox

Magnavox Consumer Electronics Co.
1700 Magnavox Way
Fort Wayne, Indiana 46804

Mitsubishi

Melco Sales, Inc.
3030 E. Victoria St.
Compton, California 90221

Panasonic

Northeast
Panasonic Co.
50 Meadowlands Parkway
Secaucus, New Jersey 07094
Southeast
Panasonic Co.
#3 Mecca Way
Norcross, Georgia 30093
Midwest
Panasonic Co.
425 E. Algonquin road
Arlington Heights, Illinois 60005
Southwest
Panasonic Co.
1825 Walnut Hill Lane
Irving, Texas 75062

Philco

Philco Video Products
Public Affairs Department
Entertainment Products Group
GTE Products Corporation
700 Ellicott Street
Batavia, New York 14020

Quasar

Quasar Company
Advertising Communications
9401 West Grand Avenue
Franklin Park, Illinois 60131
Attention: Mr. David Carlson

RCA

RCA Consumer Electronics
600 North Sherman Drive
Indianapolis, Indiana 46201

Sanyo

Sanyo Electronic, Inc.
1200 West Artesia Boulevard
Compton, California 90220

Sears

Sears Betavision
Home Entertainment Center
Sears Retail Stores or see the
Sears General Catalog

Sharp

Sharp Electronics Corporation
10 Keystone Place
Paramus, New Jersey 07652
Attention: Mr. Bob Garbutt

Sony

Sony Corporation of America
9 West 57th Street
New York, New York 10019

Sylvania

Sylvania Video Products
Public Affairs Department
Entertainment Products Group
GTE Products Corporation
700 Ellicott Street
Batavia, New York 14020

Zenith

Zenith Video Products
Roel, Inc.
1011 West Irving Park Road
Bensonville, Illinois 60106

Toshiba

Toshiba America, Inc.
280 Park Avenue
New York, New York 10017

AUTHOR INDEX

A

Abell, R. G., 6, 39
Acker, C. W., 270
Aderman, D., 38, 39
Agras, W. S., 7, 41
Aiduk, R., 17, 18, 23, 28, 30, 39
Alberti, R. E., 212, 213, 214, 220, 221
Alger, I., 5, 6, 7, 8, 33, 39, 269
Alker, H. A., 21, 22, 23, 24, 25, 26, 33, 35, 39
Alkire, A., 7, 8, 10, 23, 39
Amolsch, T., 76
Andrews, J., 50, 73
Annon, J. S., vii, xi, 163, 171, 172, 174, 176, 178
Arbuckle, S., 31, 45
Arnkoff, D. B., 17, 18, 20, 23, 30, 35, 40
Arkowitz, H., 35, 43
Armstrong, R. C., 6, 40
Arnheim, R., 85, 86, 92
Arsenian, J., 6, 40
Austin, N., 210, 214, 215, 221
Authier, J., 150, 161

B

Bach, R. C. R., 221
Backup, C. E., 21, 42
Baer, J., 158, 160, 213, 214, 220, 222
Bailey, K. G., 5, 6, 7, 14, 15, 17, 21, 23, 30, 35, 40, 77, 159, 160
Bailey, W., 51, 63
Baker, T. B., 11, 12, 23, 25, 30, 40, 53, 73
Baldinger, M., 242, 243
Ball, P. G., vii, xii, 209, 211, 221
Bandura, A., 20, 25, 33, 36, 37, 40, 44, 47, 48, 49, 59, 60, 62, 63, 65, 66, 67, 68, 73, 74, 147, 149, 151, 153, 154, 160, 269
Barab, P., 48, 49, 59, 60, 73
Barbach, L. S., 166, 178
Bardwick, J. M., 221

Barnett, J. T., 158, 161
Barrington, H., 269
Bart, P. B., 221
Bates, H. D., 214, 220
Bateson, G., 96, 117
Bellack, A. S., 5, 42, 58, 67, 75
Bem, D. H., 221
Bem, S. L., 221
Benschoter, R. A., 269, 276, 284, 302
Berger, M. M., 7, 14, 16, 29, 31, 40, 126, 145, 291, 302
Berman, A. L., 14, 15, 23, 29, 30, 40
Bernal, M. E., 7, 9, 40
Berne, E., 141, 145, 193, 206
Bernstein, D. A., 67, 70, 71, 74, 76
Bernstein, P. L., 114, 117
Bishop, P., 190, 207
Black, J. L., 35, 44
Blanchard, E., 49, 73
Blanchard, W., 109, 117
Blank, J. E., 166, 179
Bloom, B. S., 275, 302
Bloom, L. Z., 212, 220
Bloomfield, H. H., 221
Blount, H. P., 17, 18, 20, 33, 35, 40
Bolles, R. N., 222
Boszormenyi-Nagy, I., 141, 145
Bower, G. H., 222
Bower, S. A., 222
Boyd, H. S., 33, 34, 40
Brandon, J. R., 269
Braucht, G. N., 14, 15, 34, 40
Brehm, S. S., 38, 39
Brenman, M., 31, 42
Britton, G., 223
Brodsky, S. L., 207
Brooks, V., 313, 315
Bruch, M., 61, 74
Brunse, A. J., 7, 8, 10, 23, 39
Bryan, J., 50, 59, 77
Burck, H. D., 41
Burgoyne, R. W., 303

321

SUBJECT INDEX

A

Acting out, 226
Actor's studio, 249
Addictions, 54 (*also see* Drug dependent adolescents)
Addison Gallery, 79, 80, 87, 88
Affect simulation vignettes, 282, 301
Affective reactions, 22
Aggression, 212, 216
Alcoholics
  behavior rehearsal and videotape simulated interactions with, 199-201
  symbolic modeling with, 53
  videotaped psychodrama with, 267
  videotape recorded playback with, 10-14, 267
Anorexia Nervosa, 20
Anxiety
  being taped as source of, 284-286
  dating, symbolic modeling for, 51
  dental/medical, symbolic modeling for, 50-51, 55-56
  test, symbolic modeling for, 50, 55
  videotaped recorded playback and, 31
Art therapy (*see* Expressive therapy)
Assertive behavior
  vs aggression, 211-215
  definition of nonassertive and, 212-213
  nonverbal components of, 215-217, 219
  vs sex-role socialization, 209-211
Assertiveness training
  methods of, 211
  model use and selection in, 218-219
  Rathus assertiveness scale in, 192
  rationale for, 210-211
  and re-entry female college students, 190-193
  stimulus-modeling tape development for, 151
  and symbolic modeling, 52-53, 56, 66-67, 218-219

therapist/trainer interaction in, 215
Attributions of causality, 34-35

B

Behavior rehearsal
  and alcoholics, 199-201
  and assertiveness training, 190-192
  coaching during, 185
  for confrontation management, 182-190
  diagram of videotape simulations for, 185
  effects of, pre-post difference measures as, 189-190, 192-193
  filming techniques for, 185-186, 187, 190, 196-197, 199-201
  and police cadet training, 182, 188, 190
  and success in tennis, fear of, 194, 197
  and re-entry college women, 190-193
  and social skills training, 201-204
  and stressful situations, 187-190
  and success, fear of, 193-199
  and symbolic modeling, 52-53, 57
  as step in symbolic-modeling formats, 155
  and therapist interaction, 186-187, 205-206, 215
Biomedical Communications Department, 227

C

Camarillo State Hospital, 257, 259, 261, 267
Camera (*see* Video equipment, use of)
Carkhuff Gross Rating Scale, 301
Character disorder, 226
Child-parent interaction (*see* Parent-child interaction)
Clinical photographer, 97, 100, 108
Cognitive behavior therapy, 36-38
Conflict Resolution Inventory, 192